Intellectual Property Policy, Law and Administration in Africa

This book examines the harmonization of Intellectual Property (IP) policy, law and administration in Africa.

Two recent developments have brought this topic to the fore. The first is the escalation of long-standing efforts to establish a Pan-African Intellectual Property Organization (PAIPO), a continental initiative. The second is the current sub-regional attempt to operationalize the IP provisions of the Southern African Development Community (SADC)'s Protocol on Trade (articles 9b and 24) and its Protocol on Science, Technology and Innovation (article 2m).

Intellectual Property Policy, Law and Administration in Africa discusses the viability of such initiatives with particular reference to the current socio-economic status of Africa's nations. With a view to contributing to future developments in Africa at both a continental and sub-regional level, the author considers this issue through the lens of advancing the public interest in IP. Ncube argues that harmonization initiatives ought to be crafted in a way that is supportive of the development aspirations of African states. Consequently, she urges due consideration of individual states' unique conditions and aspirations in any harmonization venture, a necessity outlined in article 7 of the Agreement on Trade Related Aspects of Intellectual Property Rights.

This book will be of great relevance to scholars and policy makers with an interest in IP law and African law in general.

Caroline B. Ncube is a Professor in the Department of Commercial Law at the University of Cape Town, South Africa.

Routledge Research in Intellectual Property

Intellectual Property Policy, Law and Administration in Africa
Exploring continental and sub-regional co-operation
Caroline B. Ncube

Intellectual Property Rights and Competition in Standard Setting
Objectives and tensions
Valerio Torti

Re-thinking Intellectual Property
The political economy of copyright protection in the digital era
YiJun Tian

The Development of Intellectual Property Regimes in the Middle East
David Price

Intellectual Property, Community Rights and Human Rights
The biological and genetic resources of developing countries
Marcelin Tonye Mahop

Intellectual Property in Global Governance
The crisis of equity in the knowledge economy
Chidi Oguamanam

Intellectual Property Overlaps
Theory, strategies, and solutions
Robert Tomkowicz

Private Copying
Stavroula Karapapa

The Law and Economics of Intellectual Property in the Digital Age
The limits of analysis
Niva Elkin-Koren and Eli Salzberger

The Politics of Patent Law
Crafting the participatory patent bargain
Kali Murray

Copyright Industries and the Impact of Creative Destruction
Copyright expansion and the publishing industry
Jiabo Liu

Health Technologies and International Intellectual Property
A precautionary principle
Phoebe Li

Intellectual Property, Traditional Knowledge and Cultural Property Protection
Cultural signifiers in the Caribbean and the Americas
Sharon Le Gall

Intellectual Property and Traditional Knowledge in the Global Economy
Translating geographical indications for development
Teshager W. Dagne

Forthcoming:

Intellectual Property and Conflict of Laws
Moral rights and alternatives to the copyright qualifications
Hanan Almawla

The Object of Copyright
A conceptual history of originals and copies in literature, art and design
Stina Teilmann-Lock

Well-Known Trade Marks
A comparative study of Japan and the EU
Hiroko Onishi

Intellectual Property Policy, Law and Administration in Africa

Exploring continental and sub-regional co-operation

Caroline B. Ncube

Routledge
Taylor & Francis Group
LONDON AND NEW YORK

First published 2016
by Routledge
2 Park Square, Milton Park, Abingdon, Oxon, OX14 4RN

and by Routledge
711 Third Avenue, New York, NY 10017

Routledge is an imprint of the Taylor & Francis Group, an informa business

British Library Cataloguing in Publication Data
A catalogue record for this book is available from the British Library

Library of Congress Cataloging-in-Publication Data
Ncube, Caroline B., author.
Intellectual property policy, law and administration in Africa : exploring continental and sub-regional co-operation / by Caroline B. Ncube.
pages cm. -- (Routledge research in intellectual property)
Includes bibliographical references and index.
ISBN 978-1-138-82073-9 (hardback : alk. paper) -- ISBN 978-1-315-74371-4 (ebook : alk. paper)
1. Intellectual property--Africa. I. Title.
KQC370.N37 2015
346.604'8--dc23
2015018421

ISBN: 978-1-138-82073-9 (hbk)
ISBN: 978-1-315-74371-4 (ebk)

Typeset in Baskerville MT Pro by
Servis Filmsetting Ltd, Stockport, Cheshire

MIX
Paper from responsible sources
FSC® C013604

Printed and bound by CPI Group (UK) Ltd, Croydon, CR0 4YY

Contents

List of abbreviations ix
Acknowledgements xiii
Preface xiv
Foreword xv

1 Introduction **1**
The Intellectual Property landscape in Africa 1
Overview and history of national IP laws 2
IP and the public interest 5
African states' diversity and the need for flexible and nuanced IP systems 10
African states' contribution to the articulation and formulation of the Development Agenda at WIPO 12
TRIPS implementation by African states 14
Book overview 31

2 IP policy frameworks in Africa **40**
Introduction 40
The importance of IP policies in Africa 43
Factors affecting IP policy design 44
Technical assistance 46
REC IP policies 51
Country profiles 52
Conclusion 60

3 Sub-regional trade co-operation and integration **68**
Introduction 68
Theories of regionalism 69
The AU and the AEC 73
The relationship between community laws and national laws 76
COMESA 78
EAC 79
ECOWAS 82
SADC 83

T-FTA 86
Conclusion 90

4 Sub-regional IP co-operation **97**
Introduction 97
ARIPO 98
OAPI 109
Conclusion 121

5 Continental IP co-operation: PAIPO **126**
Introduction 126
Historical overview of the AU's efforts to establish PAIPO 126
How PAIPO will function 131
Policy imperatives – the PAIPO statute and the WIPO development agenda 139
Conclusion 139

6 Key considerations in the development of IP harmonization models **145**
Introduction 145
IP co-operation 146
Harmonization 153
Lessons from existing harmonization efforts 160
Conclusion 165

7 General conclusions **176**

Index 181

List of abbreviations

ABS	Access Benefit Sharing
ACTRIPS	Advisory Council on Trade-Related Innovation Policies
AEC	African Economic Community
ALI	The American Law Institute
AMCOST	African Ministerial Conference on Science and Technology
APEC	Asia-Pacific Economic Cooperation
ARIPO	African Regional Intellectual Property Organisation
ASEAN	Association of South East Asian Nations
ASPEC	ASEAN Patent Search and Examination Cooperation
AU	African Union
AU-STRC	Scientific, Technical and Research Commission
AWGIPC	ASEAN Working Group on IP Co-operation
BRICS	Brazil Russia India China South Africa
CCM	MERCOSUR Council of the Common Market
CDIP	WIPO Committee on Development and Intellectual Property
CDR	Community Design Regulation
CEN-SAD	Community of Sahel-Saharan States
CEPA	UN's Committee of Experts in Public Administration
C-FTA	Continental Free Trade Area
CMA	MERCOSUR Common Market Group
CMG	Common Market Group
CMTR	Community Trade Mark Regulations
COHRED	Council on Health Research for Development
COMESA	Common Market for Eastern and Southern Africa
CSO	Civil Society Organization
CTI	Committee on Trade and Investment
CTM	Community Trademark
CU	Customs Union
DA	Development Agenda
DAG	Development Agenda Group
DFID	UK Department for International Development
DPADM	UN Division for Public Administration and Development

	Management
DRC	Democratic Republic of the Congo
DST	South Africa's Department of Science and Technology
DTI	South Africa's Department of Trade and Industry
EAC	East African Community
ECCAS	Economic Community of Central African States
ECJ	European Court of Justice
ECOWAS	Economic Community of West African States
ECSA-HC	East, Central and Southern African Health Community
EFTA	European Free Trade Association
EPA	Economic Partnership Agreement
EPO	European Patent Office
ESARIPO	Industrial Property Organization for English-speaking Africa
EU	European Union
FDI	Foreign Direct Investment
FTA	Free Trade Agreement/Free Trade Area
GATS	General Agreement on Trade in Services
GATT	General Agreement on Tariffs and Trade
GR	Genetic Resources
HIV/AIDS	Human Immunodeficiency Virus/Acquired Immune-Deficiency Syndrome
HRS&T	AU Human Resources, Science and Technology
ICT	Information and Communications Technology
IGAD	Intergovernmental Authority on Development
IGC	Intergovernmental Committee
IGOs	Intergovernmental Organizations
IK/IKS	Indigenous Knowledge/Indigenous Knowledge System
INPI	French National Patent Rights Institute
IOC	Indian Ocean Commission
IP/IPR	Intellectual Property/Intellectual Property Right
IPDP	Intellectual Property Development Plan
IPEG	IPR-Experts Group
IPR-GT	Intellectual Property Rights Get Together
JPO	Japan Patent Office
LDC	Least Developed Country
MERCOSUR	Mercado Común del Sur (Common Market of the South)
MTC	MERCOSUR Trade Commission
NEPAD	New Partnership for Africa's Development
NRS	National Recordal System
OAMPI	L'Office Africaine et Malgache de la Propriété Industrielle
OAPI	Organisation Africaine de la Propriété Intellectuelle (African Intellectual Property Organization)
OAU	Organization of African Unity
OECD	Organisation for Economic Co-operation and Development

OHADA	L'Organisation pour l'Harmonisation en Afrique du Droit des Affaires (Organization for the Harmonization of Business Law in Africa)
OHIM	EU Office for Harmonization in the Internal Market
PAIPO	Pan-African Intellectual Property Organization
PBR	Plant Breeders Rights
PCT	Patent Cooperation Treaty
PRA	Property Rights Alliance
PSA	Partial Scope Agreements
PTA	Preferential Trade Agreement
PVP	Plant Variety Protection
R&D	Research and Development
REC	Regional Economic Community
RIA	Regional Integration Arrangement
RISDP	Regional Indicative Strategic Development Plan
RSTI	Research, Science, Technology and Innovation
RTA	Regional Trade Agreement
SACU	Southern African Customs Union
SADC	Southern African Development Community
SADCC	Southern African Development Co-ordination Conference
SARPAM	Southern Africa Regional Programme on Access to Medicines and Diagnostics
SCCP	APEC Sub-Committee on Customs Procedures
SIPO	State Intellectual Property Office of the People's Republic of China
SME	Small and Medium Enterprises
STI	Science, Technology and Innovation
STISA	Science, Technology and Innovation Strategy
T-FTA	Tripartite Free Trade Area
TIDCA	Trade Investment and Development Cooperation Agreement
TK	Traditional Knowledge
TMD	Trademark Directive
TRIPS	Agreement on Trade Related Aspects of Intellectual Property Rights, Including Trade in Counterfeit Goods
UMA/AMU	Arab Maghreb Union
UNCITRAL	United Nations Commission on International Trade Law
UNCTAD	United Nations Conference on Trade and Development
UNDP	United Nations Development Program
UNECA	United Nations Economic Commission for Africa
UNESCO	United Nations Educational, Scientific and Cultural Organization
UNIDO	United Nations Industrial Development Organization
UNIDROIT	International Institute for the Unification of Private Law
UPOV	International Union for the Protection of New Varieties of Plants

USPTO	United States Patent and Trademark Office
WHO	World Health Organization
WIPO	World Intellectual Property Organization
WTO	World Trade Organization

Acknowledgements

I would like to express my deep gratitude to my family Phenias, Vuyo and Wandile and my sister Heather for their support; my colleagues and students who served as a sounding board for many of my ideas and to Charlene Musiza for her editorial assistance.

Preface

This book seeks to examine efforts to harmonize IP policy, law and administration in Africa. The last several years have seen heightened interest in IP matters as they pertain to Africa. Two recent developments spurred me to write this book. The first is the current sub-regional attempt to operationalize the IP provisions found in the Southern African Development Community (SADC)'s Protocol on Trade (1998) and its Protocol on Science, Technology and Innovation (2008). SADC's efforts are augmented by the SADC, East African Community (EAC) and Common Market for Eastern and Southern Africa (COMESA) Tripartite Free Trade Agreement (T-FTA) and its IP Agenda, as contained in an Annex to the T-FTA Agreement. The T-FTA was launched in June 2015 and is slated to merge with the Economic Community of West African States (ECOWAS), as a major step towards the establishment of a continental FTA (C-FTA). These regional economic communities have already incorporated IP into their integration agendas, making IP a focal point for sub-regional and regional integration. Any further IP initiatives emanating from the C-FTA will have an impact on the 35 African states that constitute it.

The second development is the escalation of long-standing efforts to establish a Pan-African Intellectual Property Organization (PAIPO), a continental initiative. The AU has passed a decision for its creation and an offer has been made by Tunisia to host its Secretariat. Therefore, all indications are that PAIPO will be operationalized in the short-to-medium term. This will create a continental IP organization. If it eventuates, IP will take a new continental significance. In view of these far-reaching developments, this is an opportune time to evaluate African states' approach to IP and its alignment to their development aspirations. Such an evaluation will proffer some suggestions as how best to manage both developments in a way that ensures that socio-economic development on the continent is not compromised.

Unless where indicated otherwise, this book discusses the law and events, as known to the author, as at 1 March 2015.

Foreword

Caroline B. Ncube has written an important and most welcome book. It is the first comprehensive examination of the substantive intellectual property (IP) regimes and institutional as well as policy frameworks in Africa. It examines efforts at the sub-regional and continental levels to harmonize and cooperate around IP issues. In so doing, Professor Ncube has made visible the tensions and trade-offs in pursuing substantive harmonization of IP regimes, on the one hand, and unification, on the other. She also examines how these regimes, institutions and policies are suited to the many varied African conditions and the challenges harmonization and cooperation raises in light of the differing legal traditions, for example civil as opposed to common law, overlapping sub-regional trading frameworks and competing sub-regional IP regimes. For some regimes such as the Organisation Africaine de la Propriété Intellectuelle, (OAPI), and the Organization for the Harmonization of Business Laws in Africa (OHADA), unification has been the choice. That is why the book endorses 'malleable harmonization models' as opposed to unification and in the process recommends looking to the ASEAN region for inspiration for structuring such a process of enabling 'appropriate calibration of national IP systems.' The author also critically explores the divergence between the support African countries have given to the World Intellectual Property Organization's Development Agenda with what she considers to be their surprising support of proposed Pan-African Intellectual Property Organization (PAIPO) that has no similar developmental objectives.

A major strength of the book is the way in which it examines the extent to which existing IP regimes, institutions and policies are appropriate fits for different African experiences. Ncube argues that to suit IP regimes, policies and institutions to these diversity of circumstances requires 'policy and legislative space for national nuancing.' The overall framework the book adopts is based on viewing the international IP regime complex as anchored in the WTO as one in which there is a balance between the rights of IP holders and the interests of IP users. That balance, reflected in various flexibilities embodied in the TRIPS Agreement and related instruments inspires the manner in which the book discusses IP regimes in Africa. Understandably therefore the book raises the question of why many African LDCs have already adopted WTO TRIPS type laws even though they are not yet legally required to do so. That question is all the more poignant because the book shows that many African national IP regimes have colonial origins and their development has continued to be transplants of European and American IP regimes rather than adapting them to fit local circumstances and priorities. Perhaps the efficacy of these transplanted regimes can only be as effective as they reflect local circumstances and priorities. As Funmi Arewa has recently shown, the rise of digital technologies resulted in the rise of a global movie industry in Nigeria at a time when there was very weak copyright protection there. Entrepreneurs, pirates and creators worked together in ways that have now created opportunities to monetize this industry that has a global reach. Ncube's book contributes to how the interests and concerns of creators, users and society ought to be taken into account in IP regimes. For taking this perspective, the book is a welcome, refreshing and important addition to understanding IP regimes in Africa. The book represents a new generation on IP scholarship that takes seriously and as a central objective the interests and concerns of a broad swath of stakeholders in the IP regime complex in Africa. Others must follow suit and take forward the research agenda this book wonderfully sets out.

James Thuo Gathii
Wing-Tat Lee Chair in International Law and Professor of Law
Loyola University Chicago School of Law

1 Introduction

The Intellectual Property landscape in Africa

> *Africa is not a country: it is a very heterogeneous continent comprised of . . . nations with great variations in physical, economic, political, and social dimensions.*[1]

This book considers the viability of the creation of a harmonized African continental and sub-regional Intellectual Property (IP) framework, keeping in sight the fact that African states[2] have different socio-economic, cultural and political contexts.[3] Their history is diverse, albeit with the widely held common experience of colonization[4] and the legal transplants it brought with it. Unsurprisingly, they each have unique national IP environments, which are comprised of statute and case law, policies and practices.[5] It is important to point out, at the outset, that the African IP landscape is multi-layered. In addition to relevant global and national frameworks, there are regional and sub-regional IP frameworks to consider, located either in an IP sub-regional organization or a Regional Economic Community (REC). This terrain is further complicated by the multiplicity of RECs, which currently number about 14,[6] of which only eight are recognized by the African Union as constituent elements of the African Economic Community (AEC).[7]

1 Broadman and Isik (2007) p. 5.

2 Africa has 57 states, 54 of which are members of the African Union (AU). Morocco is not an AU member state. The two disputed states – the Sahrawi Arab Democratic Republic and Somaliland – are also not AU member states. For a history of the Sahrawi Arab Democratic Republic see Jensen (2005) and Shelley (2004).

3 Collins and Burns (2013) p. 4.

4 With the exception of Ethiopia and Liberia, all of Africa was colonized by 1914 per Boahen (1990) p. 1. Liberia had been a colony of the United States from 1820–1847 per Kongolo (2014) pp. 163, 168.

5 Armstrong, de Beer, Kawooya, Prabhala and Schonwetter (2010) p. 5.

6 Kolbeck (2014) p. 3; African Union (AU) Study for the Quantification of RECs: Rationalization Scenarios, 2009 p. 34.

7 Kolbeck (2014) p. 3; Gathii (2011) p. 362; AU Decision on the Moratorium on the Recognition of RECs DOC.EX.CL/278 (IX). AU Doc. Assembly/AU/Dec. 111–132 (VII). The eight RECS are the Arab Maghreb Union (AMU/UMA); Community of Sahel-Saharan States (CEN-SAD); Common Market for Eastern and Southern Africa (COMESA); East African Community (EAC);

Many African states are members of more than one REC,[8] which compounds the situation.

The book adopts Akokpari's conceptualization of a region as consisting of states in geographical proximity[9] and uses the word interchangeably with 'continental', to refer to Africa. The term 'sub-regional' refers to various continental sub-groupings. Legal harmonization is the approximation of legal standards across a defined community that permits national divergence, whilst unification is the imposition of exactly the same standards with no scope for national variances.[10] Whilst both approaches are currently in use in Africa, the African Union (AU)'s preferred approach is harmonization. This preference is shared by some RECs such as the Common Market for Eastern and Southern Africa (COMESA), the East African Community (EAC), the Economic Community of West African States (ECOWAS) and the Southern African Development Community (SADC). Similarly, harmonization is the mode of choice for the African Regional IP Organization (ARIPO), one of the continent's two sub-regional IP organizations. In contrast, the other sub-regional IP organization, the African Intellectual Property Organization, *Organisation Africaine de la Propriété Intellectuelle* in French (OAPI) and the Organization for the Harmonization of Business Laws in Africa (OHADA) have taken the unification approach.

This introductory chapter will provide an overview of existing IP laws in Africa and their historical development. The chapter will then introduce the concept of the public interest in IP and highlight African countries' unique challenges with an emphasis on the diversity of circumstances across the continent. This wide range of diversity necessitates an IP framework that permits sufficient flexibility to enable the appropriate calibration of national IP systems and equally malleable harmonization models. It will then turn to an overview of African states' contribution to the articulation and formulation of the Development Agenda (DA) at the World IP Organization (WIPO) which signaled a commitment to advancing the public interest in IP. Finally, it will briefly outline the status of African states' implementation of the Agreement on Trade Related Aspects of Intellectual Property Rights (TRIPS), with particular emphasis on how this implementation has been nuanced to meet African circumstances and needs through the use of flexibilities.

Overview and history of national IP laws

Most African states currently have separate statutes providing for the different types of IP rather than one piece of omnibus legislation catering for all types of

Economic Community of Central African States (ECCAS/CEEAC); Economic Community of West African States (ECOWAS); the Inter-Governmental Authority of Development (IGAD); and Southern African Development Community (SADC).

8 Gathii (2011) p. 65.

9 Akokpari (2008) p. 88.

10 Rachlitz (2014) p. 50.

IP. OAPI member states share the same body of IP laws as provided for in the Bangui Agreement Relating to the Creation of an African Intellectual Property Organization of 1977. The Bangui Agreement includes a series of Annexes that regulate copyright, patent, trademarks and designs, amongst other types of IP protection. OAPI's Anglophone counterpart, ARIPO's Protocols, do not have direct application in member states and have to be domesticated by party states. Consequently, each ARIPO member state has its own national IP framework. A detailed overview of the content of OAPI's Bangui Agreement and its Annexures, ARIPO's Protocols and the rest of Africa's individual IP laws has been given elsewhere[11] and thus falls outside the ambit of this book. Select laws are considered, as examples, where appropriate throughout the text.

The history of IP law in Africa is inextricably linked to colonial history. Some of the first iterations of African states' IP laws were legal transplants introduced by former colonialists well before the conclusion of the Paris and Berne conventions.[12] In other cases, the first colonial IP legislation was introduced after the conclusion and entry into force of these conventions.[13] The precise method of the enactment of these laws was comprised of two steps. The first entailed the submission, by the colonizing state, of a declaration of the application of the applicable international agreement to the colonized state. Declarations of the application of the Berne Convention were made in accordance with article 19 of the original text of the convention.[14] Declarations of the applicability of the Paris Convention were made in terms of article 16 bis (1)–(2) of the London Act of 1934 and the Lisbon Act of 1958 of the convention.[15] Second, the declaration of applicability of the international conventions was then followed by the extension of the colonizing state's copyright or patent legislation to the colony, or the enactment of legislation applicable only to the colonized territory.[16] In either case the law was created by the colonizing, rather than the colonized, state. Therefore, the goals and interests of the former, rather than the latter state, informed these IP laws.[17]

Many African states continued to adhere to these colonial laws after their independence[18] and the relevant international agreement upon which they were based. However, in some instances, after their independence some states did not immediately accede to the Berne Convention and enacted their own copyright law that repealed the colonial copyright legislation. A case in point is Ghana, which enacted its first post-independence Copyright Act in 1961 and chose to accede to the Universal Copyright Convention in 1962 instead of the Berne Convention, to which it only acceded in 1991.[19] The drafting of post-independence copyright

11 du Plessis (2012).
12 Okediji (2003a) p. 323.
13 Kongolo (2014) pp. 168–170; Kongolo (2013b) pp. 115–116.
14 Kongolo (2014) p. 165.
15 Kongolo (2013b) p. 107.
16 Kongolo (2013b) p. 106.
17 Kongolo (2013a) p. 1.
18 Kongolo (2013a) p. 1; Joireman (2001) p. 576.
19 Kongolo (2014) p. 173.

laws was informed to a large extent by the UN Educational, Scientific and Cultural Organization (UNESCO)–WIPO Tunis Model Copyright Law for Developing Countries, 1976.[20]

Since their independence African states have, to varying degrees, sought to revise existing IP laws[21] or to enact their own IP laws.[22] However, in some ways these post-independence efforts have been constrained by the current international IP framework, primarily through the Agreement on Trade-Related Aspects of Intellectual Property Rights (TRIPS).[23] The TRIPS framework has served as 'a powerful mechanism for transplanting European and American law'[24] and some scholars characterize it as a 'device that drives economic neo-colonialism forward.'[25] Whilst African states participated in its negotiation and conclusion, they did so at a disadvantage, lacking adequate representation and resources (human and otherwise) to ensure that the agreement was truly to their benefit.[26]

In spite of these disadvantages African and other developing states successfully lobbied for the inclusion of some provisions in the agreement which seek to meet their unique circumstances. Of these, articles 7 and 8 are discussed further below in this chapter. Another important mechanism was the inclusion of a transition period for the full implementation of TRIPS by least developed countries (LDCs). This period, initially set to expire in 2005, has been extended twice and is currently set at 1 July 2021 or sooner if a country ceases to become an LDC before that date.[27]

In their revision or crafting of IP laws, African states have relied upon technical assistance from the World Trade Organization (WTO), the World IP Organization (WIPO) and other United Nations specialized agencies such as UNESCO and the World Health Organization (WHO). However, as noted by Ndulo, such assistance can become a Trojan horse that brings in detrimental ideas.[28] Therefore the nature, scope and content of such assistance need to be carefully structured and developed because it may exacerbate existing problems. Many UN agencies subscribe to progressive development theories that are informed by human rights considerations. However, concerns have been raised about whether WIPO shares this common developmental approach. These concerns culminated in the adoption of the WIPO DA that it is hoped will realign the organization's approach by making it more development-orientated.

20 Kongolo (2014) pp. 172–173.

21 Kongolo (2013a) pp. 1, 9.

22 Okediji (2003a) p. 335.

23 Agreement on Trade-Related Aspects of Intellectual Property Rights, including Trade in Counterfeit Goods (1994) 33 ILM 81 (TRIPS).

24 Seuba (2014) p. 3 citing Dreyfuss (2004) p. 21.

25 Rahmatian (2009) pp. 41–42.

26 Kongolo (2013a) p. 2; Watal (2011) p. 25.

27 WTO Decision of the Council for Trade-Related Aspects of Intellectual Property Rights *Extension of the Transition Period under Article 66.1 for Least Developed Country Members* (11 June 2013) IP/C/64. For an overview of the genesis and extent of the original extension period as well as the latest extension request made in 2012, see Abbott (2013).

28 Ndulo (2007) p. 333.

In many cases the post-TRIPS IP legislation of many states is still not properly attuned to prevailing socio-economic conditions. It is only in the last few years that some African states have articulated IP policies that will be used to calibrate their IP laws to suit their national priorities, within the confines of the international, regional, sub-regional and bilateral agreements to which they are party. In addition to IP legislation and policies (where they exist), there are specific state and industry implementation practices that are yet to be comprehensively studied or reported upon. For example, an IP statute may provide for criminal sanctions for infringement, yet in practice no prosecutions ever take place. Thus, a study of the legislation only may not provide a full picture of the real situation. It is necessary to look at other constituent parts of the legal environment which include case law (where it exists), and prevailing 'perceptions of the [IP] framework, and norms, social conditions and market dynamics that affect how people access and use [IP protected works].'[29] The analysis of these other constituent elements falls beyond the scope of this book which confines itself to a discussion of laws and policies and whether or not they serve the public interest.

IP and the public interest

The public interest, sometimes referred to as public welfare,[30] is distinct from public policy. Public policy is a statement of a government's chosen approach to specific matters which gives guidance to relevant persons, including government itself, on how certain goals are to be set and achieved.[31] It is crafted as part of a political process within a national legal and administrative framework. The goal of public policy should be to 'further [or serve] the public interest.'[32] Achieving this end is 'the highest standard of governmental action, the measure of the greatest wisdom or morality in government.'[33]

Despite contestations about its value and its exact meaning,[34] the public interest is a useful concept. The general definition adopted for purposes of this text is Ho's *ex ante* analysis which is premised on the position of the representative individual.[35] Under this approach, before selecting a policy direction, 'vested interests' would be eliminated or reduced by the consideration of policy options by reference to an 'imaginary person' who 'could be anyone.'[36] The outcome that would best cater for this individual would be in the public interest. In the IP context, I have argued elsewhere that serving the public interest would be to

29 African Copyright and Access to Knowledge Project (ACA2K) (2008) p. 7.
30 Okediji (1999), (2003b) and (2014).
31 Belohlavek (2012) p. 118. Also see Dye (1972) p. 2; Hogwood and Gunn (1984) pp. 23–24; Wilson (2006) p. 1.
32 Ho (2012) pp. 1, 19. Also see Smith (2006) p. 730.
33 Souraf (1957) p. 616.
34 Box (2007) p. 586; Held (1970) p. 1; Storing (1964); Friedrich (1962); Schubert (1960) p. 224; Sorauf (1957).
35 Ho (2012) p. 13.
36 Ho (2012) p. 7.

'equitably balance the interests of creators and users in a manner that is beneficial to society generally.'[37] However, as I have also noted elsewhere, utilizing the metaphor of balance presents some conceptual difficulties.[38] These include the definition of balance, the determination of the conceptual tool or device to be used to calibrate it and the selection of appropriate means to achieve it. These difficulties with the twin concepts of the public interest and balance can be ameliorated by careful articulation of their meanings hence their continued usage in IP discourse.

One way of carefully articulating these concepts is by differentiating normative claims according to IP right and national context. Discussions of the public interest are normally held at macro-level that is to explore what would be in the public interest generally with regard to all IP. Whilst such high-level discussions are valuable they cannot replace the deliberate consideration of the public interest with regard to each type of IP right.[39] Examples of the articulation of carefully nuanced IP type specific public interest goals include the Adelphi Charter[40] and the Washington Declaration on IP and the Public Interest.[41] As stated above, the national and continental context is also important, [42] hence this text's specific focus on Africa. However, engaging in a comprehensive discussion of the public interest in relation to all types of IP rights is beyond the scope of this work. Where appropriate IP right specific public interest recommendations will be made, particularly in relation to patents and public health as well as the protection of traditional knowledge (TK). The following two sub-sections speak to the geo-political context of the public interest.

A global public interest?

Okediji states that both global and national welfare are the aim and result of 'market based efficiencies that simultaneously promote and reflect the pursuit of self-interest' on a global and national stage respectively.[43] She also notes that the concept of global welfare or global public interest is by no means settled and that there are at least two ways of understanding this concept.[44] First, it may be conceived of as an aggregation, of various states' national public interest which is reached by compromise and adherence to which is dependent on mutual co-operation. Alternatively, it may be viewed as a standard derived from international norms or doctrines to which individual states comply without regard to the position taken, or compliance thereof, by other states. The second scenario is the one which prevails because the current international IP framework provides

37 Ncube (2013) p. 374.
38 Ncube (2015) pp. 54–56.
39 Okediji (2004) p. 233.
40 Royal Society of Arts (RSA) (2006).
41 Global Congress on Intellectual Property and the Public Interest (2011).
42 Okediji (2004) p. 234.
43 Okediji (1999) p. 123.
44 See for example, Okediji (2014) p. 4.

a public interest standard which individual states interpret and implement differently in their territories.

Whilst the concept of the global public interest is not well developed, it has been articulated to a certain extent in international IP agreements. For example, articles 7 and 8 of TRIPS take a normative stance with regard to the welfare goals of IP standards agreed upon in the agreement.

Article 7 provides:

> The protection and enforcement of intellectual property rights should contribute to the promotion of technological innovation and to the transfer and dissemination of technology, to the mutual advantage of producers and users of technological knowledge and in a manner conducive to social and economic welfare, and to a balance of rights and obligations.

This provision takes cognisance of the competing interests of producers and users of technological knowledge and calls for an equitable balancing of these interests. However, its meaning and import is contestable, and has created a 'crisis of confidence and jurisprudence in its relation to the application of the global IPR rules that developing countries have continued to grapple with.'[45] For example, it has been pointed out that the transfer and dissemination of technological knowledge is upon the terms dictated by the IP right-holders who tend to be from developed states.[46] Further, although the compulsory licensing provisions in TRIPS are 'relatively generous' in theory, in practice their benefits have only been marginally realized with regard to patents[47] whilst they have so far yielded limited results in relation to copyright[48] and are not applicable to trademarks.[49]

Article 7's pro-development position is reinforced by article 8 which in part provides:

> 1. Members may, in formulating or amending their laws and regulations, adopt measures necessary to protect public health and nutrition, and to promote the *public interest* in sectors of vital importance to their socio-economic and technological development, provided that such measures are consistent with the provisions of this Agreement.
> 2. Appropriate measures, provided that they are consistent with the provisions of this Agreement, may be needed to prevent the abuse of intellectual

45 Adewopo (2012) p. 29. The Doha Development Agenda was established by the Doha WTO Ministerial Declaration (adopted 14 November 2001) Doc. WT/MIN(01)/DEC/1 20 November 2001.

46 Rahmatian (2009) p. 52.

47 Article 31 TRIPS and the 2003 Doha Decision on the implementation of par 6 of the Doha Declaration Doc. WT/L/540 and Corr.1 (1 September 2003). For a discussion of the use of flexibilities in relation to patents for pharmaceuticals see Matthews and Correa (2011); Matthews (2005); Avafia, Berger and Hartzenberg (2006).

48 Articles 9(1) and 13 TRIPS.

49 Article 21 TRIPS; Rahmatian (2009) pp. 52–53.

> property rights by right holders or the resort to practices which unreasonably restrain trade or adversely affect the international transfer of technology. [emphasis added]

Article 8 'formulates the general guidelines to be observed by WTO members when they adopt exceptions to the exclusive rights conferred by IPRs.'[50] To this end, it provides for the permissible 'political objective' of the state and for the twin restraints of necessity and consistency that must guide the state.[51]

These two articles are particularly significant because they articulate the goal of IP law formulation, protection and enforcement as the promotion of the public interest and socio-economic welfare. They have been characterized as being 'aspirational'[52] and as being the lens through which TRIPS must be viewed or interpreted.[53]

These provisions have been deployed powerfully by developing countries to achieve significant gains for the development cause. A case in point is how they have been credited as the foundation of the Doha Development Agenda[54] and its outcomes such as the Doha Declaration on the TRIPS Agreement and Public Health.[55] A second example is how they provided pivotal support for developing countries' successful proposal for the adoption of the WIPO DA[56] which is discussed further below.

The meaning of the global public interest concept has been canvassed elsewhere at length by others who have argued that the way in which it is articulated in the TRIPS Agreement has some detrimental effects for the global south/developing world.[57] Therefore it will not be the focus of this chapter. Instead, the next section considers how the national public interest has been defined and deployed by African states, at international, continental, sub-regional and national levels.

A national public interest?

Internally, each state sets its own national priorities through prescribed processes such as ministerial or departmental drafting followed by necessary approvals, perhaps through parliament. For example, South Africa categorises certain industrial sectors such as tourism as priority sectors. Any national regulatory scheme, including IP, would therefore have to be supportive of growth and development in these sectors. A state will also have certain obligations to its citizenry to provide essential

50 Rodrigues Jr. (2012) p. 45.
51 Rodrigues Jr. (2012) p. 45.
52 Dreyfuss (2004) p. 22.
53 Gervais (2003) pp. 120, 122; Kapczynski (2009).
54 Adewopo (2012) p. 38.
55 Doha Declaration on the TRIPS Agreement and Public Health (adopted 14 November 2001), Doc. WT/MIN(01)/DEC/2 (20 November 2001). For a detailed discussion see Kongolo (2013a) pp. 199–219, 285.
56 Yu (2009).
57 Gana (1996) p. 744; Harris (2007) pp. 203–204.

services and facilitate the attainment of their constitutional or human rights such as the right to health[58] and a basic education.[59] Consequently, while IP is only one of the factors that impact the attainment of these rights, it is significant and ought to be given due weight. When IP policies and laws are being debated and crafted, the public interest is served when the concerns and rights of creators, users and society generally are all taken into account and are appropriately provided for. In some cases, constitutional rights serve as a tie-breaker of these contesting interests.[60] For instance in discussions of patents and access to medicines or copyright and access to learning materials, the right to health and a basic education, respectively, acquire a great significance.

In its role as custodian and driver of this process, the state ought to be 'a guardian of welfare for all its subjects'. However, unfortunately, in certain cases the state's focus is captured, and driven, by the lobbying of a segment of society.[61] Sadly, examples of this are easy to find. It has been pointed out by many scholars that in the United States, copyright holders have captured copyright legislative processes through extensive and entrenched lobbying.[62] Some of these right-holders have extended their reach and influence to developing countries through local chapters or branches of international right-holder organizations.[63]

The same phenomenon is evident in the field of patents. For example early in 2014, a strategy proposed to the Innovative Pharmaceutical Association of South Africa (IPASA) to capture the national IP policy drafting process was unveiled by the local and international press.[64] It was reported that the pharmaceutical companies intended to work with a US lobbying group, Public Affairs Engagement, and a local 'front-man' to ensure that the policy protected their interests.[65] The front man was required to give the campaign a local face and veil the fact that there was foreign, US-based strategic direction being given to the campaign. The Minister of Health was livid at these revelations and went as far as to call these plans genocide. Thereafter the plan was quickly disavowed[66] and some organizational changes were implemented at the pharma organization.[67] At the time of writing, March 2015, the national IP policy was still not finalized.

The capture of legislative and policy making processes by industry players or IP right holders is often detrimental to the interests of users as users frequently lack the same level of resources and organizational capacity to forcefully advance their interests. Consequently, only one voice is heard and the other is disregarded, resulting in inequitable IP regimes. Watching this scenario unfold in African states

58 For a discussion see Helfer and Austin (2011) pp. 90–170.
59 For a discussion see Helfer and Austin (2011) pp. 315–363.
60 Ncube (2013) pp. 378–381.
61 Okediji (2003b).
62 Loren (2008) p. 37; Samuelson (2013).
63 Deere-Birbkeck (2008) pp. 111, 114–115.
64 de Wet (2014a); Motsoeneng (2014).
65 See Public Affairs Engagement (PAE) (2014).
66 de Wet (2014b).
67 Kahn (2014).

is very distressing because, as shown below, on the international plane African states have consistently called for nuanced systems which are best achieved through the prudent use of flexibilities and policy space in the national sphere.

African states' diversity and the need for flexible and nuanced IP systems

An analysis of statements by African states indicates that their vision for IP laws in the public interest is for appropriately calibrated laws that are fitting for a state's current conditions. For example, at WIPO meetings and discussions, the African Group[68] and the Development Agenda Group (DAG)[69] have repeatedly said that an appropriately balanced or nuanced system is one that takes a country's socio-economic conditions and development goals into account and not one that is based on a 'one size fits all' and 'IP as an end itself' perspective. These views are clearly articulated in para 7 of the African proposal for the establishment of a DA for WIPO as follows[70]:

> IP is just one mechanism among many for bringing about development. It should be used to support and enhance the legitimate economic aspirations of all developing countries including LDCs, especially in the development of their productive forces, comprising of both human and natural resources. IP should therefore, be complimentary [sic] and not detrimental to individual national efforts at development, by becoming a veritable tool for economic growth.

The same perspective was expressed in para 1 of the DAG's Guiding Principles where the DAG applauded the adoption of the DA as[71]:

> a milestone in achieving the historic aspiration of developing countries for a paradigm shift in the international perspective of intellectual property (IP): a shift from viewing IP as an end in itself, to viewing it as a means to serve the larger public goals of social, economic and cultural development. This vision has refuted the universal applicability of 'one size fits all IP protection models' or the advisability of the harmonization of laws leading to higher protection standards in all countries irrespective of the levels of development.

68 Shabalala (2007).

69 The DAG consists of countries that subscribe to the agreed guiding principles stated in the DAG Guiding Principles Paper WIPO Doc CDIP/5/9 Rev. As at 26 April 2010 this group comprised of Algeria, Brazil, Cuba, Djibouti, Ecuador, Egypt, Guatemala, India, Indonesia, Iran (Islamic Republic of), Malaysia, Pakistan, Philippines, South Africa, Sri Lanka, Sudan, Uruguay and Yemen.

70 African proposal for the establishment of a development agenda for WIPO Doc IIM/3/2 Rev, 31 July 2005.

71 WIPO Doc CDIP/5/9 Rev, 26 April 2010.

Chapter 5 will consider the continental effort to establish the Pan-African IP Organization (PAIPO) against the backdrop of this pro-development position taken by African states at WIPO. It will consider whether, having won a hard-fought battle with the adoption of the DA at WIPO, African states have remained true to that vision in the Draft PAIPO Statute.

As stated above, African states exhibit extensive diversity in their national socio-economic, political and cultural profiles. The categorization of states as either developing countries or LDCs illustrates this starkly. As at June 2013, 34 of the AU's 54 member states were classified as LDCs.[72] The other 20 ranked as developing countries. However, there are disparities in their levels of development. For example, in 2013, under the more nuanced Human Development Index (HDI) calibration, Libya, Mauritius, Seychelles, Tunisia and Algeria were classified as having 'high human development' making them the highest-ranking African states on the HDI for 2013.[73]

The above developing country/LDC and HDI classifications are indicators of economic development, the understanding of which has evolved over time.[74] The classic definition is that economic development is 'the process by which per capita income and economic welfare of a country improve over time.'[75] Working from this definition, economic development would then be measured by tracking gross domestic product (GDP) trends. There has been a definitive movement in the comprehension of how economic development happens and how it should be measured.[76] The more progressive conceptualization is that measurement of real growth in economic welfare ought to concern itself with more than just the growth of GDP.[77] Sen argues that economic development is not confined to 'formal economic opportunities that are available (such as free markets, open trade, transactional facilities), but ultimately about the effective freedoms and capabilities that people have . . . to have basic economic needs fulfilled.'[78] Therefore we should be more concerned about 'human development accounting' which 'involves a systematic examination of a wealth of information about how human beings in each society live.'[79] Working from this premise, the United Nations Development Program (UNDP) has been publishing human development indices annually since 1990.

African states require flexible and nuanced or 'fine tuned'[80] IP systems in view of their differing national conditions and their stated desire for appropriately nuanced solutions. The following sections detail contribution to the development of the WIPO DA and their efforts to domesticate patent related TRIPS flexibilities.

72 Merso (2013) p. 1.
73 UNDP (2014) pp. 160–161.
74 Adelman (1961) p. 1; Arndt (1989) pp. 1–5.
75 Jain et al (2008) p. 2.
76 Sen (1997) pp. 1–2, 26.
77 Anand and Sen (2000) p. 2032.
78 Sen (2000a).
79 Sen (2000b) p. 18.
80 Kilic (2015) p. 209.

African states' contribution to the articulation and formulation of the Development Agenda at WIPO

> *WIPO's Development Agenda is the most significant IP matter to confront the international community since the TRIPS Agreement and perhaps ever.*[81]

The events and discussions leading up to the adoption of the WIPO DA have been well documented and analysed elsewhere,[82] hence this section will only offer a brief synopsis. The adoption of the agenda was initiated by a proposal from Argentina and Brazil.[83] This initiative garnered the support of other developing states (collectively known as the Group of Friends of Development)[84] and after a series of meetings,[85] a seminar culminated in the establishment of a Provisional Committee on Proposals related to the WIPO DA (PCDA) which drafted proposals which it refined over time.[86] Ultimately in 2007, 45 recommendations were agreed upon by member states.[87] Soon thereafter, organizational changes were made at WIPO to ensure the management and implementation of the DA. The Committee on Development and Intellectual Property (CDIP) and its secretariat, the DA Coordination Division (DACD) were created. Since then the CDIP has met annually[88] and a number of projects have been implemented,[89] some of which have been subjected to external review.[90] The CDIP reports annually to the General Assembly on its progress on its following mandate[91]:

81 de Beer (2009) pp. 2–3.

82 See for example Sell (2011); Netanel (2009) p.1; de Beer (2009); May (2008, 2007).

83 WIPO (n.d.); Proposal by Argentina and Brazil for the Establishment of a Development Agenda for WIPO, WO/GA/31/11.

84 Proposal to Establish a Development Agenda for WIPO: An Elaboration of Issues Raised in Document WO/GA/31/11 WIPO Doc IIM/1/4. (Group of Friends Elaboration Document IIM/1/4). The members of the group were Argentina and Brazil, Bolivia, Cuba, the Dominican Republic, Ecuador, Egypt, Iran, Kenya, Peru, Sierra Leone, South Africa, Tanzania and Venezuela; Shabalala (2007) p. 24, n18.

85 For example, see WIPO Inter-Sessional Intergovernmental Meeting on a Development Agenda for WIPO, First Session, Geneva, April 11 to 13, 2005 Report. (IIM/1/6).

86 WIPO Provisional Committee on Proposals Related to the WIPO Development Agenda (PCDA) First Session, February 20–24 2006 (PCDA 1/6 Prov 2); WIPO PCDA Fourth Session, June 11–15 2007 (PCDA /4/3) WIPO PCDA Fourth Session, June 11–15 2007. (PCDA/4/3. Annex).

87 Assemblies of the Member States of WIPO, Forty-Third Series of Meetings, Geneva, September 24 to October 3, 2007, WIPO General Assembly Report A/43/16 (November 12, 2007).

88 Details of meetings and documents are available at <http://www.wipo.int/meetings/en/topic.jsp?group_id=241>.

89 List of projects and progress reports are available at <http://www.wipo.int/ip-development/en/agenda/projects.html>.

90 For example the 'Project on Enhancement of WIPO's Results-Based Management (RBM) Framework to Support the Monitoring and Evaluation of the Impact of the Organization's Activities on Development' which included the implementation of Development Agenda Recommendations 33, 38 and 41 was evaluated in Deere-Birkbeck and Roca (2011).

91 CDIP <http://www.wipo.int/policy/en/cdip/>.

1. develop a work-program for implementing the 45 adopted DA recommendations;
2. monitor, assess, discuss and report on the implementation of all recommendations adopted; and for that purpose to co-ordinate with relevant WIPO bodies; and
3. discuss IP and development-related issues as agreed by the Committee, as well as those decided by the General Assembly.

At the adoption of the DA, its normative impact was difficult to predict due to its non-binding status in relation to both WIPO[92] and its member states.[93] However, it was clear that it could not be ignored due to its moral effect.[94] Indeed, immediate organizational restructuring was carried out at WIPO, which was followed by the roll-out of projects as described above.

Several years after its adoption and some implementation, as initially predicted, the WIPO DA has proven to be complex and not easy to define.[95] Its distinctive features have been identified as its 'malleability, complexity, opportunity and gravity.'[96] It is said to be malleable because it contains ambiguities which it is hoped will be interpreted in a manner consistent with the socio-economic condition of developing states. It owes its complexity to the diverse nature of its stakeholders and the availability of other fora where it may be advanced or thwarted ('forum proliferation').[97] Despite such complexity and malleability it continues to present WIPO with an amazing opportunity to redeem itself and recreate itself as an organization that truly advances the socio-economic development of its member states through a 'calibrated' approach to IP that is country-context sensitive.[98] Sell notes that although some articulated cautionary views[99] and others were carefully optimistic[100] about the DA's ability to actually bring about real change, there have been glimmers of fulfilled promise through meaningful scrutiny of WIPO's delivery of technical assistance.[101]

In its rejection of an 'IP-centric view',[102] the WIPO DA is in essence 'an attempted paradigm shift' at WIPO from the furtherance of IP centric goals to a move to the prioritization of the 'public policy aspects of IP rights.'[103] It was clear from experience, that technology transfer and FDI did not always follow from TRIPS compliance, as Dreyfuss notes the reality was that 'it had not happened.'[104]

92 de Beer (2009) p. 11.
93 de Beer (2009) p. 11.
94 de Beer (2009) p. 12.
95 de Beer (2009) p. 3.
96 de Beer (2009) pp. 9–17.
97 de Beer (2009) p. 13.
98 de Beer (2009) p. 15.
99 Maksus (2009) p. 163.
100 Okediji (2009).
101 Sell (2011) p. 20.
102 Netanel (2009) p. 2.
103 de Beer (2009) pp. 2–3.
104 Dreyfuss (2004) p. 29.

It acknowledges that the impact of undifferentiated application of strong IP regimes globally is not always an increase in the various facets of creative and economic progress.[105] Instead, it is based on the premise that what is required is a calibrated approach that allows developing countries to benefit from a robust public domain and make use of flexibilities in their national policy space.[106] This exposition of the position taken by African states on the international plane will be used as a comparator for the positions these states have taken on the continent. For example, is the current push towards the creation of PAIPO congruent with the stated African position at WIPO?

TRIPS implementation by African states

TRIPS implementation involves domesticating the agreement's minimum IP standards whilst making appropriate use of its flexibilities to cater for a jurisdiction's unique socio-economic conditions. Developing countries and LDCs struggle with both aspects of TRIPS implementation,[107] and those in Africa are no exception. This is largely because the TRIPS deal was not concluded in their best interests and some of the agreement's minimum standards are not tenable for them. Indeed, Deere comments that its conclusion was 'a victory for those multinational companies determined to raise international IP standards and boost IP protection in developing countries.'[108] She also notes that developing countries had sounded concern that the agreement would hinder the achievement of their developmental goals and would be unlikely to yield significant benefits for them.[109] Further, the very process of domestication is fraught with difficulty for developing countries and LDCs as they have limited technical expertise and are thus hampered in this task.[110] Experience has shown that these misgivings were well founded as the implementation of TRIPS has had mixed results for some African states[111] and is still nowhere near attainable for LDCs. The following section considers to what extent flexibilities have been utilized by African states.

TRIPS flexibilities

The term 'TRIPS flexibilities' refers to those provisions in TRIPS that provide some policy space for party states to calibrate their domestic IP regimes.[112] A basic

105 Netanel (2009) p. 2.
106 Ibid.
107 Kapczynski (2009).
108 Deere (2009) p. 1.
109 Deere (2009) p. 1.
110 Musungu, Villanueva and Blasetti (2004) p. 24.
111 For example see the analysis of Francophone Africa's experiences of implementation from 1995–2007 in Deere (2009) pp. 240–286.
112 For discussion of the development of the phrase see Blakeney and Mengistie (2011) pp. 243–244. Also see Patent Related Flexibilities in the Multilateral Legal Framework and their Legislative Implementation at the National and Regional Levels (2010) CDIP/5/4 rev. para 33–34.

categorization of flexibilities is the distinction between transition periods and flexibilities that pertain to the actual content of substantive provisions.

Various transition periods were provided for to enable the implementation of TRIPS by WTO member states. All WTO members were afforded a year after the coming into force of TRIPS before they became obliged to comply with it.[113] In addition, developing countries were afforded an additional 4 years' transition period out of recognition of their disadvantaged position.[114] However, they were required to comply with articles 3, 4 and 5 which pertain to non-discrimination. This meant that they did not have to apply TRIPS in full until 1 January 2000. Further, they could postpone pharmaceutical and agricultural chemicals patent protection until 1 January 2005.[115] If they did so, they were required to permit the filing of patent applications as from 1 January 1995 which would then be examined at the time when that country began to issue these patents.[116] If the product was marketing during the transition period, exclusive marketing rights were to be granted to the patent applicant.[117] LDCs were granted an initial transition period that ran to 1 January 2006.[118] The LDC transition period was extended to 1 July 2013 and most recently to 1 July 2021 or sooner if a country ceases to become an LDC before that date.[119]

Other transition periods pertain to the grant of pharmaceutical patents, which LDCs are not expected to grant before 1 January 2016.[120] The pharmaceutical transition period is two-fold in the sense that it originates from two decisions, namely TRIPS Council Decision, IP/C/25, on product patent and data protections, and General Council Decision, WT/L/478, on exclusivity rights under Article 70(9).[121]

The exact status of this pharmaceutical transition period has been debated since the extension of the LDC transition period to 2021. The debate pertains to whether the 2016 pharmaceutical patent waiver has now been subsumed into the 2021 transition period. It has been argued that this is not the case and that LDCs would have to motivate for an extension of this waiver otherwise they would be required to begin issuing patents for pharmaceuticals after 1 January 2016. Indeed, in October 2014 LDCs notified the TRIPS Council that they would be formally requesting an extension of this transition period at the 2015 TRIPS Council.[122]

113 Article 65(1) TRIPS.
114 Article 65(2) TRIPS.
115 Article 65(4) TRIPS.
116 Article 70(8) TRIPS.
117 Article 70 (9) TRIPS.
118 Article 66(1) TRIPS.
119 WTO Decision of the Council for Trade-Related Aspects of Intellectual Property Rights Extension of the Transition Period under Article 66.1 for Least Developed Country Members (11 June 2013) IP/C/64. For an overview of the genesis and extent of the original extension period as well as the latest extension request made in 2012, see Abbott (2013).
120 Article 66(1) TRIPS; paragraph 7 Doha Declaration on TRIPS Agreement and Public Health (WT/MIN(01)/DEC/2).
121 Baker (2015) p. 1.
122 Baker (2015).

In addition to the distinction between transitional and substantive flexibilities, further distinctions can be made according to:

1. the IP right the flexibilities are associated with;
2. their purpose[123]; and
3. the timing of the availability of the flexibility.

The first classification categorizes flexibilities according to the type of IP they apply to, for example as a copyright-related flexibility or a patent-related flexibility. The second categorization goes to the reason why a state may resort to a particular flexibility. For example, it may be to meet public health goals by making pharmaceuticals more readily available at lower prices or to curb anti-competitive activities. Under the third manner of categorization listed above, a flexibility is classified according whether it is available[124]:

(i) in the process of the acquisition of the right;
(ii) defining the scope of the right; and
(iii) in the process of enforcing the right.

Here the question being asked is at what stage in the life cycle of the IP right the flexibility is applicable. It may be when it is being created or acquired and expressed through formal or substantive requirements for application and grant. For example, it may relate to how much information is required to be disclosed by the applicant in the application.[125] In the definition of the scope of rights, flexibilities pertain to exactly what is protected by IP and which uses are permitted in the public interest. Exceptions to IPRs, compulsory licenses and provisions pertaining to parallel imports are included in this category.[126] In relation to enforcement, party states have some leeway in their domestic provision for remedies for infringement. For example, they may provide for punitive damages in instances of wilful or flagrant infringement.[127]

These classifications can be used simultaneously to characterize a single flexibility. For example, one could categorize compulsory licenses as patent related flexibilities that serve public health goals and are available post patent grant. The main patent-related flexibilities are outlined below. It is important to stress that the following is not a comprehensive or exhaustive statement of flexibilities.

123 Correa (2013) p. 418.

124 Patent Related Flexibilities in the Multilateral Legal Framework and their Legislative Implementation at the National and Regional Levels (2010) CDIP/5/4 rev. para 36.

125 Patent Related Flexibilities in the Multilateral Legal Framework and their Legislative Implementation at the National and Regional Levels (2010) CDIP/5/4 rev. para 37.

126 Patent Related Flexibilities in the Multilateral Legal Framework and their Legislative Implementation at the National and Regional Levels (2010) CDIP/5/4 rev. para 38.

127 Patent Related Flexibilities in the Multilateral Legal Framework and their Legislative Implementation at the National and Regional Levels (2010) CDIP/5/4 rev. para 39.

A. Definition of invention and other patent grant related flexibilities

Article 27.1 of TRIPS provides

> Subject to the provisions of paragraphs 2 and 3, patents shall be available for any inventions, whether products or processes, in all fields of technology, provided that they are new, involve an inventive step and are capable of industrial application. Subject to paragraph 4 of Article 65, paragraph 8 of Article 70 and paragraph 3 of this Article, patents shall be available and patent rights enjoyable without discrimination as to the place of invention, the field of technology and whether products are imported or locally produced.

Whilst party states are obliged to extend patent protection to inventions in all fields of technology, they have leeway when it comes to defining what constitutes an invention. This flexibility can be used to prohibit the patenting of second or new uses of pharmaceuticals,[128] a practice commonly known as ever-greening. Typically, it plays itself out as follows: a patent subsists in a pharmaceutical compound that is used for the treatment of a certain condition, perhaps in particular dosage and in combination with another compound. A few years before the expiry of the patent, the patent holder discloses that that use of the compound is no longer effective and it now has to be used in combination with another compound or in a different dosage or changes its pharmaceutical composition slightly. Alternatively a new use could be found for the medication (second medical indication). A patent is then registered over the 'new' compound, combination or use, thus further extending the patent holder's economic exclusivity or 'ever-greening' the patent. In order to avert or curb this practice, national legislation could provide that new uses of compounds are excluded from patentability.[129]

In addition to policy space pertaining to the definition of an invention, states may also regulate the following in a flexible way[130]:

- the determination of what constitutes an inventive step;
- the disclosure that is required to sustain a successful patent application;
- the examination of patent applications; and
- whether or not substances existing in nature are patentable.

It has been suggested that a strict test for inventive step that references a 'person highly skilled in the art' instead of the commonly used ordinary skill standard ought to be introduced in order to ensure that stronger patents are registered.[131] It has also been suggested that states should require the disclosure of 'all modes' of implementing an invention, an 'express indication of the best mode for carrying

128 Musungu, Villanueva and Blasetti (2004) p. 15.
129 Musungu, Villanueva and Blasetti (2004) p. 15.
130 Correa (2013) pp. 419–423; Sibanda (2013).
131 EAC TRIPS Policy p. 13; Park, Prabhala and Berger (2013).

out an invention by experts skilled in the art, who reside in the respective' jurisdiction and information pertaining to related foreign patent applications and the grant thereof.[132] The substantive examination of patents would also weed out sub-patentable inventions. Finally, it has been recommended that natural substances should be excluded from patentability.[133]

B. Parallel imports

Parallel importation occurs when goods that are lawfully available in one market (A) are purchased there and imported into another jurisdiction (B) without the authorization of the holder of IP rights in the goods and are thereafter traded on the open market in B, in competition with the IP right-holder or his licensees.[134]

The TRIPS provision that grants party states policy space to provide for parallel importation in their domestic laws is article 6 which provides[135]:

> For the purposes of dispute settlement under this Agreement, subject to the provisions of Articles 3 and 4 nothing in this Agreement shall be used to address the issue of the exhaustion of intellectual property rights.

An IP right-holder's rights are exhausted when the protected goods have been lawfully sold or distributed. If a jurisdiction subscribes to the principle of national exhaustion then the rights are exhausted when the product is first distributed on the national market. Where international exhaustion applies, then its distribution anywhere in the world exhausts the right-holders' rights.

As is clear from article 6 above, each WTO member state is at liberty to select either the national or international regime of exhaustion. Where international exhaustion applies a citizen or resident of that country is then able to purchase the product from another market and then import it into their country of residence for further trade or distribution. This is a very useful way of accessing products from another market when they are not available or are unaffordable in a person's country of residence and has been used in various contexts for example by South African activists to procure generic medication for HIV/AIDS.[136]

C. Compulsory licenses and government use

'A compulsory license is a license granted by an administrative or judicial body to a third party to exploit an invention without the authorization of the patent

132 EAC TRIPS Policy p. 17.

133 EAC (2013) p. 13.

134 Musungu, Villanueva and Blasetti (2004) p. 13.

135 Also see para. 5(d) of the Doha Declaration on the TRIPS Agreement and Public Health WT/MIN (01)/DEC/W/2, 14 November 2001.

136 For example see Heywood (2001) for an account of how activists brought HIV/AIDS medication into South Africa.

holder.'[137] Such licenses may be issued to permit the production and distribution of generic medication[138] which is often cheaper than patented and branded medication. Article 31 of TRIPS provides a series of conditions under which such licenses may be issued. Examples of these conditions include the following: article 31(h) provides that satisfactory remuneration must be paid to the patent-holder paying consideration to the 'economic value of the license.' Article 31(f) provides that use of the medicines manufactured under compulsory license shall be 'predominantly for the supply of the domestic market.' This limitation prevents countries with the capacity to make generics under compulsory licenses from exporting a significant amount of those generics to other countries which is to the detriment of countries who would seek to import generics from them. It has since been 'softened' by the 'paragraph 6 solution' of the 2003 Waiver Decision which was then incorporated into TRIPS as article 31 bis by the 2005 amendment of the Agreement. The amendment will come into force after its acceptance by two-thirds of WTO members and in the interim the Waiver Decision applies.[139] This solution is a rule-based waiver of the article 31(f) requirement. It removed the limits on exports under compulsory license to WTO member states with limited pharmaceutical products manufacturing capacity, provided that the relevant member states met certain conditions. For example, both the exporting and importing countries have to issue compulsory licenses and advise the TRIPS Council of the import and export. However, this solution is complex and impracticable[140] and has only been used once, by Rwanda and Canada.[141]

D. Exceptions

Article 30 of TRIPS provides:

> Members may provide limited exceptions to the exclusive rights conferred by a patent, provided that such exceptions do not unreasonably conflict with a normal exploitation of the patent and do not unreasonably prejudice the legitimate interests of the patent owner, taking account of the legitimate interests of third parties.

This provision contains the so-called Three Step Test which made its first appearance in the Berne Convention. Examples of exceptions under this provision include

137 Musungu, Villanueva & Blasetti (2004) p. 12.

138 Ncube (2009) p. 681 defines generics as 'medication that consists of the same active medicinal substance as an originator pharmaceutical product and because they act in the same way in the human body, they are interchangeable with the originator product'.

139 WTO (n.d.); General Council Amendment of the TRIPS Agreement – Fourth Extension of the Period for the Acceptance by Members of the Protocol Amending the TRIPS Agreement, Decision of 26 November 2013, WT/L/899.

140 For a detailed statement of its working see WHO, WIPO and WTO (2012) pp. 224–228.

141 For commentary see Nkomo (2013); Outterson (2010); Ncube (2009) pp. 686–687; Andemariam (2007); Abbott and Reichman (2007).

the research and experimentation exception and the early working exception, which is also known as the Bolar provision.[142] The research and experimentation exception allows creators and manufacturers scope to use patented technology (e.g. product or pharmaceutical) in an experimental manner in order to create alternatives.[143] Bolar provisions enable competitors to use or otherwise exploit patented pharmaceuticals to make a generic version, then to obtain 'the regulatory approval and registration of a generic product before the expiry of the patent term.'[144]

The next section considers how African states have utilized these flexibilities.

African states' use of transition periods

Generally, many African LDCs have benefitted from using transition periods. However, pharmaceutical patents are granted by many LDCs despite existence of the LDC transition period for granting these patents until January 2016. For example, LDC SADC member states grant such patents.[145] Similarly, LDC OAPI member states voluntarily subscribed to TRIPS standards in 2002 via the revised Bangui Agreement, well before the expiry of the initial LDC compliance transition period.[146] This development has been rightly criticized by some scholars and commentators for being both inappropriate and premature as the socio-economic conditions in these states did not warrant it.[147] Deere ascribes the LDC OAPI member states' decision to the following five factors[148]:

1. limited technical knowledge of IP matters and TRIPS standards coupled with a heavy reliance on technical assistance that promoted such early adoption;
2. strong pro-IP external pressure exerted on isolated, poorly resourced and inadequately networked national IP offices;
3. the domination of national IP offices by a relatively powerful OAPI Secretariat, which unfortunately was also vulnerable to external pro-IP influences;
4. the compromise of OAPI's decision-making by a combination of the above factors and the application of external pressure by donors and the providers of technical assistance; and
5. a susceptible political environment that had been persuaded to adopt an unquestioning commitment to uncalibrated early TRIPS compliance.

It has been argued that a robust TRIPS and TRIPS-plus legal framework is a necessary pre-condition to economic development. If this assertion is correct, then one would expect that OAPI's LDCs would by now have achieved some

142 Musungu, Villanueva and Blasetti (2004) p. 17.

143 Musungu, Villanueva and Blasetti (2004) p. 17. *Canada – Patent Protection of Pharmaceutical Products*, Report of the Panel adopted on April 7, 2000 (WT/DS114/R, of March 17, 2000).

144 Musungu, Villanueva and Blasetti (2004) p. 17.

145 Musungu (2012) p. 9.

146 Deere (2009) p. 240.

147 Deere (2009) p. 240.

148 Deere (2009) pp. 241–242.

demonstrable economic progress, which could partially be ascribed to their early adoption of TRIPS standards. However, more than a decade after their adoption of TRIPS standards, none of them has managed to make significant economic development gains, let alone transition to developed country status. One obvious reason for this may be that whilst they have domesticated TRIPS, they are yet to fully apply and enforce it due to various resource and capacity constraints. Paradoxically, the existence of these constraints is the very reason why they should not have been early adopters of these standards.

It has been argued that OAPI member states caved in to external pressure to adopt TRIPS standards earlier than they were obliged to, to alleviate the pressure they were under, knowing full well that they would not be in a position to fully apply and enforce them.[149] If this is indeed the case, then OAPI and its member states would have acted in bad faith. However, if any moral blameworthiness is to be ascribed, it ought to also extend to those parties who exerted pressure on OAPI to make this decision, when it was not yet legally required and member states' national conditions were not conducive to, and would not benefit from, such a robust IP regime. Whilst such claims are difficult to substantiate and test, it is certainly true that any attempt to resort to any available WTO TRIPS enforcement avenue against non-performing resource-constrained LDCs would be reprehensible.

African states' use of substantive patent-related flexibilities

African states are yet to make full use of substantive patent-related TRIPS flexibilities. Although continuing efforts are being made, with technical assistance from UNDP and other UN agencies, to achieve this.[150] There are several significant international and continental developments that are relevant to these endeavours. These include the WHO's Global Strategy and Plan of Action on Public Health, Innovation and IP, the African Union Health Strategy and Pharmaceutical Manufacturing Plan for Africa (PMPA), 2007 and the initiative on Strengthening Pharmaceutical Innovation Africa, which has the endorsement of the African Ministerial Conference on Science and Technology (AMCOST).[151] In 2012 the AU Heads of State endorsed the PMPA Business Plan (PMPA BP) which was jointly developed by the AU Commission (AUC) and UNIDO. The PMPA BP reiterates the reasons for African states' failure to utilize flexibilities noted above and makes this stark call:

> Africa therefore faces a simple choice in the next four years – to fully exploit the TRIPS flexibilities and accelerate the ongoing negotiations for an extension to the 2016 transition period or face the prospect of paying more for drugs in the future.[152]

149 Deere (2009) p. 241.
150 For example see Republic of Botswana (2013).
151 Berger et al (2010) p. 7.
152 AU PMPA BP (2012) p. 50.

It then details options for implementation at various levels. Notably, it stresses that RECs and ARIPO have a role to play in leading and supoorting their member states' efforts to domesticate and implement flexibilities.[153]

RECs have responded to this call and initiated sub-regional initiatives to realise the meaningful use of patent-related flexibilities in tandem with Pharmaceutical Business Plans. For example, the EAC Regional Pharmaceutical Manufacturing Plan of Action (2012–2016) and SADC's Pharmaceutical Business Plan (2007–2013). The EAC has developed policies and protocols on the incorporation of patent-related TRIPS flexibilities into national laws, whilst SADC is in the process of creating such frameworks. African inter-governmental organizations (IGOs) are also involved in efforts to implement these flexibilities. A case in point is the East, Central and Southern Africa Health Community (ECSA-HC).[154] The current membership of this community comprises Kenya, Lesotho, Malawi, Mauritius, Seychelles, Swaziland, Tanzania, Uganda, Zambia and Zimbabwe.

The following section outlines how EAC, ECOWAS and SADC member states are currently utilizing transition and substantive patent-related flexibilities.

A case study of EAC, ECOWAS and SADC member states' use of TRIPS patent-related flexibilities

The membership of these three RECs is tabulated below, together with an indication of each state's developing country (DC) or LDC status and an indication of their sub-regional IP organization membership.

Table 1.1

EAC (5)		*ECOWAS (15)*		*SADC (15)*	
Burundi (LDC)	N/A	Benin (LDC)	OAPI	Angola (LDC)	N/A
Kenya (DC)	ARIPO	Burkina Faso (LDC)	OAPI	Botswana (DC)	ARIPO
Rwanda (LDC)	ARIPO	Cabo Verde	N/A	Democratic	N/A
Tanzania (LDC)	ARIPO	Cote D'Ivoire (DC)	OAPI	Republic of	
Uganda (LDC)	ARIPO	Ghana (DC)	ARIPO	Congo (LDC)	ARIPO
		Guinea (LDC)	OAPI	Lesotho (LDC)	ARIPO
		Guinea Bissau	OAPI	Madagascar (LDC)	N/A
		(LDC)	ARIPO	Malawi (LDC)	ARIPO
		Liberia (LDC)	OAPI	Mauritius (DC)	N/A
		Mali (LDC)	OAPI	Mozambique	ARIPO
		Niger (LDC)	OAPI	(LDC)	ARIPO
		Nigeria (DC)	N/A	Namibia (DC)	N/A
		Senegal (LDC)	ARIPO	Seychelles (DC)	N/A
		Sierra Leone (LDC)	ARIPO	South Africa (DC)	ARIPO
		The Gambia (LDC)	OAPI	Swaziland (DC)	ARIPO
		Togolese Republic	OAPI	Tanzania (LDC)	ARIPO
		(LDC)		Zambia (LDC)	
				Zimbabwe (DC)	

153 AU PMPA BP (2012) pp. 77, 79–80.

154 See for example, EQUINET and ECSA HC (2011).

This is a significant grouping of 35 states. Tanzania is the only state that is a member of two RECs of the three RECs under study. For purposes of the following discussion, it is important to note that whilst there are five EAC member states, there are in fact six legal systems to consider because Tanzania has two legal systems – Tanzania-Mainland and Tanzania-Zanzibar.

EAC, ECOWAS and SADC member states, with the exception of Liberia and Seychelles, are WTO members and are bound by the TRIPS Agreement. Both have commenced accession procedures. Seychelles is scheduled to become a member of the WTO by 1 June 2015,[155] whilst Liberia is also working towards attaining membership by the end of 2015.[156]

A. Definition of invention and other patent grant related flexibilities

EAC

Of the LDC states only Rwanda excludes pharmaceutical products from patent protection.[157] The other three have prematurely provided patent protection for pharmaceuticals.[158] Burundi and Tanzania-Zanzibar provide for data protection. Burundi, Rwanda and Tanzania-Zanzibar exclude the patenting of new uses for known products, whilst Tanzania-Mainland legislation is silent on the issue.[159] Kenyan legislation expressly permits such patents but provides for 'case by case exclusion for public health reasons' and the Ugandan legislation seems to permit such patents.[160] Burundi, Rwanda and Tanzania-Zanzibar exclude natural substances from patentability whilst Kenya and Uganda are silent on new substances.

ECOWAS

The OAPI member states grant pharmaceutical patents.[161] None of the ECOWAS member states' current legislation explicitly provides for provisions that may eliminate or reduce ever-greening, although draft amendment bills in Ghana and Nigeria include provisions that cover 'novelty and non-recognition of new uses' and other relevant aspects.[162]

155 WTO (2014a).
156 WTO (2014b).
157 EAC Regional Intellectual Property Policy on the Utilization of Public Health-Related WTO-TRIPS Flexibilities and the Approximation of National Intellectual Property Legislation, 2013 (EAC TRIPS Policy) p. 29.
158 EAC TRIPS Policy p. 29.
159 EAC TRIPS Policy p. 30.
160 EAC TRIPS Policy p. 30.
161 ECOWAS Development of a Harmonized TRIPS Policy for Adoption by ECOWAS Member States that Employ TRIPS Flexibilities to Improve Access to Medicines in the Region, 2012 (ECOWAS TRIPS Policy) p. 30.
162 ECOWAS TRIPS Policy p. 30.

SADC

SADC member states, including LDCs, grant pharmaceutical patents.[163] Only Malawi, Namibia and Zambia prohibit the patenting of new uses of pharmaceutical compounds.[164]

B. Parallel importation

EAC

Burundi, Kenya, Rwanda, Tanzania-Mainland and Tanzania-Zanzibar all have an international exhaustion regime for patent law whilst the meaning of the Ugandan patent provisions remains unclear.[165] In addition, Burundi and Tanzania-Zanzibar also extend this regime to trademarks.[166] Trademark rights may be declared to be exhausted in certain circumstances and measures may be taken to limit the use of marks to secure 'access to generic pharmaceutical products and medical devices.'[167]

ECOWAS

OAPI member states provide for a regional regime of exhaustion, whilst Cape Verde, Liberia, Nigeria and The Gambia all provide for a national exhaustion regime.[168] Ghana provides for international exhaustion and Sierra Leone has no applicable provisions.[169]

SADC

Most SADC member states do not have an international exhaustion regime so parallel importation is not possible. Three SADC countries have national exhaustion regimes, namely Madagascar, Mozambique and Tanzania.[170] Five member states have an international exhaustion regime, namely Botswana, Mauritius, Namibia, South Africa and Zimbabwe.[171]

163 Musungu (2012) p. 9.
164 Musungu (2012) p. 9.
165 EAC TRIPS Policy p. 32.
166 EAC TRIPS Policy p. 32.
167 EAC TRIPS Policy p. 32.
168 ECOWAS TRIPS Policy p. 32.
169 ECOWAS TRIPS Policy p. 32.
170 Musungu (2012) p. 10.
171 Musungu (2012) p. 10.

C. Compulsory licenses

EAC

All five member states have compulsory license provisions in their patent legislation that expressly reference the public interest and are broad enough to encompass public health needs.[172] As noted above, Rwanda has used the paragraph 6 solution to import generics from Canada.

ECOWAS

OAPI member states' provisions on ex-officio licenses are not broad enough to encompass the importation of medicines whilst Cape Verde, Ghana, Liberia, Nigeria and The Gambia have provisions that may enable this.[173] Sierra Leone does not have any applicable provisions.[174]

SADC

All SADC member states have provisions for compulsory licenses in their laws.[175] However, only a few SADC member states have issued compulsory licenses. In 2002 Zimbabwe declared a Period of Emergency to enable the government to issue licenses for a period of 6 months for the import of generic HIV/AIDS medication.[176] This period was extended for 5 years in 2003 and ran until 31 December 2008. During this period the government commenced local manufacture of generics medication through Varichem Pharmaceuticals (Private) Ltd. In 2004 Zambia issued a compulsory license to a local company (Pharco) to manufacture generic HIV/AIDS medication, namely lamivudine, stavudine and nevirapine with a 2.5 per cent royalty.[177] In the same year Pharco Moz Ltd was issued with a compulsory license to manufacture 3TC, D4T and nevirapine with the total amount of royalties set at 2 per cent of total turnover. It is important to note that there are many practical and capacity problems that attach to the local manufacture of generics.[178]

172 EAC TRIPS Policy p. 33.
173 ECOWAS TRIPS Policy p. 37.
174 ECOWAS TRIPS Policy p. 37.
175 Musungu (2012) p. 10.
176 Sibanda (2013).
177 Sibanda (2013).
178 For example see Owoeye (2014); UNCTAD (2011).

D. Exceptions

EAC

All member states have a research exception for scientific purposes but it only extends to commercial purposes in Tanzania-Zanzibar and Uganda.[179] Burundi, Rwanda, Tanzania-Zanzibar and Uganda provide for Bolar exceptions for obtaining market approvals worldwide.[180] Kenya limits the exception to national approvals granted by the Kenya Industrial Property Institute whilst Tanzania-Mainland does not provide for the Bolar exception at all.[181]

ECOWAS

Only Ghana, Liberia and Nigeria have provisions pertaining to research and experimental use exceptions.[182] Ghana's provision is wide enough to include use for commercial purposes.[183]

SADC

Madagascar and Swaziland have provision for exceptions that are broad enough to cover research, however these provisions are vague and do not cover commercially driven research.[184] Botswana, DRC, Lesotho, Mauritius, Mozambique, Namibia and Tanzania have specific research exemption provisions.[185] The other SADC member states have no provisions that cover research exemptions. Only Botswana, Namibia, South Africa and Zimbabwe have early working (Bolar) exceptions.[186]

In view of the above identified gaps in the implementing TRIPS flexibilities, the EAC, ECOWAS and SADC have ramped up their efforts to ensure better implementation by their member states. In particular, the EAC and ECOWAS have adopted policies, which are outlined below.

EAC's policy and protocol on TRIPS flexibilities

In 2013 the EAC adopted a Regional IP Policy on the Utilization of Public Health-Related WTO-TRIPS Flexibilities and the Approximation of National IP Legislation. This policy is based on the analysis of the EAC Partner States' national legislation and it aims to assist these states to meaningfully domesticate

179 EAC TRIPS Policy p. 31.
180 EAC TRIPS Policy p. 31.
181 EAC TRIPS Policy p. 31.
182 ECOWAS TRIPS Policy p. 27.
183 ECOWAS TRIPS Policy p. 27.
184 Musungu (2012) p. 10.
185 Musungu (2012) p. 10.
186 Musungu (2012) p. 10. See Ncube (2009) supra 685 for an outline of South Africa's Bolar exception provision – s 69A Patents Act.

and implement TRIPS Flexibilities. To this end it makes the eleven policy statements which are summarized below. Member states ought to:

1. 'take advantage of the 2016 transition period' and abolish any mailbox provisions in their laws.[187]
2. 'strictly define' patentability criteria specifically with regard to novelty, inventive step and industrial application. These aims are to be achieved in the following ways:

   'a. Considering a wide concept of prior art consisting of everything disclosed to the public whether by use, in written or oral form, including patent applications, information implied in any publication or derivable from a combination of publications, which are published anywhere in the world and which can be actually or theoretically accessed by the general public;
   b. Clearly define the inventive step standard by referring to a 'highly' skilled person;
   c. Strictly apply the industrial application requirement and limit the patentability of research tools to only those for which a specific use has been identified.'[188]

3. a. Exclude the following from patentability:

   'i. Natural substances including micro-organisms, even if purified or otherwise isolated from nature;
   ii. New medical uses of known substances including micro-organisms; EAC Partner States seeking to consider new medical uses principally patentable as processes under the patentability criteria, shall strictly apply the patentability requirements on a case-by-case basis;
   iii. Derivatives of medical products that do not show significantly enhanced therapeutic efficacy/significant superior properties.
   b. EAC Partner States, in order to protect small-scale innovations, e.g. in the areas of traditional medicines or genetic resources, shall reward such inventors with a right to compensation from third parties who use the inventions for follow-on improvements (use-and-pay/compensatory liability).'[189]

4. Provide for research exceptions that:

   'a. Explicitly authorise research for scientific, non-commercial and commercial purposes. The preponderant purpose of commercial research must be the generation of new knowledge of the patented substance.
   b. Provide a right to claim a non-exclusive licence for the use of patented research tools against payment of compensation.'[190]

187 EAC TRIPS Policy p. 12.
188 EAC TRIPS Policy pp. 12–13.
189 EAC TRIPS Policy p. 14.
190 EAC TRIPS Policy p. 15.

5. Provide for a Bolar exception that permits the 'use [of] patented substances for acts 'reasonably related' to the development and submission of information required for marketing approvals.'[191]
6. Upon the expiry of relevant transition periods, protect 'test and other data' in a way that enables the continued reliance on original test data by medicines regulatory authorities in their evaluation of generics. Further, patents and marketing authorization should not be connected in a manner that inhibits or prevents the grant of marketing approvals for generics during the validity of the relevant patent.[192]
7. Require the disclosure of all modes, including the best mode, of implementing an invention by 'experts skilled in the art who reside in EAC partner states' in patent applications. In addition, the applicant must disclose 'the International Non-proprietary Name (INN) of a pharmaceutical substance or an active pharmaceutical ingredient as soon as it is available.'[193]
8. Provide for 'effective pre- and post-grant administrative patent opposition procedures.' ARIPO member states are required to discuss the amendment of the Harare Protocol to provide for opposition procedures and a possible extension of the six month period within which national patent offices have to approve ARIPO patents.[194]
9. Provide for international exhaustion in relation to patent, copyright and trademark laws.[195]
10. Provide for compulsory licenses that enable 'the export of up to 100% of pharmaceuticals' to countries without adequate manufacturing capacity; adopt relevant guidelines or regulations to enable such import and export of pharmaceuticals and 'waive remuneration for import compulsory licenses' in specified circumstances.[196] They are also required to enact legislative provisions that:

    - cap remuneration at 4 per cent and consider anti-competitive behaviour in setting such remuneration;
    - limit the license negotiation period to 90 days, after which the potential licensee may apply for a compulsory license;
    - permit the waiver of prior negotiation periods 'in case of national emergency, other situations of extreme urgency, public non-commercial use [or] government use, and to remedy anti-competitive behaviour of the patent right-holder.' In addition, an 'institutional monitoring mechanism' must be operationalized in order to monitor the implementation of this provision.

191 EAC TRIPS Policy p. 16.
192 EAC TRIPS Policy p. 16.
193 EAC TRIPS Policy p. 17.
194 EAC TRIPS Policy p. 18.
195 EAC TRIPS Policy p. 18.
196 EAC TRIPS Policy p. 20.

- preclude the use of interdicts as a remedy where government use licenses are in issue.[197]

Finally, the grant of compulsory licenses is to be an administrative, rather than a judicial, function.[198]

11. Enumerate licensing terms 'that may be considered unjustified restrictions of competition, and authorise the patent registrar to refuse the registration of such licensing contracts.' Such terms are to be based on existing statutory provisions under Kenyan, Rwandese, Tanzanian-Mainland and Ugandan laws.[199]

In addition, the EAC has adopted the Regional Protocol on Health-Related WTO-TRIPS Flexibilities that gives the above recommendations force of law. However, the protocol needs to go to a signature and ratification process before it becomes effective.[200]

ECOWAS' TRIPS policy and guidelines

ECOWAS's health related initiatives are led by the West African Health Organization (WAHO), an ECOWAS specialized institution which was created in 1987. Its constitutive Protocol merged the West African Health Community (WAHC) and the Organisation de Co-ordination et de Co-operation pour la Lutte contre les Grandes Endemies (OCCGE) to create it.[201] WAHO was operationalized in 2000 following a decision made by the Heads of State to select the seat of the institution and appoint a Director and Deputy Director of the organization.[202] A Supplementary Protocol[203] amending its constitutive protocol is yet to come into force.

WAHO prepared a TRIPS Policy[204] and Guidelines[205] for ECOWAS, which were adopted in October 2012. The policy's primary objectives are to enhance access to essential medicines through the provision of 'legal and technical guidance for the development and marketing of medicines' and 'for implementing TRIPs compliant national legislations or regulations.'[206] To this end, a review of member states' relevant legislation was undertaken. The findings of this review then informed the following patent legislation specific recommendations made by the policy:

197 EAC TRIPS Policy p. 20.
198 EAC TRIPS Policy p. 20.
199 EAC TRIPS Policy p. 21.
200 Article 151(3) Treaty for the Establishment of the EAC.
201 Article II Protocol A/P.2/7/87 on the Establishment of a West African Health Organization.
202 ECOWAS Heads of State Decision A/Dec.9/10/98.
203 Supplementary Protocol A/SP.1/01/06 amending Articles VI-C, VI-L, IX-8, XI-2 and XII of Protocol A/P2/7/87 on the Establishment of the WAHO.
204 ECOWAS TRIPS Policy.
205 Guidelines for Implementation of TRIPS Flexibilities in National Legislation to Improve Access to Medicines in the West African Region (2012).
206 ECOWAS TRIPS Policy pp. 11–12.

1. Dishonest and unfair commercial use of test data must be prohibited, taking care to ensure that 'protection of test data should not unreasonably prevent or hamper the development of generic medicines.'[207]
2. Experimental (research) and Bolar exceptions ought to be provided for.[208]
3. The disclosure of the 'best mode' of implementation of inventions must be required from applicants for patents.[209]
4. Ever-greening ought to be curbed by 'preventing the extension of existing patents and patenting of trivial and/or non-efficacious variants of existing chemical substances. Product derivatives of a known chemical substance should be patentable only if, when compared to the original substance, they show significant improvements in therapeutic efficacy.'[210]
5. International exhaustion should be provided for.[211]
6. TRIPS articles 31(b) and (k) should be domesticated.[212]

These recommendations are reiterated in the accompanying guidelines which give direction to ECOWAS member states on how to incorporate them into national legislation and provide an implementation action plan for the sub-region for the period 2012–2015.

SADC's work on TRIPS flexibilities

SADC's Pharmaceutical Business Plan (2007–2013) prioritizes the use of the TRIPS flexibilities as a strategy to make quality medicines more affordable to citizens in member states. The Trade, TRIPS and Access to Medicines (TTAtM) project is being run with the Southern Africa Regional Programme on Access to Medicines and Diagnostics (SARPAM) supported by funding from the UK Department for International Development (DFID) and UK Aid. The project has a Technical Working Group. So far it has undertaken a number of activities that include national stakeholder meetings including in Zimbabwe in January 2014 and in Lesotho in August 2014, the preparation of briefing papers[213] and reports.[214]

Consequent to the above work, SARPAM's key recommendations to SADC member states include:

- the domestication of article 31 bis of the TRIPS Agreement to create a larger market for the regional pharmaceutical manufacturing industry;
- the finalization of IP policies to inform legislative reform; and

207 ECOWAS TRIPS Policy pp. 25–26.
208 ECOWAS TRIPS Policy p. 28.
209 ECOWAS TRIPS Policy p. 28.
210 ECOWAS TRIPS Policy p. 30.
211 ECOWAS TRIPS Policy p. 32.
212 ECOWAS TRIPS Policy p. 37.
213 Bannenberg (2012).
214 Musungu (2012).

- the review of legislation and policies that are relevant to IP to ensure 'that they are in line with international IP obligations, incorporate TRIPS flexibilities and give effect to national developmental aspirations'.[215]

The above overview shows that meaningful progress is being made to domesticate TRIPS flexibilities. One may argue that 10 years after the entry into force of TRIPS, it is too little, too late. However, the better view is that such developments are welcome no matter how late they are. African states ought to be encouraged to continue in the efforts and to give priority to the acceptance of the 2003 Waiver by 31 December 2015 deadline. So far only the following African states have done so[216]:

- Botswana (18 June 2014)
- Egypt (18 April 2008)
- Mauritius (16 April 2008)
- Rwanda (12 December 2011)
- Senegal (18 January 2011)
- Uganda (12 July 2010)
- Zambia (10 August 2009)

Book overview

Against the above background, the book will proceed as follows:

Chapter 2 discusses national and REC IP policies and evaluates to what extent, if any, they serve the public interest. Chapter 3 discusses IP harmonization efforts by RECs, with a view to evaluating their public interest goals and achievements. Chapter 4 considers the harmonization and unification of IP frameworks by ARIPO and OAPI, respectively through a similar lens. Chapter 5 outlines the historical development of plans to establish PAIPO and canvasses some public interest concerns that are raised by such development. Chapter 6 considers the various legal harmonization models in play in Africa and beyond, with a view to making recommendations for the AU in relation to PAIPO. Chapter 7 concludes the text by discussing the viability of current and future IP harmonization initiatives with reference to the current socio-economic status of African states. It asks whether such harmonization efforts would be in the public interest and urges due consideration of individual states' unique conditions and aspirations in any harmonization venture.

215 SARPAM (2014, 2013).
216 WTO (n.d.).

References

Primary sources: agreements, decisions and official documents

AU

AU Commission and UNIDO Pharmaceutical Manufacturing Plan for Africa Business Plan (2012).

Decision on the Moratorium on the Recognition of Regional Economic Communities (RECs) DOC.EX.CL/278 (IX). AU Doc. Assembly/AU/Dec. 111–132 (VII). Assembly of the African Union. Seventh Ordinary Session. 1–2 July 2006. Banjul, The Gambia.

Health Strategy and Pharmaceutical Manufacturing Plan for Africa (2007).

Study for the Quantification of Regional Economic Communities (RECs): Rationalization Scenarios (Provisional Report) (2009). Online. Available HTTP: <http://www.au.int/en/sites/default/files/Rationalisation%20study%20%28English%29.2.pdf>, accessed 15 March 2015.

EAC

Health Protocol on Public Health Related WTO-TRIPS Flexibilities (2013).

Regional Pharmaceutical Manufacturing Plan of Action (2012–2016).

Regional Intellectual Property Policy on the Utilization of Public Health-Related WTO-TRIPS Flexibilities and the Approximation of National Intellectual Property Legislation (2013).

Treaty for the Establishment of the EAC (1999).

ECOWAS

Development of a Harmonized TRIPS Policy for Adoption by ECOWAS Member States that Employ TRIPS Flexibilities to Improve Access to Medicines in the Region (2012).

Guidelines for Implementation of TRIPS Flexibilities in National Legislation to Improve Access to Medicines in the West African Region (2012).

Protocol A/P2/7/87 on the Establishment of a West African Health Organization (1987).

Supplementary Protocol A/SP.1/01/06 amending Articles VI-C, VI-L, IX-8, XI-2 and XII of Protocol A/P2/7/87 on the Establishment of the WAHO (2006).

OAPI

Bangui Agreement Relating to the Creation of an African Intellectual Property Organization, 1977.

SADC

Draft Agreement Establishing the COMESA, EAC AND SADC T-FTA (revised 2010).

Pharmaceutical Business Plan (2007–2013).

Protocol on Science, Technology and Innovation (2008).

Protocol on Trade (1996).

WHO

Global Strategy and Plan of Action on Public Health, Innovation and Intellectual Property (2008).

WIPO

African Proposal for the Establishment of a Development Agenda for WIPO Doc IIM/3/2 Rev, 31 July 2005.
Assemblies of the Member States of WIPO, Forty-Third Series of Meetings, Geneva, September 24 to October 3, 2007, WIPO General Assembly Report A/43/16 (November 12, 2007).
Berne Convention for the Protection of Literary and Artistic Works (1986) 1161 U.N.T.S. 3.
Information on the Development Agenda Group Guiding Principles WIPO Doc CDIP/5/9 Rev, 26 April 2010.
Paris Convention for the Protection of Industrial Property 21 U.S.T. 1583, 828 U.N.T.S. 305.
Patent Related Flexibilities In The Multilateral Legal Framework And Their Legislative Implementation At The National And Regional Levels (2010) CDIP/5/4 rev para 33–34.
Proposal of Argentina and Brazil, for the establishment of a development agenda for WIPO, 27 August 2004, document WO/GA/31/11.
Proposal to Establish a Development Agenda for WIPO: An Elaboration of Issues Raised in Document WO/GA/31/11 WIPO Doc IIM/1/4 (Group of Friends Elaboration Document IIM/1/4).
Universal Copyright Convention (Paris Act/Text, 1971) 25 U.S.T. 1341, 943 U.N.T.S. 178.
WIPO Inter-Sessional Intergovernmental Meeting on a Development Agenda for WIPO, First Session, Geneva, 11–13 April, 2005 Report (IIM/1/6).
WIPO Provisional Committee on Proposals Related to the WIPO Development Agenda (PCDA) First Session, February 20–24 2006 (PCDA 1/6 Prov 2).
WIPO PCDA Fourth Session, June 11–15 2007 (PCDA /4/3).
WIPO PCDA Fourth Session, June 11–15 2007 (PCDA/4/3. Annex).

WTO

Agreement on Trade-Related Aspects of Intellectual Property Rights, including Trade in Counterfeit Goods (1994) 33 ILM 81 (TRIPS).
Amendment of the TRIPS Agreement – Fourth Extension of the Period for the Acceptance by Members of the Protocol Amending the TRIPS Agreement, Decision of 26 November 2013, WT/L/899.
Doha Decision on the implementation of par 6 of the Doha Declaration (2003). Doc. WT/L/540 and Corr.1
Doha Declaration on the TRIPS Agreement and Public Health (adopted 14 November 2001), Doc. WT/MIN(01)/DEC/2 (20 November 2001).
Doha WTO Ministerial Declaration (adopted 14 November 2001) Doc. WT/MIN(01)/DEC/1 (20 November 2001).
Panel Report, Canada Patent Protection of Pharmaceutical Products, f 7.23, WT/DS114/R (17 March, 2000).

WTO Decision of the Council for Trade-Related Aspects of Intellectual Property Rights *Extension of the Transition Period under Article 66.1 for Least Developed Country Members* (11 June 2013) IP/C/64.

Secondary sources

Abbott, F.M., 2013. *Technical Note: The LDC TRIPS Transition Extension and the Question of Rollback*, Policy Brief No 15. Geneva: International Centre for Trade and Sustainable Development.

Abbott, F.M. and Reichman, J.H., 2007. The Doha Round's Public Health Legacy: strategies for the production and diffusion of patented medicines under the amended TRIPS provisions, *Journal of International Economic Law*,10, 921–987.

Adelman, I., 1961. *Theories of Economic Growth and Development.* Stanford, CA: Stanford University Press.

Adewopo, A., 2012. *According To Intellectual Property: A Pro-Development Vision Of The Law And The Nigerian Intellectual Property Law And Policy Reform In The Knowledge Era.* Lagos: Nigerian Institute of Advanced Legal Studies.

African Copyright and Access to Knowledge Project (ACA2K), 2008. *Methodology Guide.* Johannesburg: International Development Research Centre (IDRC), Shuttleworth Foundation and LINK Centre, University of the Witwatersrand.

Akokpari, J., 2008. 'Dilemmas of regional integration and development' in Akokpari et al. (eds) *The African Union and its Institutions.* Auckland Park: Fanele, 85–110.

Anand, S. and Sen, A., 2000. Human development and economic sustainability, *World Development*, 28(12), 2029–2049.

Andemariam, S.W., 2007. The cleft-stick between anti retroviral drug patents and HIV/AIDS victims: an in-depth analysis of the WTO's TRIPS Article 31 bis Amendment proposal of 6 December 2005, *Intellectual Property Quarterly*, 4, 414–466.

Armstrong, C., de Beer, J., Kawooya, D., Prabhala, A. and Schonwetter, T., 2010. 'Introduction' in Armstrong, C., de Beer, J., Kawooya, D., Prabhala, A. and Schonwetter, T. (eds) *Access to Knowledge in Africa: The Role of Copyright.* Cape Town: UCT Press.

Arndt, H.W., 1989. *Economic Development: The History of an Idea.* United States: University of Chicago Press.

Avafia, T., Berger, J. and Hartzenberg, T., 2006. *The Ability of Select Sub-Saharan African Countries to Utilize TRIPS Flexibilities and Competition Law to Ensure a Sustainable Supply of Essential Medicines: A Study of Producing and Importing Countries.* Stellenbosch: ICTSD, UNCTAD and TRALAC.

Baker, B., 2015. 'LDC members' entitlement to and need for a further extension of their pharmaceutical transition period'. infojustice.org. Online. Available HTTP: <http://infojustice.org/archives/33969>, accessed 1 March 2015.

Bannenberg, W., 2012. *Briefing Paper: Trade, TRIPS and Access to Medicines: Challenges and Options for the SADC Region.* Gaborone: SADC.

Belohlavek, A.J., 2012. 'Public policy and public interest in international law and EU law' in Belohlavek, A. and Rozehnalova, N. (eds) *CYIL: Czech Yearbook of International Law: Public Policy and Ordre Public* Vol. III. Huntington, New York: Juris Publishing Inc., 117–147.

Berger, M., Murugi, J., Buch, E., IJsselmuiden C., Moran, M., Guzman, J., Devlin, M. and Kubata, B., 2010. *Strengthening Pharmaceutical Innovation in Africa.* Geneva: Council on Health Research for Development (COHRED); New Partnership for Africa's Development (NEPAD).

Blakeney, M. and Mengistie, G., 2011. Intellectual property and economic development in Sub-Saharan Africa, *Journal of World Intellectual Property*, 14(3/4), 238–264.

Boahen, A.A., ed. 1990. *General History of Africa VII: Africa Under Colonial Domination. 1880–1935.* London: James Currey Publishers.

Box, R.C., 2007. Redescribing the public interest, *The Social Science Journal*, 44(4), 585–598.

Broadman, H.G. and Isik, G., 2007. *Africa's Silk Road: China and India's New Economic Frontier.* Washington DC: World Bank.

Collins, R.O. and Burns, J.M., 2013. *A History of Sub-Saharan Africa.* 2nd edition. Cambridge: Cambridge University Press.

Correa, C.M., 2013. 'Multilateral agreements and policy opportunities' in: Cimoli, M., Dosi, G., Maskus, K.E., Okediji, R.L. and Reichman, J.H. (eds) *Intellectual Property Rights: Legal and Economic Challenges for Development.* Oxford: Oxford University Press, 417–438.

de Beer, J., 2009. 'Defining WIPO's development agenda' in Jeremy de Beer (ed.) *Implementing the World Intellectual Property Organisation's Development Agenda.* Waterloo, Ontario: International Development Research Centre and Wilfrid Laurier University Press.

de Wet, P., 2014a. Motsoaledi: Big pharma's 'satanic' plot is genocide. *Mail & Guardian*, 17 January 2014.

de Wet, P., 2014b. How the big 'pharma' plot died an early death. *Mail & Guardian*, 18 January 2014.

Deere, C., 2009. *The Implementation Game: The TRIPS Agreement and the Global Politics of Intellectual Property Reform in Developing Countries.* New York: Oxford University Press.

Deere-Birkbeck, C., 2008. 'The politics of intellectual property reform in developing countries: the relevance of the World Intellectual Property Organization' in Netanel, N.W. (ed.) *The Development Agenda: Global Intellectual Property and Developing Countries.* Oxford: Oxford University Press, 111–131.

Deere-Birkbeck, C. and Roca, S., 2011. *An External Review of WIPO Technical Assistance in the Area of Cooperation for Development.* Geneva, Switzerland: WIPO. Online. Available HTTP: <http://www.wipo.int/edocs/mdocs/mdocs/en/cdip_8/cdip_8_inf_1-annex1.pdf>, accessed 19 February 2015.

Dreyfuss, R.C., 2004. TRIPS-Round II: should users strike back? *University of Chicago Law Review*, 71(1), 21–35.

du Plessis, E. ed. 2012. *Adams & Adams Practical Guide to Intellectual Property in Africa.* Pretoria: Pretoria University Law Press.

Dye, T., 1972. Understanding public policy. Englewood Cliffs, NJ: Prentice Hall.

EQUINET and ECSA-HC, 2011. *Preventing Substandard, Falsified Medicines and Protecting Access to Generic Medicines in Africa. Supporting Global Health Diplomacy in East, Central and Southern Africa Policy Series No. 24.* equinetafrica.org.

Friedrich, C.J. ed. 1962. *Nomos V: The Public Interest. Yearbook of the American Society for Political and Legal Philosophy.* New York: Atherton Press.

Gana, R.L., 1996. Prospects for developing countries under the TRIPs Agreement, *Vanderbilt Journal of Transnational Law*, 29, 735–755.

Gathii, J.T., 2010. African regional trade agreements as flexible legal regimes, *North Carolina Journal of International Law and Commercial Regulation*, 35(3), 572–668.

Gathii, J.T., 2011. *African Regional Trade Agreements as Legal Regimes.* Cambridge: Cambridge University Press.

Gervais, D., 2003. *The TRIPS Agreement: Drafting History and Analysis.* 2nd edition. London: Sweet and Maxwell.

Global Congress on Intellectual Property and the Public Interest, 2011. 'The Washington declaration on intellectual property and the public interest'. infojustice.org. Online. Available HTTP: <http://infojustice.org/washington-declaration>, accessed 1 March 2015.

Harris, D.P., 2007. TRIPS and Treaties of Adhesion Part II: Back To The Past Or A Small Step Forward? *Michigan State Law Review*, 185–214.

Held, V., 1970. *The Public Interest and Individual Interests.* New York: Basic Books.

Helfer, L. and Austin, G.W., 2011. *Human Rights and Intellectual Property: Mapping the Global Interface.* New York: Cambridge University Press.

Heywood, M., 2001. 'Debunking 'Conglomo-talk': A case study of the amicus curiae as an instrument for advocacy, investigation and mobilization, *Law, Democracy & Development*, 5(2), 133–162.

Ho, L.S., 2012. *Public Policy and the Public Interest.* Abingdon: Routledge

Hogwood, B.W. and Gunn, L., 1984. *Policy Analysis for the Real World.* Oxford: Oxford University Press

Jain, T.R., Bajaj, B.K., Gupta, A. and Sandhu, A.S., 2008. *Development Economics.* New Delhi: VK Publications.

Jensen, E., 2005. *Western Sahara: Anatomy of a Stalemate.* London: Lynne Rienner Publishers.

Joireman, S.F., 2001. Inherited legal systems and effective rule of law: Africa and the colonial legacy, *Journal of Modern African Studies*, 39(4), 571–596.

Kahn, T., 2014. IPASA axes committee in wake of patents row, *Business Day*, 7 February 2014.

Kapczynski, A., 2009. Harmonization and its discontents: A case study of TRIPS implementation in India's pharmaceutical sector, *California Law Review*, 97(6), 1571–1649.

Kilic, B., 2015. *Boosting Pharmaceutical Innovation in the Post-TRIPS Era.* Cheltenham and Northampton: Edward Elgar.

Kolbeck, B., 2014. *Legal Analysis on the Relationship between the AU/AEC and RECs: Africa Lost in a 'Spaghetti Bowl' of Legal Relations?* Thesis (LLM). Cape Town: University of Cape Town.

Kongolo, T., 2013a. *African Contributions in Shaping the Worldwide Intellectual Property System.* Farnham, Surrey: Ashgate.

Kongolo, T., 2013b. Historical developments of industrial property laws in Africa, *WIPO Journal*, 5(1), 105–117.

Kongolo, T., 2014. Historical evolution of copyright legislation in Africa, *WIPO Journal* 5(2), 163–175.

Loren, L.P., 2008. The Pope's copyright? Aligning incentives with reality by using creative motivation to shape copyright protection, *Louisiana Law Review*, 69, 1–41.

Maksus, K.K., 2009. 'The WIPO development agenda: A cautionary note' in Netanel, N.W. (ed.) *The Development Agenda: Global Intellectual Property and Developing Countries.* Oxford: Oxford University Press.

Matthews, D., 2005. TRIPS flexibilities and access to medicines in developing countries: the problem with technical assistance and free trade agreements, *European Intellectual Property Review*, 27(11), 420–427.

Matthews, D. and Correa, C., 2011. *The Doha Declaration Ten Years on and Its Impact on Access to Medicines and the Right to Health.* New York: United Nations Development Programme.

May, C., 2007. *The World Intellectual Property Organization: Resurgence and the Development Agenda.* Abingdon, Oxford: Routledge.

May, C., 2008. The World Intellectual Property Organisation and the Development Agenda, *Global Society*, 22(1), 97–113.

Merso, F., 2013. *IP Trends in African LDCs and the LDC TRIPS Transition Extension.* Policy

Brief no 16. Geneva, Switzerland: International Centre for Trade and Sustainable Development.

Motsoeneng, T., 2014. Big Pharma may threaten to cut S. Africa investment in generics row. *Reuters*, 17 January 2014.

Musungu, S.F., 2012. *Pharmaceutical Patents, TRIPS Flexibilities and Access to Medicines in SADC*, Gaborone: SADC.

Musungu, S.F., Villanueva, S. and Blasetti, R., 2004. *Utilizing Trips Flexibilities For Public Health Protection Through South-South Regional Frameworks*. Geneva, Switzerland: South Centre.

Ncube, C.B., 2009. Enforcing patent rights against goods in transit: a new threat to trans-border trade in generic medicines, *South African Mercantile Law Journal*, 21, 680–694.

Ncube, C.B., 2013. Harnessing Intellectual Property for Development: Some Thoughts on an Appropriate Theoretical Framework, *Potchefstroom Electronic Law Journal*, 16(4), 369–487.

Ncube, C.B., 2015. 'Fair is as fair does: contractual normative regulation of copyright user contracts in South Africa' in: Dinwoodie, G.B. (ed.) *Intellectual Property and General Legal Principles: Is IP a Lex Specialist?* Cheltenham: Edward Elgar, 49–68.

Ndulo, B.J., 2007. 'The evolution of global development paradigms and their influence on African economic growth' in: Ndulo, B.J., O'Connell, S.A., Bates, R.H., Collier, P. and Soludo, C.C. (ed.) *The Political Economy of Economic Growth in Africa, 1960–2000*. Cambridge: Cambridge University Press.

Netanel, N.W., 2009. 'The WIPO Development Agenda and its development policy context' in Netanel, N.W. (ed.) *The Development Agenda: Global Intellectual Property and Developing Countries*. Oxford: Oxford University Press.

Nkomo, M., 2013. Rwanda's new intellectual property law and compulsory licensing for export under the WTO: not quite a panacea, *African Journal of International and Comparative Law*, 21(2), 279–294.

Okediji, R.L., 1999. Copyright and public welfare in global perspective, *Indiana Journal of Global Legal Studies*, 7(1), 117–189.

Okediji, R.L., 2003a. The international relations of intellectual property: narratives of developing country participation in the global intellectual property system, *Singapore Journal of International & Comparative Law*, 7, 315–385.

Okediji, R.L., 2003b. Public welfare and the role of the WTO: reconsidering the TRIPs Agreement, *Emory International Law Review*, 17, 819–918.

Okediji, R.L., 2004. Africa and the global intellectual property system: beyond the agency model, *African Yearbook of International Law*, 12, 207–251.

Okediji, R.L., 2009. 'History lessons for the WIPO development agenda' in: Netanel, N.W. (ed.) *The Development Agenda: Global Intellectual Property and Developing Countries*. Oxford: Oxford University Press, 137–162.

Okediji, R.L., 2014. 'Public welfare and the international patent system' in: Okediji, R.L and Bagley, M.A. (eds) *Patent Law in Global Perspective*. Oxford: Oxford University Press, 1–50.

Oppong, R.F., 2011. *Legal Aspects of Economic Integration in Africa*. Cambridge: Cambridge University Press.

Outterson, K., 2010. 'Disease-based limitations on compulsory licenses under Articles 31 and 31 bis' in: Correa, C. (ed.) *Research Handbook on the Protection of Intellectual Property under WTO Rules*. Cheltenham: Edward Elgar, 673–697.

Owoeye, O.A., 2014. Compulsory patent licensing and local drug manufacturing capacity in Africa, *Bulletin of the World Health Organisation*, 92, 214–219.

Park, C., Prabhala, A. and Berger, J., 2013. *Using Law to Accelerate Treatment Access in South Africa: An Analysis of Patent, Competition and Medicines Law.* New York: UNDP.

Public Affairs Engagement. 2014. *Campaign to Prevent Damage to Innovation from the Proposed Draft National IP Policy in South Africa.* Proposal Prepared for PhRMA and IPASA. Online. Available HTTP: <http://cdn.mg.co.za/content/documents/2014/01/16/skmbt36314011511040.pdf>, accessed 19 January 2015.

Rahmatian, A., 2009. Neo-colonial aspects of global intellectual property protection, *The Journal of World Intellectual Property*, 12(1), 40–74.

Rachlitz, R., 2014. Effective private law harmonization: A comparative analysis of the EU Draft Regulation on Common European Sales Law and the OHADA Uniform Acts, *Journal of Comparative Law in Africa*, 47–65.

Republic of Botswana, 2013. *Implementation of TRIPS Flexibilities in National IP Legislation for Strengthening Access to Medicines in Botswana.* Gaborone: UNDP-SARPAM-Botswana Government Workshop Report.

Rodrigues Jr., E.B., 2012. *The General Exception Clauses of the TRIPS Agreement: Promoting Sustainable Development.* New York: Cambridge University Press.

Royal Society of Arts, 2006. *Adelphi Charter on Creativity, Innovation and Intellectual Property. Promoting Innovation and Rewarding Creativity: A Balanced Intellectual Property Framework for the Digital Age* 4–5.

Samuelson, P., 2013. Is copyright reform possible? *Harvard Law Review,* 126, 740–779.

SARPAM, 2013. Report on SARPAM TTAtM work. Online. Available HTTP: <www.sarpam.net>, accessed 1 March 2015.

SARPAM, 2014. Review of the SADC Pharmaceutical Business Plan underway. March to May 2014, SARPAM Newsletter. Online. Available HTTP: <http://www.sarpam.net/sarpam-newsletter-march-may-2014>, accessed 1 March 2015.

Schubert, G., 1960. *The Public Interest: A Critique of the Theory of a Political Concept.* Glencoe: The Free Press.

Sell, S.K., 2011. Everything old is new again: the development agenda then and now, *The WIPO Journal,* 3(1), 17–23.

Sen, A. 1997. *Development Thinking at the Beginning of the 21st Century.* LSE STICERD Research Paper No. DEDPS 02. DEDPS, 2. Suntory and Toyota International Centres for Economics and Related Disciplines, London School of Economics and Political Science, London, UK. Online. Available HTTP: <http://sticerd.lse.ac.uk/>, accessed 22 March 2015.

Sen, A., 2000a. What is the role of legal and judicial reform in the development process? The role of legal and judicial reform in development, *World Bank Legal Conference,* Washington DC, 5 June 2000.

Sen, A., 2000b. A decade of human development, *Journal of Human Development,* 1(1), 17–23.

Seuba, X., 2014. *International Regulation of Pharmaceuticals, Codification by Means of Legal Transplantation,* Information Note, Programme on Innovation, Technology and Intellectual Property, Geneva: International Centre for Trade and Sustainable Development, 3.

Shabalala, D., 2007. *A Citizen's Guide to WIPO.* Geneva: CIEL.

Shelley, T., 2004. *Endgame in the Western Sahara: What Future for Africa's Last Colony?* London: Zed Books.

Sibanda, M., 2013. *Patent-related Flexibilities in Multilateral Treaties and their Importance for Developing countries and LDCs.* 2nd WIPO Inter-Regional Meeting on South-South Cooperation on Patents, Trademarks, Geographical Indications, Industrial Designs and Enforcement, May 2013.

Smith, K.B., 2006. 'Economic techniques' in Moran, M., Rein, M., Goodin, R.E., (eds.) *The Oxford Handbook of Public Policy*. New York: Oxford University Press, 729–745.

Souraf, F., 1957. The public interest reconsidered. *Journal of Politics*, 19, 616–639.

Storing, H.J., 1964. Review: the crucial link: public administration, responsibility, and the public interest. *Public Administration Review*, 24(1), 39–46.

UNCTAD, 2011. *Using Intellectual Property Rights to Stimulate Pharmaceutical Production in Developing Countries: A Reference Guide*. Geneva: UNCTAD.

UNDP, 2014. *Human Development Report 2014 Sustaining Human Progress: Reducing Vulnerabilities and Building Resilience*. New York: UNDP.

UNECA, 2014a. *Annual Report*. Addis Ababa: UNECA.

UNECA, 2014b. *Opportunities and Challenges in Using the Intellectual Property (IP) Systems to Strengthen Regional Cooperation Through Policy Harmonization in SADC*. Addis Ababa: UNECA

Watal, J., 2011. From Punta Del Este to Doha and beyond: lessons from the TRIPs negotiating processes, *WIPO Journal*, 3(1), 24–35.

WHO, WIPO and WTO, 2012. *Promoting Access to Medical Technologies and Innovation: Intersections between Public Health, Intellectual Property and Trade*. Geneva: WHO, WIPO and WTO.

Wilson, R., 2006. 'Policy analysis as policy advice', in Moran, M., Rein, M. and Goodin, R.E. (eds) *The Oxford Handbook of Public Policy*. New York, NY: Oxford University Press, 152–168.

WIPO, n.d. 'WIPO development agenda: background (2004–2007)'. WIPO. Online. Available HTTP: <http://www.wipo.int/ip-development/en/agenda/background.html>, accessed 1 March 2015.

WTO, n.d. 'Members accepting amendment of the TRIPS agreement'. WTO. Online. Available HTTP: <http://www.wto.org/english/tratop_e/trips_e/amendment_e.htm>, accessed 17 January 2015.

WTO, 2014a. 'Accessions: General Council approves Seychelles' WTO membership, only ratification left' (10 December, 2014) Online. Available HTTP: <http://www.wto.org/english/news_e/news14_e/acc_syc_10dec14_e.htm>, accessed 7 January, 2015.

WTO, 2014b. 'Accession of Liberia. WTO Accessions Newsletter', 30 October 2014. Available HTTP: <https://www.wto.org/english/thewto_e/acc_e/nl_e/2014_10_acc_newsletter_e.pdf>, accessed 7 January 2015.

Yu, P.K., 2009. A Tale of Two Development Agendas, *Ohio Northern University Law Review*, 35, 465–573.

2 IP policy frameworks in Africa

Introduction

It is apt to begin this chapter on IP policies with a clarification of terminology. In the discourse on IP policy, the phrases one encounters most frequently are IP strategy, IP policy and IP plan. A recent external evaluation of WIPO technical assistance pointed out that WIPO and some of its member states appear to use these terms interchangeably even though there is a clear divergence in what the users of each term meant by it.[1] It is therefore necessary to define these terms before embarking on a substantive discussion to avoid replicating the shortcoming identified in WIPO documents and to ensure that the discussion proceeds from a point of clarity.

IP policy

The definition of public policy is nebulous and several formulations have been suggested over the years.[2] This work adopts the UN's Committee of Experts in Public Administration (CEPA) and the Division for Public Administration and Development Management (DPADM) conceptualization of public policy as:

1. The organizing framework of purposes and rationales for government programs that deal with specified societal problems.
2. The complex of programs enacted and implemented by the government.[3]

From this, one can deduce that an IP policy is the over-arching framework, consisting of aims and objectives for government programs that are directed at issues affected by, and affecting, IP. Such a policy would be cross-cutting, implicating issues of culture, education, health, scientific innovation and trade.

1 Deere-Birkbeck and Roca (2011) p. 80.

2 Dye (1972) p. 2; Anderson (1984) p. 3; Hogwood and Gunn (1984) pp. 23–24; Wilson (2006) p. 154. Simon (2007) p. 1.

3 UN (n.d.).

IP strategy

In ordinary parlance a strategy is simply 'a planned series of actions for achieving something.'[4] In policy discourse, a strategy is defined as a 'high-level plan or course of action that will be taken to bring change'[5] or to implement a policy. An IP strategy would therefore be a government's processes and procedures set to accomplish its IP policy objectives. WIPO advances the following two definitions of IP strategy[6]:

> A set of measures formulated and implemented by a government to encourage and facilitate the effective creation, development, management and protection of IP at national level.

> A comprehensive national document which outlines how all policy developments related to IP, and the implementation of these developments, should take place in a co-ordinated manner within a national framework.

IP plan

An IP plan is at one level below a strategy. It arises out of the strategy and is one of its constituent parts as is clear from its definition as 'a set of actions for achieving something in the future, especially a set of actions that has been considered carefully and in detail.'[7] Plans are more 'strategic or directive' than policies.[8] A series of plans constitute a strategy. Based on the above definitions, to speak about IP plans is to take a very detailed approach that focuses on implementation. This book focuses on a higher level and discusses IP policies that are at the highest level of abstraction when compared to strategies and plans.

IP development plan

Another term that is also frequently encountered in WIPO literature is 'IP Development Plan' (IPDP). This is a document that serves as a memorandum or an agreement between WIPO and a state that sets out the technical assistance that WIPO will render to the state. For example a WIPO Press Release stated the following with regard to an IPDP that it had concluded with Ghana:

> The IP Development Plan covers a range of activities including legislative advice and workshops on strategic use of different aspects of the IP system targeting various stakeholders including small and medium-sized enterprises,

4 *Longman Dictionary of Contemporary English* (2003).
5 Sykes (2011) p. 4.
6 *WIPO Methodology for the Development of National Intellectual Property Strategies: Tool 1: The Process.*
7 *Longman Dictionary of Contemporary English* (2003).
8 Howlett and Lejano (2013) p. 359.

research and development institutes, and the judiciary. It also includes support and advice to promote the development of creative industries, electronic commerce, copyright collective management, traditional knowledge, agricultural development and plant varieties. The plan further seeks to enhance the country's IP infrastructure through modernizing and automating national IP administration to ensure high quality service delivery, extensive training and public awareness programs and the development of a national IP strategy to support economic growth and development.[9]

Policy design, governance and public administration

The process of crafting or formulating policy is known as policy design which is defined as:

> The effort to more or less systematically develop efficient and effective policies through the application of knowledge about policy means gained from experience, and reason, to the development and adoption of courses of action that are likely to succeed in attaining their desired goals or aims.[10]

The policy design process unfolds in the context of governance and public administration, which is a field that has been the subject of sustained scholarship for a long time.[11] Olowu notes that there are several definitions of governance and the concept is contested.[12] However, there are broadly two main core definitions. The first is used by the UN and conceives of governance as an intra-governmental leadership matter or 'the manner in which (state) political leaders manage or use (or misuse) power – whether it promotes social and economic development or pursues agendas that undermine such goals'.[13] The second category of definitions conceives of governance as 'multi-organizational' and broader than governmental leadership because it 'focuses on the sharing of authority for public management between state and non-state organizations'.[14] The second definition has more currency and is more broadly accepted by scholars in the field.[15] For instance, it is clearly expressed in Howlett and Lejano's following definition of governance as[16]:

> the broadening of the notion of 'government' away from a state-centered concept toward more diffuse, often boundary-spanning, networks of governmental and nongovernmental actors. . . . In its broadest sense, 'governance'

9 WIPO (2008).
10 Howlett and Lejano (2013) p. 359.
11 Olowu (2002) p. 345
12 Olowu (2002) p. 345.
13 Olowu (2002) p. 346.
14 Olowu (2002) p. 346.
15 Olowu (2002) p. 346.
16 Howlett and Lejano (2013) pp. 365–366.

> is a term used to describe the mode of co-ordination exercised by state actors in their interactions with societal actors and organizations.

The scope of this chapter does not extend to a detailed discussion of governance and public administration. Rather, having stated its working definitions above, it proceeds by first considering the significance of IP policies in Africa, thereafter it considers the role of technical assistance in policy design. Finally the chapter ends with an overview of REC IP policies and country profiles of IP policies in Africa.

The importance of IP policies in Africa

As briefly shown in Chapter 1, in the last decade African states have become more involved in the global IP law system, with their most auspicious moment being the adoption of the WIPO DA in 2007.[17] Since the adoption of the WIPO DA several projects have been initiated in Africa with a view to enhancing development through appropriately calibrated IP systems. These systems are crafted through legislation thus making IP legislation and the policies that inform it the focal area for analysis of IP systems.

In an ideal world, legislation is informed by a thoroughly researched policy that has been comprehensively consulted upon. Many African states' reality is far from this ideal as they have IP legislation that they inherited from their colonizers and have had to review to comply with TRIPS without the benefit of meaningful policy formulation. Many African states are only embarking on policy formulation now, some with the assistance of WIPO under the rubric of WIPO DA Recommendation 10 which mandates WIPO:

> To assist Member States to develop and improve national intellectual property institutional capacity through further development of infrastructure and other facilities with a view to making national intellectual property institutions more efficient and promote [sic] fair balance between intellectual property protection and the public interest. This technical assistance should also be extended to sub-regional and regional organizations dealing with intellectual property.

This then is an important moment which should enable African states to reset the course of their IP environments (strategies, policies, law and practices) in alignment with their developmental goals. Therefore technical assistance has to be carefully conceptualized and delivered to ensure that this opportunity is well used. In particular, the manner in which African states are leveraging technical assistance from WIPO and other developmental agencies in the furtherance of their socio-economic goals is of great significance. An external review and an evaluation of WIPO's technical assistance with respect to IP policy have been

17 de Beer (2009) p. 15; Musungu (2010); May (2007).

conducted at the organization's behest.[18] It is not possible for this chapter to undertake a similar evaluation because the documents detailing the legislative and policy advice provided by WIPO and other relevant information are held in confidence.[19] Therefore the following sections discuss WIPO technical assistance in relatively abstract terms without reference to the minutiae of the agreements between it and its member states nor the full detail of the activities carried out thereunder.

Factors affecting IP policy design

Deere-Birkbeck states that national IP policy formulation and law reform processes are significantly shaped by a trio of factors, namely:

(i) the degree of public engagement;
(ii) the internal capacity of governments on IP matters; and
(iii) the degree of government co-ordination.[20]

Pugatch identifies the same three factors although he merges (ii) and (iii) and creates a new third factor of 'global influences on decision-making regarding IP policies'.[21] The following few paragraphs of this chapter discuss these four factors, namely Deere-Birkbeck's three factors and Pugatch's fourth factor.

Where these four factors are in deficit, the resultant policy or reforms are sub-optimal. To put it differently, policy or reform that has been hampered by limited public consultation, low levels of governmental capacity on IP and co-ordination and a policy space that has been shrunk by international norms invariably fails to deliver outcomes that are in the public interest. Consequently, these policies or reforms fail to advance the national socio-economic and developmental goals.

Amongst the many factors that negatively affect public consultation, perhaps the key factor is the tendency to frame IP matters as technical issues upon which only appropriately trained individuals can comment. Such perceptions are bolstered by the use of jargon in consultative documents that then places the debate beyond those not schooled in the jargon and legalese. In addition, the failure to properly contextualize these IP matters as having a wider societal significance also adds to the discouragement of public engagement with them. In some cases this approach may be intentional and adopted with a view to avoiding public engagement and in others it may be an unintended consequence of the adoption of an overly technical approach. Public engagement may be encouraged by the involvement of civic society.

18 Deere-Birkbeck and Roca (2011); WIPO CDIP: Tenth Session. Geneva, November 12 to 16, 2012. *Evaluation Report on the Project on Improvement of National, Sub-regional and Regional IP Institutional and User Capacity*. CDIP/10/7.

19 WIPO (n.d.a).

20 Deere (2009) p. 113.

21 Pugatch (2011) p. 72.

In relation to governmental capacity, the most important determinant factors are 'the level of technical IP capacity in governments, the strength and efficiency of government institutions, and the relative autonomy of IP offices responsible for TRIPS implementation'.[22] Unfortunately, most governmental institutions are weak and capacity resides in a few technocrat IP office staffers who receive significant levels of technical training from WIPO. The manner in which technical assistance is rolled out, in such contexts, is significant primarily because the sometimes IP-centric message of WIPO[23] gets fed without nuance to developing country officials who imbibe the message and translate it into national positions, without the necessary further calibration.[24] One of the reasons for this failure to factor in public interest considerations is that these technocrat national IP office staffers often have no training in public policy.[25] Consequently, their focus remains national compliance with international obligations rather than the appropriate nuancing of policy and law.[26] Due to their expertise, these staffers tend to be autonomous and are often tasked with policy design through to legislative drafting with little input from outside a closed circle of IP attorneys and right-holder groups. Legislatures rely heavily on the expertise of these staffers and, feeling out of their depth, frequently simply pass these laws without any input of their own or of others outside the circle. This type of IP regulation has been aptly labeled 'insider governance'.[27]

This unfortunate state of affairs can be remedied in at least three ways. One is to revise the WIPO message so that it is not primarily IP-centric and generic but includes context-specific advice that is development oriented. Indeed, this is one of the aims of the WIPO DA. The second way is to capacitate IP office and government department staffers so that they are more appreciative of the developmental and public interest relevance of IP, and are skilled in aligning IP laws and policies to these wider goals. The third way is to open up the insider governance model so that other players who may be more public interest oriented are included in deliberations on policy formulation and/or reforms.

The third factor affecting IP reforms and policies, government co-ordination, is affected by the relationship between government departments, those departments with the relevant country's Geneva representatives and between third parties such as international organizations and donor agencies.[28] Here, national departments may have different positions on certain aspects. For example, a department of trade and industry may be more IP-centric and right-holder focused in its approach whilst a department of arts and culture or health may be more user, patient or creator friendly and thus be less IP-centric in its views. If one of

22 Deere (2009) p. 115.
23 For example, WIPO technical assistance has been faulted for not incorporating flexibilities: see Abdel Latif (2011) p. 37; Netanel (2009) p. 7.
24 Deere (2009) pp. 114–115.
25 Deere (2009) p. 115.
26 Deere (2009) p. 116.
27 Deere (2009) p. 116.
28 Deere (2009) p. 117.

these departments is seized with IP policy making, it may do so in a manner that sidelines the approach of the other departments. A country's Geneva based representatives may be more in tune with public interest views due to their proximity to, and interaction with, international civic groups. Therefore, they may advance more pro-development positions on behalf of a country at international fora that do not seem to be taken up at national level. At national level, right-holders may have more influence over IP offices and government departments due to funding models that see IP offices deriving most of their income from right-holder fees. IP offices and government departments are also heavily influenced by WIPO in a way that has been characterized as 'a combination of material enticements and socialization.'[29]

The fourth factor, of global influences, is in turn a coalescence of three other considerations.[30] First, states are obliged to comply with binding international IP agreements to which they are party. As noted in Chapter 1, this will invariably include TRIPS. Secondly, they may also be bound to regional, sub-regional and bi-lateral trade agreements that limit their policy choices. Policy space is often whittled down by concessions made in trade agreements.[31] Finally, as a result of globalization, they may have to factor in the interests of non-citizen parties.

Technical assistance

IP-specific technical assistance may be rendered to developing countries and LDCs directly by developed states, the WTO and WIPO, other UN specialized organizations, civic society or any other interested parties. The provision of legal/technical assistance to its member states is one of WIPO's core functions.[32] Following the entry into force of TRIPS, WIPO and WTO entered into a co-operation agreement regarding their mutual provision of legal-technical assistance and technical co-operation to each other's developing country member states.[33] More recently, WIPO, WTO and WHO have hosted trilateral symposia and published studies on public health, intellectual property and trade.[34]

Developed countries are required to provide technical assistance to developing and LDC WTO members to aid their efforts to implement TRIPS standards by article 67 of the TRIPS which provides:

> In order to facilitate the implementation of this Agreement, developed country Members shall provide, on request and on mutually agreed terms and conditions, technical and financial co-operation in favour of developing and

29 Deere (2009) p. 125.

30 Pugatch (2011).

31 Correa (2006); Sell (2007); Frankel (2008).

32 Article 4(v) Convention Establishing the WIPO.

33 Article 4 Agreement between the WIPO and the WTO. For commentary see Salmon (2003).

34 WIPO (n.d.b).

> least-developed country Members. Such co-operation shall include assistance in the preparation of laws and regulations on the protection and enforcement of intellectual property rights as well as on the prevention of their abuse, and shall include support regarding the establishment or reinforcement of domestic offices and agencies relevant to these matters, including the training of personnel.

This requirement is amplified by the annex to the protocol amending the TRIPS of 8 December 2005 (WT/L/641), which provides:

> 5. With a view to harnessing economies of scale for the purposes of enhancing purchasing power for, and facilitating the local production of, pharmaceutical products, it is recognized that the development of systems providing for the grant of regional patents to be applicable in the Members described in paragraph 3 of Article 31 bis should be promoted. To this end, developed country Members undertake to provide technical co-operation in accordance with Article 67 of this Agreement, including in conjunction with other relevant intergovernmental organizations.

The process which has been followed to meet this obligation has included the submission of status updates and detailed requests for assistance by LDCs to the TRIPS Council, technical assistance fora and the implementation of some projects.[35] Technical assistance has been rendered to developing states and LDCs pursuant to this process. There are numerous instances of the provision of technical assistance. However, for purposes of this discussion, the following two initiatives are of immediate interest:

a) Improvement of National, Sub Regional and Regional IP Institutional and User Capacity (Development Agenda Project DA_10_05).
b) The WIPO Director General led Framework on Designing National IP Strategies[36] under which WIPO has recently rolled out an IP Policy Toolkit.

These initiatives are outlined below.

The WIPO DA Project DA_10_05

This three-year project was initiated in April 2009 under Recommendation 10 of the WIPO DA. It was initially intended to be completed in two years with five pilot countries, namely the Dominican Republic, Mongolia, Moldova, Tanzania

35 Blakeney and Mengistie (2011) p. 250, referring to an IP Technical Assistance Forum, sponsored by the UK Department for International Development (DFID) in 2006 and a pilot project flighted by the ICTSD Program on IPRs and Sustainable Development in collaboration with Saana Consulting in 2007.

36 http://www.wipo.int/ipstrategies/en/.

and Mali.[37] Its objective was the creation of tools to be used in the policy making cycle[38] by

> provid[ing] an integrated set of policies and strategies, institutional and enterprise level interventions, including tools and mechanisms, directed at IP administrations, at the national, sub regional and regional levels, and to enterprise support institutions, the aim being to enhance both the efficiency and utilization of the IP system in developing LDCs, as well as countries in transition, by fulfilling their development objectives.[39]

For purposes of implementation, the project was divided into the following three distinct rungs[40]:

a) to develop and pilot a standard methodology for IP policy/strategy development and institutional reform;
b) to promote work sharing or other co-operation mechanisms, with a focus on the Caribbean region; and
c) to develop and/or improve IPR support services for SMEs, through developing and piloting standardized methodology for surveys/studies on IP and SMEs, training of trainers and further developing IP Panorama.

The first of these three sub-projects is of relevance to this section. A sixth pilot country, Algeria, was included in the project as from May 2011.[41] This project was externally reviewed along with other WIPO technical assistance projects in the 2008–2010 biennium and a final review report was issued in August 2011.[42] This report found that the project implementation process was iterative and responsive but that the audit and benchmarking tools which had been developed were 'imperfect'.[43] It pointed out specific inadequacies in the benchmarking questionnaire and lamented the fact that the toolkit did not provide countries with implementation, monitoring and evaluation support after their adoption of IP policies.[44] In May 2012 the DAG group and the Africa Group proposed that

37 WIPO CDIP: Eighth Session. Geneva, November 14 to 18, 2011. Progress Reports on Development Agenda Projects. CDIP/8/2 Annex VIII p. 2–3.

38 WIPO Methodology and Tools for the Development of National IP Strategies (2014). Also see WIPO; CDIP. Project Documents for Implementation of Recommendations 2, 5, 8, 9 and 10. CDIP/3/INF/2. (2009); CDIP Progress Report on Projects for Implementation of Recommendations 2, 5, 8, 9 and 10. CDIP/4/2 Annex VIII (2009).

39 WIPO CDIP: Sixth Session. Geneva, November 22 to 26, 2010. Progress Reports on Development Agenda Projects. CDIP/6/2 Annex IX p. 1.

40 WIPO CDIP: Tenth Session. Geneva, November 12 to 16, 2012. *Evaluation Report on the Project on Improvement of National, Sub-regional and Regional IP Institutional and User Capacity*. CDIP/10/7 p. 8.

41 WIPO. CDIP: Eighth Session. Geneva, November 14 to 18, 2011. Progress Reports on Development Agenda Projects. CDIP/8/2 Annex VIII p. 3.

42 Deere-Birkbeck and Roca (2011).

43 Deere-Birkbeck and Roca (2011) p. 82.

44 Deere-Birkbeck and Roca (2011) pp. 83–84.

Secretariat should publish the 'tools, methodologies and other relevant documentation' that were developed under this project.[45] Consequently, the toolkit was published on the WIPO website and may be used by any country. It consists of the following four tools:

> Tool 1 – The Process [46]
> Tool 2 – Baseline Questionnaire [47]
> Tool 3 – Benchmarking Indicators [48]
> Tool 4 – National IP Strategies (NIPS) Online Survey.[49]

Following the completion of the project and the publication of the toolkit, WIPO undertook its own review of the project, under the leadership of an external expert. This review found that its implementation process was sufficiently consultative and responsive to the needs of member states.[50] The review also found that the toolkit is both 'replicable and adaptable' as evidenced by its use by at least 10 other countries.[51] However, it found that a 'baseline analysis' ought to have been conducted in Tanzania prior to the commencement of work on a single IP policy for the country's bifurcated legal regime.[52] Work seems to be continuing on Tanzania's IP policy as evidenced by the fact that at the end of 2014, WIPO reported that it was still in consultation with Tanzania in relation to the formulation of its IP strategy and IP policy.[53] A bifurcated national IP policy has been developed, heeding the 2012 review report's comments. The Business Registrations and Licensing Agency (BRELA) which administers IP for Tanzania-Mainland has published an action plan for the development of IP policies for the mainland and Tanzania-Zanzibar on its website.[54] However, at the time of writing (March 2015) the policies have not yet been formally adopted by Tanzania.

45 WIPO CDIP: Ninth Session. Geneva, May 7 to 11, 2012. *Joint Proposal by the Development Agenda Group and the Africa Group on WIPO's Technical Assistance in the Area of Cooperation for Development.* CDIP 9/16.

46 WIPO Methodology for the Development of National Intellectual Property Strategies: Tool 1: The Process WIPO Pub_958_1 (2014).

47 WIPO Methodology for the Development of National Intellectual Property Strategies Tool 2: Baseline Questionnaire WIPO Pub 958 2 (2014).

48 WIPO Methodology for the Development of National Intellectual Property Strategies Tool 3: Benchmarking Indicators WIPO Pub 958_3 (2014).

49 WIPO Methodology for the Development of National Intellectual Property Strategies Tool 4: National IP Strategies (NIPS) Online Survey (2014).

50 WIPO CDIP: Tenth Session. Geneva, November 12 to 16, 2012. *Evaluation Report on the Project on Improvement of National, Sub-regional and Regional IP Institutional and User Capacity.* CDIP/10/7 p. 16.

51 WIPO CDIP: Tenth Session. Geneva, November 12 to 16, 2012. *Evaluation Report on the Project on Improvement of National, Sub-regional and Regional IP Institutional and User Capacity.* CDIP/10/7 p. 17.

52 WIPO CDIP: Tenth Session. Geneva, November 12 to 16, 2012. *Evaluation Report on the Project on Improvement of National, Sub-regional and Regional IP Institutional and User Capacity.* CDIP/10/7 p. 17.

53 WIPO Committee on Development and Intellectual Property (CDIP): Thirteenth Session. Geneva, May 19 to 23, 2014. Director General's Reports on Implementation of the Development Agenda. CDIP 13/2.

54 Action Plan for Realizing the IP Potentials of Tanzania.

Likewise, Algeria is yet to adopt the IP policy that it has developed under this WIPO pilot scheme.

WIPO Framework for Developing National IP Strategies for Innovation

In 2011, in addition to the project described above, WIPO also initiated a second project, which it describes as having been established

> to create a framework to assist all countries in developing national IP strategies for innovation which directly reference and support their development needs and priorities, and take into account their specific economic circumstances and aspirations. The framework, which will provide a conceptual basis for the design of IP strategies, has strong links with project DA_10_05, which aims to develop a practical methodology, validated by a piloting process in selected countries, using a series of practical tools.[55]

The framework would be developed by 'expert working groups comprised of eminent development economists from around the world, IP experts and advisors from UN organizations, in the fields of trade, environment, culture and education, industry, health, agriculture, and science and technology.'[56] This project approached IP policy making from a different vantage point than that taken by the WIPO DA project. The former project was conceptualized as a 'high-level' expert driven initiative aimed at ministerial level whilst the latter was 'a bottom or ground up approach' aimed at giving voice to 'national stakeholders'.[57] The 2011 External Review Report noted that a clear articulation of the synergy between the two projects was required.[58] It was not possible at that stage for the external reviewers to undertake an in-depth evaluation of the Framework project as it was in very early stages of implementation.

The DAG and Africa Group echoed the external reviewers' call for clarification of the relationship between the two projects and requested that regular updates be provided to the CDIP on the Framework project's objective, purpose, methodology and outcomes.[59]

As of March 2015, it is not clear what the status of this project is because it has

55 WIPO CDIP: Eighth Session. Geneva, November 14 to 18, 2011. Progress Reports on Development Agenda Projects. CDIP/8/2 Annex VIII p. 3.

56 WIPO CDIP: Eighth Session. Geneva, November 14 to 18, 2011. Progress Reports on Development Agenda Projects. CDIP/8/2 Annex VIII p. 3. Also see WIPO General Assembly Forty-First (21ST Extraordinary) Session. Geneva, October 1 to 9, 2012. Report of the CDIP. WO/GA/41/12 Appendix III p. 4–5.

57 Deere-Birkbeck and Roca (2011) p. 84.

58 Deere-Birkbeck and Roca (2011) p. 85.

59 WIPO CDIP: Ninth Session. Geneva, May 7 to 11, 2012. *Joint Proposal by the Development Agenda Group and the Africa Group on WIPO's Technical Assistance in the Area of Cooperation for Development.* CDIP 9/16 p. 10.

not been reported upon in the Director General's Reports on Implementation of the Development Agenda and Progress Reports submitted to the CDIP at its eleventh session May 2013,[60] twelfth session in November 2013,[61] thirteenth session in May 2014,[62] and fourteenth session in November 2014.[63]

The following section focuses on the IP Policies of RECs.

REC IP policies

As stated in Chapter 1, Africa currently has at least fourteen RECs, only eight of which are recognized by the AU as building blocks of the AEC.[64] Of these eight only COMESA has a comprehensive IP policy, which is outlined below. Two others, namely the EAC and ECOWAS, have policies on patent-related TRIPS flexibilities that have been discussed in Chapter 1.

COMESA

The COMESA member states are Burundi, Comoros, DR Congo, Djibouti, Egypt, Eritrea, Ethiopia, Kenya, Libya, Madagascar, Malawi, Mauritius, Rwanda, Seychelles, Swaziland, Sudan, Uganda, Zambia and Zimbabwe. In 2011 COMESA's Council of Ministers adopted its Regional Policy on IP Rights and Cultural Industries (COMESA IP Policy) together with Guidelines for preparing a national IP policy in accordance with this policy.[65] The policy was formulated with some technical assistance from WIPO.[66] It is structured as in Table 2.1 below.

The policy is a detailed statement of the COMESA member-states' commitments to regulating and implementing IP in a particular manner. Key amongst these are their undertakings to fully exploit available flexibilities 'to facilitate access to medicines for all people particularly the marginalised of society'[67] and the pro-

60 WIPO CDIP: Eleventh Session. Geneva, May 13 to 17, 2013. *Director General's Report on Implementation of the Development Agenda*. CDIP/11/2.

61 WIPO CDIP: Twelfth Session. Geneva, November 18 to 21, 2013: Progress reports. CDIP 12/2.

62 WIPO Committee on Development and Intellectual Property (CDIP): Thirteenth Session. Geneva, May 19 to 23, 2014. *Director General's Reports on Implementation of the Development Agenda*. CDIP 13/2.

63 WIPO CDIP: Fourteenth Session. Geneva, November 10 to 14, 2014. Revised Report on the Measurement of the Millennium Development Goals (MDGs) in other United Nations Agencies and specialized Agencies, and on the Contribution to WIPO to the Implementation of the MDGs (November, 2014) CDIP/14/12 Rev. Annex II, 8; and CDIP: Fourteenth Session. Geneva, November 10 to 14, 2014. Progress Reports. CDIP/14/2.

64 Gathii (2011) p. 362.

65 COMESA Council of Ministers Decision 90 (f) (2011); *COMESA Report of the Thirtieth Meeting of the Council of Ministers* (October 2011) CS/CM/XXX/2 para 249(c) p. 61.

66 WIPO Technical Assistance Database: Visit to WIPO headquarters by three senior officials from COMESA, October 2011 and Technical Assistance Database: COMESA – Comments on draft model law on IP policy and draft model law on IP, October 2011.

67 Para 39(d) Part A.

Table 2.1

Part A: 'COMESA Policy on Intellectual Property Rights'	*Part B: The COMESA Policy on copyright and copyright related industries*
Introduction (para 1–3)	Introduction (para 1–4)
Overview of IP (para 4–8)	Situation analysis (para 5–7)
Opportunities created by IP (para 9–10)	Policy objectives (para 8–9)
IP and economic development (para 11–14)	Applicability (para 10)
IP and trade (para 15–20)	Benefits (para 11)
IP and cultural industries (para 21–26)	Role of the COMESA Secretariat (para 12)
IP and TK and expressions of folklore (para 27–30)	Copyright (para 13–14)
IP and ICT (para 31–32)	Publishing (para 15–16)
IP Audit and valuation (para 33–34)	Media and Advertising (para 17–19)
Copyright and related rights (para 35–37)	Computer Software (para 20–22)
Industrial property (para 38–39)	Music (para 23–25)
	Film (para 26–28)
	Theatre and performing arts (para 29–31)
	Collective management organisations (para 32–33)
	Expressions of traditional cultural expressions (para 34–35)
	Valuation of copyright (para 36–37)
	Legal Framework (para 39)
	Commercialisation of copyright works (para 40)

motion of a harmonized IP legislative framework.[68] In relation to copyright the main policy objective is to 'encourage and promote copyright protection for socio-economic development within the COMESA member States, recognising that copyright is a major component of intellectual property.'[69] There is no express commitment to using available flexibilities to achieve other public interest goals like education or access to knowledge. The Guidelines for preparing a national IP policy are not publicly available so it is not possible to discuss them substantively.

Country profiles

This section summarizes the findings of a survey of African states' IP policies conducted primarily online through searching WIPO's online repository of national IP laws and related literature, WIPO Lex,[70] WIPO's technical assistance database,[71] the relevant states' government websites and a general internet search for news and other reports.[72] The aims of the survey were to:

1. determine if a country has an IP policy in place;

68 Para 39(e) Part A.

69 Para 8 Part B.

70 http://www.wipo.int/wipolex/en/index.jsp?tab=3

71 http://www.wipo.int/tad/en/

72 Ncube (2013–2015).

2. if there is a policy in place, to review the policy; and
3. if there is no policy, to establish if there is any publicly available information on the preparation of such a policy.[73]

Where an IP policy is both in place and publicly available, a brief commentary on its contents is given. However, in many cases policies were not publicly available. Some states have science, technology and innovation (STI) policies that include IP. Where these are publicly available, their contents will be briefly highlighted.

A major limitation of the survey was the lack of publicly available official information about national IP policies. States seem to prefer maintaining their policies in confidence and WIPO is bound by its terms of engagement not to disclose the substantive content of technical legal advice. Some, but not all, relevant activities are captured in its technical assistance database. The details pertaining to those activities that are listed are also scant. All that is usually provided is a meeting title, without an agenda or content related documents.[74] The picture that emerged from the survey is thus limited. However, it is useful to the extent that it maps IP policy related developments in Africa.

The findings of the survey are tabulated below in Table 2.2 which indicates the existence of relevant REC IP policies and classifies the states into three categories, namely:

(a) those with IP policies;
(b) those with policies that are under formulation; and
(c) those with neither an existing policy nor one under development.

The table is followed by a narrative summary which provides further information on those states that have IP policies and those that are currently engaged in policy formulation.

States with national IP policies

1. Ghana's National IP Policy and Strategy (NIPPS) was formulated under the auspices of the Swiss Ghana IP Project which was a partnership between Ghana's Ministry of Trade and Investment, Ministry of Justice and the Swiss Federal Institute of IP.[75] The policy was developed with assistance from the US Commercial Law Development Program[76] and WIPO under an IPDP concluded in 2008.[77] However, it remains unclear whether the NIPPS has

73 Ncube (2013a).
74 For a similar finding see Deere-Birkbeck and Roca (2011) p. 95.
75 Hopeson (2013); Swiss Federal Institute of Intellectual Property (2011).
76 US Commercial Law Development Program (n.d.).
77 Mould Iddrisu (2010); WIPO (2008).

Table 2.2

	REC IP policy coverage	
COMESA IP POLICY Burundi, Comoros, DR Congo, Djibouti, Egypt, Eritrea, Ethiopia, Kenya, Libya, Madagascar, Malawi, Mauritius, Rwanda, Seychelles, Swaziland, Sudan, Uganda, Zambia and Zimbabwe	EAC TRIPS Policy Burundi Kenya Rwanda Tanzania Uganda	ECOWAS TRIPS Policy Benin, Burkina Faso, Cape Verde, Côte d'Ivoire, The Gambia, Ghana, Guinea, Guinea-Bissau, Liberia, Mali, Niger, Nigeria, Senegal, Sierra Leone and Togo
	National IP policies in place (10)	
1. Ghana 2. Liberia 3. Malawi	4. Mauritius* 5. Mozambique 6. Rwanda * a new policy is under formulation	7. Senegal 8. Seychelles 9. Tunisia 10. Zambia
	National IP policies under formulation (19)	
11. Algeria 12. Botswana 13. Burundi 14. Central African Republic 15. Chad 16. The Gambia	17. Kenya 18. Lesotho 19. Madagascar 20. Mali 21. Nigeria 22. Sao Tome & Principe 23. Sierra Leone	24. South Africa 25. Swaziland 26. Tanzania 27. Togo 28. Uganda 29. Zimbabwe
	No information on policy formulation (25)	
30. Angola 31. Benin 32. Burkina Faso 33. Cameroon 34. Cape Verde 35. Comoros 36. Congo 37. Cote d'Ivoire	38. Democratic Republic of the Congo 39. Djibouti 40. Egypt 41. Equatorial Guinea 42. Eritrea 43. Ethiopia 44. Gabon 45. Guinea	46. Guinea-Bissau 47. Libya 48. Mauritania 49. Morocco 50. Namibia 51. Niger 52. Somalia 53. Sudan 54. South Sudan

been formally adopted by the government. Some reports state it has been adopted,[78] whilst others state the contrary.[79]

2. Liberia obtained technical assistance from WIPO with regard to the formulation of its IP policy, the terms of which are partially captured in an IPDP needs evaluation report prepared in 2009.[80] In 2013 WIPO reported that an

78 Swiss State Secretariat for Economic Affairs (SECO) (2013) p. 14.

79 GhanaWeb Business News (2014).

80 *WIPO Intellectual Property Development Plan for the Republic of Liberia: Final Report on the Needs Evaluation* (2009).

'IP strategy' was already under implementation in Liberia.[81] However, this strategy is not publicly available.

3. Malawi has a draft IP policy[82] however it is not clear whether this policy has been finalized, approved by Cabinet and come into effect yet. According to some reports, it was still under formulation in 2013[83] and there have been no further public updates as to its status as of March 2015.
4. Mauritius's IP policy was formulated with technical assistance from WIPO per an IPDP dated 2009.[84] This policy had been adopted and was under implementation by the end of 2011.[85] In March 2014, it was reported that an IP Council would be set up to co-ordinate and lead national IP initiatives and that a new IP policy would be formulated 'to mainstream IP into . . . economic and social development and to further promote innovation and creativity through a more holistic approach to IP matters'.[86]
5. Mozambique's 10-year IP Strategy (2008–2018) is available on WIPO Lex.[87] The Strategy articulates the following vision:

> 'The Mozambican government regards intellectual property as an instrument for stimulating and protecting creativity and innovation to promote the country's economic, scientific, technological and cultural development'. Its overall goal is 'to create the basic preconditions for promoting creativity, the results of scientific and technological research and local innovative capacity, thereby furthering the use of the intellectual property system for the benefit of the scientific, technological, economic, cultural and social development of the country'.

The Strategy cross-references several relevant national policies. It canvasses the current IP laws of the country; discusses the significance of IP and presents a strategic framework. This framework targets the following seven areas: dissemination of IP; education and IP; scientific and technological research; innovation and competitiveness in industry; traditional knowledge and biodiversity; creativity and development of the cultural industry; and administration of the IP system. Annex II of the Strategy presents an IP Action Plan which outlines 25 strategic goals to which short and medium term actions are assigned. The mid-term achievement target was set as 2012.

6. Rwanda's IP policy, 2009, is also publicly available and has been under implementation for several years.[88] The policy includes an implementation time frame that scheduled the completion of all specified activities by the end of 2011. For example, joining ARIPO by February 2010 is listed as an

81 WIPO support to NEPAD in collaboration with other United Nations Agencies (2013) p. 3.
82 Chatema (2011).
83 Neba (2013) p. 10.
84 WIPO support to NEPAD in collaboration with other United Nations Agencies (2013) p. 3.
85 WIPO support to NEPAD in collaboration with other United Nations Agencies (2013) p. 3.
86 Boolell (2014).
87 http://www.wipo.int/wipolex/en/text.jsp?file_id=202233.
88 WIPO support to NEPAD in collaboration with other United Nations Agencies (2013) p. 3.

activity under the rubric of 'Facilitating access to IP based essential goods and services especially in the health and food sectors.' Rwanda joined ARIPO in 2011. The national IP policy also provides for impact assessment and periodic policy review. According to clause 7.5 of the policy the first impact assessment and review had 'to be carried out two (2) years from the time of the launch of the Policy (2011). Thereafter the assessment and review should be carried out every four years with the third impact assessment and review timed to coincide with the end of Vision 2020'. Copies of these assessments and review reports are not publicly available. However, that is not to say that they were not done. The policy has not been updated since its adoption that would indicate that the assessment and reviews have not indicated that any changes are required.

7. Senegal's IP policy has been under implementation for several years.[89] However, it is not publicly available so it is not possible to outline it or comment on it.
8. Seychelles's IP policy has been under implementation for several years.[90] However, it is not publicly available so it is not possible to outline it or comment on it.
9. Tunisia finalized a National Strategy and Action Plan on Copyright and Related Rights in 2009, with technical assistance from WIPO.[91] Information on the adoption and implementation of the strategy is not publicly available.
10. Zambia's IP policy was finalized and adopted in 2010.[92] The policy contains an overview of then current law, a statement of the country's vision and goals for IP, a synopsis of related national policies, a discussion of guiding principles and a 10-year implementation framework. The policy also discusses the country's aspirations with regard to the protection of traditional knowledge and new plant varieties.

States with national IP policies under formulation

1. Algeria is in the process of formulating an IP policy and is receiving technical assistance from WIPO under Development Agenda Project DA_10_05: Development of National IP Strategies.[93] Further, Algeria finalized a National Strategy and Action Plan on Copyright and Related Rights in 2009, with

89 WIPO support to NEPAD in collaboration with other United Nations Agencies (2013) p. 3.
90 WIPO support to NEPAD in collaboration with other United Nations Agencies (2013) p. 3.
91 WIPO Technical Assistance Database: Elaboration of National Strategies and Action Plans on Copyright and Related Rights, and a Road Map for their Finalization and Formal Adoption for Algeria, Jordan, Lebanon and Tunisia. (2009).
92 Lusaka Times (2010); WIPO support to NEPAD in collaboration with other United Nations Agencies (2012–2013). p. 3.
93 WIPO Technical Assistance Database: Development of a National IP Strategy for Algeria. Assessment Mission: 1 January–31 May 2012.

technical assistance from WIPO.[94] Information on the adoption and implementation of the strategy is not publicly available.

2. Botswana's National Competition Policy (2005) expressly excludes IP from its ambit. The country's Research, Science, Technology and Innovation (RSTI) policy (2011) states at clause 5.9.3 that a national IP policy 'needs to be developed'. Consequently, the National IPDP for the Republic of Botswana (2012) includes a report on an IP Audit and a strategy 'road map' for the development of a national IP policy. At the end of 2014, WIPO reported that it was in consultation with Botswana in relation to the formulation of its IP Strategy.[95]
3. Burundi's IP policy is under formulation[96] and a draft has been formulated.[97]
4. The Central African Republic has been working on an IP policy since 2010.[98]
5. Chad is also working on an IP policy with WIPO technical assistance.[99]
6. The Gambia has been working on an IP policy with the assistance of WIPO.[100]
7. Kenya already has a policy on TK and IP known as the National Policy on TK, Genetic Resources and Traditional Cultural Expressions, 2009. In addition, Kenya started work on an IP policy several years ago.[101]
8. Lesotho is also working on a national IP policy with technical assistance from WIPO.[102]
9. Madagascar is currently working on its own national IP policy,[103] and submitted a request for technical and financial assistance from the WTO with regard to this in February 2013.[104] This request was granted and technical assistance is being rendered by WIPO.

94 WIPO Technical Assistance Database: Development of a National IP Strategy for Algeria. Assessment Mission: 1 January–31 May 2012.

95 WIPO Committee on Development and IP (CDIP) Revised Report on the Measurement of the Millennium Development Goals (MDGs) in other United Nations Agencies and Specialized Agencies, and on the Contribution to WIPO to the Implementation of the MDGs (November, 2014) CDIP/14/12 Rev. Annex II, 8.

96 WIPO Technical Assistance Database: Expert Mission to review the Draft National Intellectual Property Policy, + Stakeholders Workshop to Validate the Draft National Intellectual Property Policy of Burundi. 29 November 2012–28 February 2013.

97 SAANA Consulting (2013).

98 WIPO Technical Assistance Database: Consolidation of Intellectual Property Development Plan of Central African Republic. 20–26 May 2010. Bangui, CAR.

99 WIPO Technical Assistance Database: Projet de plan de développement de la pI et de l'innovation technologique (PNDPI). N'Djaména, Chad. 10–13 September 2013.

100 WIPO support to NEPAD in collaboration with other United Nations Agencies (2012–2013) p. 1; Barry (2013).

101 Nzomo (2013); Opijah (2013).

102 WIPO support to NEPAD in collaboration with other United Nations Agencies (2012–2013) p. 1.

103 WIPO support to NEPAD in collaboration with other United Nations Agencies (2012–2013) p. 1.

104 WTO (2013).

10. Mali's national IP policy has been under discussion and formulation since 2011.[105]
11. Nigeria has commenced an IP policy formulation process, with technical assistance from WIPO.[106] The country's STI Policy, 2011, deals with IP in clause 3.4. which sets out strategies for:

    i. Ensuring adequate intellectual property recognition, promotion and protection of creativities, traditional knowledge, indigenous technology and other intellectual assets.
    ii. Building local capacities in intellectual property management for effective transfer of technology.
    iii. Promoting a sustainable culture on intellectual property at all educational levels.
    iv. Establishing and strengthening Technology Transfer Offices for effective management and utilization of IP Rights in the National System of Innovation.
    v. Providing appropriate incentives for creativity and innovation to stimulate creativity and innovations.
    vi. Developing a viable IP policy especially regarding royalties and ownerships mechanism for equitable distribution of benefits accruing from inventions, traditional knowledge, biodiversity resources and innovations among stakeholders.
    vii. Establishing, regularly updating and facilitating access to intellectual property data bank and portals.
    viii. Ensuring a dynamic development of the IPR system to address new and emerging creativities including initiating when appropriate, the enactment and review of IP laws to incorporate all aspects and issues relating to plant breeders' rights, traditional knowledge and genetic resources.
    ix. Encouraging partnership with International IPR systems and organizations such as WIPO, ARIPO, OAPI, USPTO, SIPO, JPO.
    x. Supporting the development of IP assets through incubation and commercialization processes.
    xi. Developing the required human capital to protect and enforce IP legislature and standards.

12. Sao Tome and Principe concluded an IPDP with WIPO for which a validation meeting was held in September 2014. [107]

105 WIPO support to NEPAD in collaboration with other United Nations Agencies (May 2011 until April 2012) p. 2 and WIPO support to NEPAD in collaboration with other United Nations Agencies (2012–2013) p. 2.

106 WIPO support to NEPAD in collaboration with other United Nations Agencies (2012–2013) p. 3.

107 WIPO Technical Assistance Database: Réunion de validation et d'appropriation du Plan national de développement de la propriété intellectuelle de la République de Sao Tomé-et-Principe. 2–9 September 2014.

13. Sierra Leone's IP policy formulation process was commenced in 2012, with an IP audit undertaken with technical assistance from WIPO.[108]
14. South Africa: In 2004 the Department of Science and Technology (DST) published the Indigenous Knowledge Systems Policy (IKS Policy).[109] This policy was then formulated through an interdepartmental process. The DST is creating *sui generis* protection for TK to complement the DTI's approach[110] and has established a National Recordal System (NRS) for indigenous knowledge (IK).[111] On 20 March 2015, it published the Protection, Promotion, Development and Management of Indigenous Knowledge Systems Bill, 2014 for public comment.

    In a parallel with the DST's approach, the Department of Trade and Industry (DTI) prepared a Framework for the Protection of Indigenous TK through the IP System (TK IP Policy).[112] This policy was published together with a draft bill, the IP Laws Amendment Act, which sought to amend existing IP laws to cater for the protection of traditional knowledge (TK). After various amendments, and the denial by the President to sign it into law in 2012, the IP Laws Amendment Act, 4 of 2013 was finally enacted in December 2013. It has not yet come into force.

    Following the TK IP Policy and the enactment of the IP Laws Amendment Act, the DTI considers its work with regard to the protection of TK done and it has moved on to other general IP law reform. As a precursor to any legislative amendments, the DTI has taken the lead in the national IP policy formulation process. Information about the DTI's internal processes, any expert or stakeholder involvement in the preparation of the draft is closely held. The draft national IP policy was released for public comment in September 2013. Numerous comments were submitted, some of which were published by their authors.[113] Since then, the DTI has hosted some stakeholder consultation meetings but the IP policy is yet to be finalized.
15. Swaziland is in the process of formulating a national IP policy with technical assistance from WIPO,[114] which it has committed to finalizing by 2020.[115]
16. Tanzania is currently working on the formulation of a national IP policy with

108 WIPO support to NEPAD in collaboration with other United Nations Agencies (2012–2013) p. 1; Kanu (2012); WIPO. CDIP: Fourteenth Session. Geneva, November 10 to 14, 2014. Revised Report on the Measurement of the Millennium Development Goals (MDGs) in other United Nations Agencies and specialized Agencies, and on the Contribution to WIPO to the Implementation of the MDGs (November, 2014) CDIP/14/12 Rev. Annex II, 8 p. 31.

109 Republic of South Africa, Department of Science and Technology (DST) (2004).

110 Seleti (2012).

111 Ncube (2013b) and Egbuonu (2013).

112 DTI Policy Framework for the Protection of Indigenous Traditional Knowledge through the Intellectual Property System and the Intellectual Property Laws Amendment Bill, 2008.

113 For example see Schonwetter et al. (2013).

114 WIPO Technical Assistance Database: National IP Policy Workshop: The Strategic use of IP for Technological Capacity Building, Economic Growth and Development. Mbabane, Swaziland. 19–20 May 2014.

115 Dlamini (2014).

technical assistance from WIPO.[116] Its policies have been discussed above within the context of technical assistance.

17. Togo commenced the IP policy formulation process in 2010, with technical assistance from WIPO.[117] There is no further publicly available information about progress on the formulation.
18. Uganda is currently working on the formulation of a national IP policy with technical assistance from WIPO.[118]
19. Zimbabwe has formulated a draft national IP policy, with technical assistance from WIPO.[119] The draft policy has not yet been published for comment.

Conclusion

This chapter shows that African states are coming to grips with the importance of establishing a well-articulated written policy stance as the foundation of IP legislative frameworks. Only a few countries have adopted national IP policies, of which at least half are not publicly available. This makes the evaluation of such policies unachievable. REC IP policies, general or specific to patent-related flexibilities, are a welcome development as they provide a policy model for individual states to follow. As they are collective in their conceptualization, they also contribute to a harmonized regional approach that aids regional cohesiveness and facilitates collaborative approaches to public interest problems such as securing access to pharmaceuticals. Since the adoption of the WIPO DA, WIPO technical assistance has become much more context sensitive and incorporates advice on the use of TRIPS flexibilities which is important for developing countries and LDCs.

References

Primary sources: national and REC policies / strategies, agreements, decisions and official documents

Republic of Botswana. Ministry of Infrastructure, Science and Technology. *Research, Science, Technology and Innovation (RSTI) policy*. Gaborone: Botswana Government Printing and Publishing Services (2011).

Republic of Botswana. Ministry of Trade and Industry. *National Competition Policy*. Gaborone: Botswana Government Printing and Publishing Services (2005).

116 WIPO support to NEPAD in collaboration with other United Nations Agencies (2012–2013). p. 3.

117 WIPO support to NEPAD in collaboration with other United Nations Agencies (2012–2013). p. 3.

118 WIPO Technical Assistance Database: Consultative Meeting and High-Level National IP Policy Meeting: the Role of Innovation and Creativity Policies and Strategies for Technological Capacity Building, Economic Growth and Development. Kampala, Uganda. 22–24 April 2013.

119 WIPO Technical Assistance Database: Finalization of the IP Policy and IP Strategy for the Republic of Zimbabwe. Harare, Zimbabwe. 4–5 November 2014.

Republic of Kenya. *The National Policy on Traditional Knowledge, Genetic Resources and Traditional Cultural Expressions* (2009). Online. Available HTTP: <http://www.wipo.int/wipolex/en/text.jsp?file_id=246993>, accessed 1 March 2015.

Republic of Mozambique. *Intellectual Property Strategy 2008–2018* (2007). Online. Available HTTP: <http://www.wipo.int/wipolex/en/text.jsp?file_id=202233, accessed 1 March 2015.

Republic of Rwanda. Ministry of Trade and Industry. *Rwanda Intellectual Property Policy* (2009). Online. Available HTTP: <http://www.wipo.int/wipolex/en/text.jsp?file_id=215632>, accessed 1 April 2015.

Republic of South Africa. Department of Science and Technology. *Indigenous Knowledge Systems*. Pretoria, South Africa: Department of Science and Technology (2004).

Republic of South Africa. Department of Trade and Industry. *Policy Framework for the Protection of Indigenous Traditional Knowledge through the Intellectual Property System and the Intellectual Property Laws Amendment Bill*. Pretoria, South Africa: Department of Trade and Industry (2008).

Republic of South Africa. Department of Trade and Industry. *Draft National IP Policy*. Pretoria, South Africa: Department of Trade and Industry (2013).

Republic of South Africa. Ministry of Science and Technology. *Protection, Promotion, Development and Management of Indigenous Knowledge Systems Bill*. Pretoria, South Africa: Ministry of Science and Technology (2014).

Republic of Tanzania. *Action Plan for Realizing the IP Potentials of Tanzania*. Online. Available HTTP: <http://www.brela-tz.org/4b.GOT_NIPS%20roadmap_Annex_15%20Dec.docx>, accessed 15 March 2015.

Republic of Zambia. *National Intellectual Property Policy* (2009).

Republic of Zimbabwe. *Draft National Intellectual Property Policy for Zimbabwe* (2014).

COMESA

Council of Ministers Decision 90(f) Official Gazette of COMESA. Vol 16. 15 October 2011.

Policy on Intellectual Property Rights and Cultural Industries (2011). Online. Available HTTP: <http://www.ip-watch.org/weblog/wp-content/uploads/2013/05/Comesa-IP-policy-May-2013.pdf>, accessed 1 March 2015.

Report of the Thirtieth Meeting of the Council of Ministers CS/CM/XXX/2 (October 2011).

EAC

Health Protocol on Public Health Related WTO-TRIPS Flexibilities (2013).

Regional Intellectual Property Policy on the Utilization of Public Health-Related WTO-TRIPS Flexibilities and the Approximation of National Intellectual Property Legislation (2013).

ECOWAS/WAHO

Development of a Harmonized TRIPS Policy for Adoption by ECOWAS Member States that Employ TRIPS Flexibilities To Improve Access to Medicines in the Region (2012).

Guidelines for Implementation of TRIPS Flexibilities in National Legislation to Improve Access to Medicines in the West African Region (2012).

Protocol A/P.2/7/87 on the Establishment of a West African Health Organization (1987). Heads of State Decision A/Dec.9/10/98 (1998).

Supplementary Protocol A/SP.1/01/06 amending Articles VI-C, VI-L, IX-8, XI-2 and XII of Protocol A/P2/7/87 on the Establishment of the WAHO (2006).

WAHO Director-General's Report January – December 2012. WAHO/XVIV AHM/2013/Doc Rep.02 Draft (2013).

WIPO

Agreement between the World Intellectual Property Organization and the World Trade Organization. (1995)

Convention Establishing the World Intellectual Property Organization (1967).

CDIP. *Project Documents for Implementation of Recommendations 2, 5, 8, 9 and 10*. CDIP/3/INF/2 (2009).

CDIP. *Progress Report on Projects for Implementation of Recommendations 2, 5, 8, 9 and 10*. CDIP/4/2 Annex VIII (2009).

CDIP: Sixth Session. Geneva, November 22 to 26, 2010. *Progress Reports on Development Agenda Projects*. CDIP/6/2 Annex IX.

CDIP: Seventh Session. Geneva, May 2 to 6, 2011. *Director General's Report on Implementation of the Development Agenda*. CIDP7/2 Annex 1.

CDIP: Eighth Session. Geneva, November 14 to 18, 2011. *Progress Reports on Development Agenda Projects*. CDIP/8/2 Annex VIII.

CDIP: Ninth Session. Geneva, May 7 to 11, 2012. *Joint Proposal by the Development Agenda Group and the Africa Group on WIPO's Technical Assistance in the Area of Cooperation for Development*. CDIP 9/16.

CDIP: Tenth Session. Geneva, November 12 to 16, 2012. *Evaluation Report on the Project on Improvement of National, Sub-regional and Regional IP Institutional and User Capacity*. CDIP/10/7.

CDIP: Eleventh Session. Geneva, May 13 to 17, 2013. *Director General's Report on Implementation of the Development Agenda*. CDIP/11/2.

CDIP: Twelfth Session. Geneva, November 18 to 21, 2013: *Progress reports*. CDIP 12/2.

CDIP: Thirteenth Session. Geneva, May 19 to 23, 2014. *Director General's Reports on Implementation of the Development Agenda*. CDIP 13/2.

CDIP: Fourteenth Session. Geneva, November 10 to 14, 2014. *Revised Report on the Measurement of the Millennium Development Goals (MDGs) in other United Nations Agencies and specialized Agencies, and on the Contribution to WIPO to the Implementation of the MDGs* (November, 2014) CDIP/14/12 Rev. Annex II, 8.

CDIP: Fourteenth Session. Geneva, November 10 to 14, 2014. *Progress Reports*. CDIP/14/2.

General Assembly Forty-First (21st Extraordinary) Session. Geneva, October 1 to 9, 2012. *Report of the CDIP*. WO/GA/41/12 Appendix III.

Intellectual Property Development Plan for the Republic of Liberia. *Final Report on the Needs Evaluation* (2009). Online. Available HTTP: <http://www.moci.gov.lr/doc/LiberiaFinalConsolidatedIPDP.pdf>, accessed 1 March 2015.

Methodology and Tools for the Development of National IP Strategies. Online. Available HTTP: <http://www.wipo.int/ipstrategies/en/methodology/>.

Methodology for the Development of National Intellectual Property Strategies. Tool 1: The Process WIPO Pub_958_1 (2014).

Methodology for the Development of National Intellectual Property Strategies. Tool 2: Baseline Questionnaire WIPO Pub 958 2 (2014).

Methodology for the Development of National Intellectual Property Strategies. Tool 3: Benchmarking Indicators WIPO Pub 958_3 (2014).

Methodology for the Development of National Intellectual Property Strategies. Tool 4:

National IP Strategies (NIPS) Online Survey (2014). Available HTTP: <http://www.wipo.int/ipstrategies/en/methodology/nips_survey.html>, accessed 1 March 2015.

Technical Assistance Database: COMESA – Comments on draft model law on IP policy and draft model law on IP, October 2011. Online. Available HTTP: <http://www.wipo.int/tad/en/activitydetails.jsp?id=2246>, accessed 16 January 2015.

Technical Assistance Database: Consolidation of Intellectual Property Development Plan of Central African Republic. 20–26 May 2010. Bangui, CAR. Online. Available HTTP: <http://www.wipo.int/tad/en/activitydetails.jsp?id=1138>, accessed 1 March 2015.

Technical Assistance Database: Consultative Meeting and High-Level National IP Policy Meeting: the Role of Innovation and Creativity Policies and Strategies for Technological Capacity Building, Economic Growth and Development. Kampala, Uganda. 22–24 April 2013. Online. Available HTTP: <http://www.wipo.int/tad/en/activitydetails.jsp?id=4934>, accessed 1 March 2015.

Technical Assistance Database: Development of a National IP Strategy for Algeria. Assessment Mission: 1 January–31 May 2012. Online. Available HTTP: <http://www.wipo.int/tad/en/activitydetails.jsp?id=2722>, accessed 1 March 2015.

Technical Assistance Database: Elaboration of National Strategies and Action Plans on Copyright and Related Rights, and a Road Map for their Finalization and Formal Adoption for Algeria, Jordan, Lebanon and Tunisia. Tunis, Tunisia. 17–21 November 2009. Online. Available HTTP: <http://www.wipo.int/tad/en/activitydetails.jsp?id=1167>, accessed 1 March 2015.

Technical Assistance Database: Expert Mission to review the Draft National Intellectual Property Policy, and Stakeholders Workshop to Validate the Draft National Intellectual Property Policy of Burundi. 29 November 2012–28 February 2013.

Technical Assistance Database: Finalization of the IP Policy and IP Strategy for the Republic of Zimbabwe. Harare, Zimbabwe. 4–5 November 2014. Online. Available HTTP: <http://www.wipo.int/tad/en/activitydetails.jsp?id=7294>, accessed 1 March 2015.

Technical Assistance Database: National IP Policy Workshop: The Strategic use of IP for Technological Capacity Building, Economic Growth and Development. Mbabane, Swaziland. 19–20 May 2014. Online. Available HTTP: <http://www.wipo.int/tad/en/activitydetails.jsp?id=6763>, accessed 1 March 2015.

Technical Assistance Database: Projet de plan de développement de la pI et de l'innovation technologique (PNDPI). N'Djaména, Chad. 10–13 September 2013. Online. Available HTTP: http://www.wipo.int/tad/en/activitydetails.jsp?id=5637, accessed 1 March 2015.

Technical Assistance Database: Réunion de validation et d'appropriation du Plan national de développement de la propriété intellectuelle de la République de Sao Tomé-et-Principe. 2–9 September 2014. Online. Available HTTP: <http://www.wipo.int/tad/en/activitydetails.jsp?id=7519>, accessed 1 March 2015.

Technical Assistance Database: Visit to WIPO headquarters by three senior officials from COMESA, October 2011. Online. Available HTTP: <http://www.wipo.int/tad/en/activitydetails.jsp?id=2283>, accessed 16 January 2015.

WIPO support to NEPAD in collaboration with other United Nations Agencies (May 2011 until April 2012). Available HTTP: <http://www.un.org/africa/osaa/2012_un_system/WIPO_NEPAD%202012.pdf>, accessed 1 March 2015.

WIPO support to NEPAD in collaboration with other United Nations Agencies (2012–2013).

WTO

WTO Council for Trade-Related Aspects of Intellectual Property Rights, 2013. *Priority Needs For Technical And Financial Cooperation: Communication From Madagascar*, 22 February 2013, IP/C/W/584.

Secondary sources

Abdel Latif, A., 2011. Change and continuity in the international intellectual property system: a turbulent decade in perspective, *WIPO Journal*, 3(2), 36–55.

Anderson, J.E., 1984. *Public-policy making: An Introduction.* 3rd ed. Boston, MA: Houghton Mifflin.

Barry, S., 2013. Justice Ministry, WIPO seminar on Madrid Agreement ends. *Daily Observer, The Gambia*, 9 May 2013. Online. Available HTTP: <http://archive.observer.gm/africa/gambia/article/justice-ministry-wipo-seminar-on-madrid-agreement-ends>, accessed 1 March 2015.

Blakeney, M. and Mengistie, G., 2011. Intellectual property and economic development in Sub-Saharan Africa, *Journal of World Intellectual Property*, 14(3/4), 238–264.

Boolell, A., 2014. 'Statement at the Opening of the Workshop on Intellectual Property Rights at the Intercontinental Hotel, Balaclava, Mauritius 5 March 2014'. Online. Available HTTP: <http://foreign.govmu.org/English/statements/Pages/default.aspx>, accessed 1 April 2015.

Chatema, Z., 2011. 'Presentation on Country Experiences in Implementation of Intellectual Property Rights – Malawi'. *WTO Symposium on LDC Priority Needs for Technical and Financial Cooperation*, Geneva, Switzerland, 19–21 October 2011. Online. Available HTTP: <https://www.wto.org/english/tratop_e/trips_e/zakeyo_chatima_malawi_presentation_e.pdf>, accessed 1 March 2015.

Correa, C.M., 2006. Implications of bilateral free trade agreements on access to medicines, *Bulletin of the World Health Organisation*, 84(5), 399–404.

de Beer, J., 2009. 'Defining WIPO's development agenda' in de Beer, J. (ed.) *Implementing the World Intellectual Property Organisation's Development Agenda.* Waterloo, Ontario: International Development Research Centre and Wilfrid Laurier University Press.

Deere-Birkbeck, C., 2008. 'The politics of intellectual property reform in developing countries: the relevance of the World Intellectual Property Organization' in Netanel, N.W. (ed.) *The Development Agenda: Global Intellectual Property and Developing Countries.* Oxford: Oxford University Press, 111–131.

Deere-Birkbeck, C. and Marchan, R., 2010. *The Technical Assistance Principles of the WIPO Development Agenda and their Practical Implementation. International Centre for Trade and Sustainable Development (ICTSD), Programme on IPRs and Sustainable Development*, Issue Paper No. 28. Geneva, Switzerland: ICTSD.

Deere-Birkbeck, C. and Roca, S., 2011. *An External Review of WIPO Technical Assistance in the Area of Cooperation for Development.* Geneva, Switzerland: WIPO. Online. Available HTTP: <http://www.wipo.int/edocs/mdocs/mdocs/en/cdip_8/cdip_8_inf_1-annex1.pdf>, accessed 19 February 2015.

Deere, C., 2009. *The Implementation Game: The TRIPS Agreement and the Global Politics of Intellectual Property Reform in Developing Countries.* New York: Oxford University Press.

Dlamini, T., 2014. Intellectual property laws, strategy operational by 2020. *The Swazi Observer*, 20 May 2014. Online. Available HTTP: <http://www.observer.org.sz/news/61977-intellectual-property-laws-strategy-operational-by-2020.html>.

Dye, T., 1972. *Understanding Public Policy*. Englewood Cliffs, NJ: Prentice Hall.

ECOWAS, 2014. *Parliamentarians Decry Non-Enforcement of the Community Court Judgments*. Press Release. 20 May 2014. Online. Available HTTP: <http://www.parl.ecowas.int/documents/session_mai_2014/pr2.pdf>, accessed 1 March 2015.

Egbuonu, K., 2013. 'Explained: South Africa's national recordal system for indigenous knowledge' Afro-IP, 12 June 2013. Online. Available HTTP: <http://afro-ip.blogspot.com/2013/06/explained-south-africas-national.html>, accessed 1 December 2014.

Frankel, S., 2008. 'The legitimacy and purpose of intellectual property chapters in FTAs' in Buckley, R.P., Lo, V.I. and Boulle, L. (eds) *Challenges to Multilateral Trade: The Impact of Bilateral, Preferential and Regional Agreements*. The Netherlands: Kluwer Law International, 185–200.

GhanaWeb Business News, 2014. 'Gov't to harmonise intellectual property laws', *GhanaWeb*, 29 July 2014. Online. Available HTTP: <http://www.ghanaweb.com/GhanaHomePage/NewsArchive/artikel.php?ID=318911>, accessed 1 March 2015.

Gathii, J.T., 2011. *African Regional Trade Agreements as Legal Regimes*. Cambridge: Cambridge University Press.

Howlett, M. and Lejano, R.P., 2013. 'Tales from the crypt: the rise and fall (and rebirth?) of policy design', *Administration & Society*, 45(3), 357–381.

Hogwood, B. W. and Gunn, L., 1984. *Policy Analysis for the Real World*. Oxford, UK: Oxford University Press.

Hopeson, D., 2013. Cooperative Approaches to IPR Protection in Ghana. *Workshop on the Practical Approaches to IP Utilization and Protection in Africa*. Dar es Salaam, Tanzania, 19–21 March, 2013.

Kanu, O., 2012. Sierra Leone Presentation on Challenges in Formulation and Implementation of National Intellectual Property Policies and Strategies. *WIPO Conference on The Role of Intellectual Property Offices (IPOs) in Promoting Innovation, Business Competitiveness and Economic Growth*. Tokyo, Japan. 2–3 February 2012. WIPO/INN/TYO/12/REF/T3SIERRA-LEONE. Online. Available HTTP: <http://www.wipo.int/edocs/mdocs/aspac/en/wipo_inn_tyo_12/wipo_inn_tyo_12_ref_t3sierra_leone.pdf>, accessed 1 March 2015.

Longman Dictionary of Contemporary English, 2003, 4th ed. Harlow, UK: Pearson Education.

Lusaka Times. 2010. Zambia: Government launches National Intellectual Property policy. *Lusaka Times*, 6 October 2010. Online. Available HTTP: <http://www.trademarksa.org/news/zambia-government-launches-national-intellectual-property-policy>, accessed 1 March 2015.

May, C., 2007. The World Intellectual Property Organization and the Development Agenda. *Global Governance*, 13, 161–170.

Mould Iddrisu, B., 2010. 'Attorney General launches Ghana's Intellectual Property Development Plan', 23 July 2010. Online. Available HTTP: <https://bettymould.wordpress.com/2010/07/23/attorney-general-launches-ghana%E2%80%99s-intellectual-property-development-plan/>, accessed 1 March 2015.

Musungu, S.F., 2010. The development agenda and the changing face of the World Intellectual Property Organization (WIPO). *Iqsensato Studies* 2 (Working Draft).

Ncube, C.B., 2013–2015. 'A-Z Series: IP policies in Africa' Afro-IP. Online. Available HTTP: <http://afro-ip.blogspot.com/>, accessed 25 March 2015.

Ncube, C.B., 2013a. 'New A–Z series: IP policies in Africa. No. 1: Algeria'. 23 August 2013. Online. Available HTTP: <http://afro-ip.blogspot.com/2013/08/new-z-series-ip-policies-in-africa-no-1.html>, accessed 1 March 2015.

Ncube, C.B., 2013b. 'RSA: national recordal system for indigenous knowledge launched'.

29 May 2013. Online. Available HTTP: <http://afro-ip.blogspot.co.uk/2013/05/rsa-national-recordal-system-for.html>, accessed 1 December 2014.

Neba, A., 2013. IPR systems and technology transfer at research institutions in southern Africa. (On file with author.)

Netanel, N.W., 2009. 'Introduction: The WIPO development and its development policy context' in Netanel, N.W. (ed.) *The Development Agenda: Global Intellectual Property and Developing Countries*. Oxford: Oxford University Press, 1–29.

Nzomo, V., 2013. 'Does Kenya really need a national intellectual property policy?' 18 January 2013. Online. Available HTTP: <https://cipitlawstrath.wordpress.com/2013/01/18/does-kenya-really-need-a-national-intellectual-property-policy/comment-page-1/>, accessed 1 March 2015.

Olowu, D., 2002. Introduction-governance and public administration in the 21st century: a research and training prospectus. *International Review of Administrative Sciences*, 68, 345–353.

Opijah, D., 2013. 'Towards a national intellectual property policy for Kenya'. 2 June 2013. Online. Available HTTP: <http://www.jdsupra.com/legalnews/towards-a-national-intellectual-property-13421/>, 1 March 2015.

Pugatch, M.P., 2011. Intellectual property policy making in the 21st century, *WIPO Journal*, 3(1), 71–80.

SAANA Consulting, 2013. 'Factual overview on technical and financial cooperation for LDCs related to TRIPS'. Online. Available HTTP: <https://www.wto.org/english/tratop_e/trips_e/ldc_overview_08.05.2013_ch3.pdf>, accessed 1 March 2015.

Salmon, P., 2003. Cooperation between the World Intellectual Property Organization (WIPO) and the World Trade Organization (WTO). *Journal of Civil Rights and Economic Development*, 17(3), 429–441.

Schonwetter, T., Vawda, Y.A., Ncube, C.B., Rens, A., Baker, B.K., Louw, A., Bernard Maister, B. and de Jonge, B., 2013. 'Academics' submissions on the Draft national IP Policy', 2013. Online. Available HTTP: <http://ip-unit.org/wp-content/uploads/2013/10/IP-Policy-Academics-Submission_final171013.pdf>, accessed 1 December 2014.

Seleti, Y., 2012. 'DST report on IKS activities: a progress report on sui generis legislation'. Online. Available HTTP: <www.pmg.org.za/report/20120613-indigenous-knowledge-systems-iks-activities-sui-genris-legislation-b>, accessed 28 February 2013.

Sell, S., 2007. TRIPS-plus free trade agreements and access to medicines, *Liverpool Law Review*, 28(1), 41–75.

Simon, C.A., 2007. *Public Policy: Preferences and Outcomes*. New York: Pearson Longman.

South African Government News Agency, 2013. 'DTI to host intellectual property policy conference'. 5 November 2013. Online. Available HTTP: <http://www.sanews.gov.za/south-africa/dti-host-intellectual-property-policy-conference>, accessed 1 December 2014.

Swiss Federal Institute of IP, 2011. 'Strengthening the intellectual property system in Ghana'. Online. Available HTTP: <https://www.ige.ch/en/legal-info/international-cooperation/country-specific-projects/ghana.html>, accessed 1 March 2015.

Swiss State Secretariat for Economic Affairs (SECO), 2013. *Swiss Economic Cooperation and Development Ghana Country Strategy Report 2013–2016*. Berne, Switzerland: SECO.

Sykes, S., 2011. 'Policy: what is it? How is it made?' in Porter, E. and Coles, L. (eds) *Policy and Strategy for Improving Health and Wellbeing*. Exeter: Learning Materials, 1–21.

UN, n.d. 'UN on-line glossary on governance and public administration'. Online. Available HTTP: <http://www.unpan.org/Directories/UNPAGlossary/tabid/928/Default.aspx>, accessed 19 February 2015.

US Commercial Law Development Program, n.d. 'Developing regional IP task force coordination action plans for Ghana, Liberia, Nigeria and Kenya', August 1–5, 2011. Washington, DC: US CLDP. Online. Available HTTP: <http://cldp.doc.gov/programs/cldp-in-action/details/954>, accessed 1 March 2015.

Wilson, R., 2006. 'Policy analysis as policy advice' in Moran, M. Rein, M. and Goodin, R.E. (eds) *The Oxford Handbook of Public Policy*. New York, NY: Oxford University, 152–168.

WIPO, n.d.a. 'Legislative assistance'. Online. Available HTTP: <http://www.wipo.int/ip-development/en/legislative_assistance/>, accessed 1 March 2015.

WIPO, n.d.b. 'WHO, WIPO, WTO trilateral cooperation on public health, IP and trade'. Online. Available HTTP: <http://www.wipo.int/policy/en/global_health/trilateral_cooperation.html>, accessed 1 March 2015.

WIPO, 2008. 'WIPO signs Intellectual Property development plan with the Republic of Ghana'. Geneva, May 8, 2008. PR/2008/551. Online. Available HTTP: <http://www.wipo.int/pressroom/en/articles/2008/article_0024.html>, accessed 1 March 2015.

3 Sub-regional trade co-operation and integration

Introduction

This chapter will give an outline of existing sub-regional trade co-operation and integration in Africa and then consider to what extent, if any, IP has been included in these schemes. There is a wealth of sound scholarship on regional economic integration generally[1] and in Africa, in particular,[2] which this chapter will not replicate. Instead, it will focus on the place of IP in the legal frameworks of these structures. Chapter 4 will discuss the harmonization and unification efforts of the ARIPO and the OAPI in relation to the IP frameworks of their member states. This chapter considers the same efforts by RECs. This raises the question of duplication and questions the necessity of REC involvement in this arena. Another pertinent enquiry is the relationship between community and national laws.

The inclusion of IP in the regulatory frameworks of RECs is motivated by a number of factors. These include the entrenchment of IP matters within the trade context to which they indisputably belong. IP is an important aspect of trade and excluding its detailed treatment from binding REC instruments is disadvantageous.[3] This is because when trade in goods and services occurs across the borders of REC member states, the affected trade partners will have to seek relevant IP protection in the different countries across which trade is occurring. This task is very onerous where the IP laws of those countries are different. For OAPI member states this problem does not arise because their IP laws are unified. However, for ARIPO member states, this is a very real problem because their IP systems are diverse and fragmented due to the fact that subscription to, and domestication of, ARIPO Protocols is uneven across the membership.[4]

Another important reason is that REC harmonization of IP would be more inclusive than those of the regional IP organizations because not all AU member

1 For example see Perdikis (2007); Matthias and Bhagwati (2002).

2 For example see Osiemo (2014); Matambalya (2014) pp.131–162; Gottschalk (2012); Oppong (2011); Gathii (2011, 2010); Kouassi (2007); Lee (2002); Asante (1997); Oyejide, Elbadawi and Collier (1997).

3 Nkomo (2014) p. 324.

4 Nkomo (2014) p. 321.

states are members of either of these organizations. Most notably, South Africa and Nigeria belong to neither.[5] This reason has been cited as the justification for the establishment of PAIPO. However, if it is also being cited as the reason for REC engagement with IP, as it is, wouldn't PAIPO's efforts then duplicate those of the RECs? A further justification for IP harmonization by RECs is that some RECs have dispute resolution fora such as Tribunals, which the regional IP organizations may lack.[6] ARIPO only has an appellate body to deal with appeals against registration decisions. As will be shown in Chapter 4, OAPI has broader enforcement and dispute resolution arrangements.

The cogency of these reasons may be questioned but the reality is that most RECs already include IP in their mandates and have some regulatory instruments that engage with IP. As stated in Chapter 1, some RECs, such as SADC, have articulated their intent to deepen their harmonization of IP amongst their member states. Several have also formulated IP policies, as shown in Chapter 2. Further, as stated in Chapter 1, COMESA, EAC and SADC have launched a T-FTA that will include an IP Agenda. The T-FTA is a significant building block of the continental FTA (C-FTA).[7] It has been proposed that the T-FTA and ECOWAS should merge as the first steps to the creation of the C-FTA.[8] Current plans are to launch the C-FTA in 2017.[9] Finally, as the establishment of the C-FTA, AEC and PAIPO continues apace, there is no doubt that IP matters will soon be firmly located in a continental trade context. It is thus important to grapple with the IP aspects of regionalism in this chapter.

This chapter proceeds as follows: It gives a general overview of regionalism as it has unfolded in Africa. Then it considers the relationship between community and national laws. This is followed by a consideration of selected RECs' regulation of IP. In particular, this consideration canvasses the IP Frameworks of COMESA, EAC, ECOWAS and SADC respectively. These RECs have been selected because they are 'indisputably, Africa's four leading RECs today'[10] and because they are the core of the C-FTA which is a critical formative phase of the AEC. The IP Agenda of the T-FTA is canvassed last, prior to a conclusion of the chapter.

Theories of regionalism

There is much intellectual debate about the precise definition of the core concepts in usage in trade related discourse and a tendency to conflate them.[11] It is thus necessary to present the definitions used in this work. Regionalization is a wide concept that includes the actions of state and non-state actors in the pursuit of their

5 Nkomo (2014) p. 333.
6 Nkomo (2014) p. 333.
7 UNECA (2012) p. 21.
8 Ngwenya (2015).
9 Mwanza (2014); AU (2011) p. 4.
10 Gottschalk (2012) p. 23.
11 Akokpari (2008) p. 86; Olivier and Olivier (2004) p. 353.

political, economic and social goals with regard to both formal and informal sectors.[12] Regionalism is narrower in that it excludes non-state actors. It is 'the adoption of a regional project by a formal regional economic organization designed to enhance the political, economic, social, cultural, and security integration and/or co-operation of member states.'[13] This definition encompasses both regional co-operation and regional integration.[14] Some authors use the two terms interchangeably, whilst others treat them as distinct. [15] This work falls in the latter camp and sets out disparate definitions of the two terms below, together with definitions of market integration, development integration and neo-functional integration.

Regional co-operation

Regional co-operation is project centered in the sense that countries collaborate on specific issues to achieve agreed social, economic and political ends. Regional co-operation is popularly viewed as the preliminary stage towards, and the means to, integration.[16] However, it is important to note that this is not always the case and states may co-operate with no intention to pursue ultimate integration.[17]

An example of regional co-operation is the formation of the Southern African Development Co-ordination Conference (SADCC) to reduce the economic vulnerability to which its members were exposed by their dependence on trade with apartheid South Africa. Once that vulnerability was reduced by the democratization of South Africa, SADCC morphed into SADC, which is discussed further below. Some scholars have argued that SADCC fits into the regional integration, development integration or neo-functional integration models, but the more persuasive view is that it does not fit into any of these models,[18] and is more aptly classified as regional co-operation.

Regional integration

Regional integration is the end-game towards which some regional co-operation strives.[19] Lee defines it as

> a process by which a group of nation states voluntarily and in various degrees [have access] to each other's markets and establish mechanisms and techniques that minimize conflicts and maximize internal and external economic, political, social and cultural benefits of their interaction.[20]

12 Afadameh-Adeyemi (2013) pp. 15–6; Akokpari (2008) p. 88.
13 Lee (2003) p. 8.
14 Mutai (2007) p. 31.
15 Afadameh-Adeyemi (2013) p. 12; Mutai (2007) p. 32; Asante (1997) p. 20.
16 Akokpari (2008) p. 86; Haas (1970) p. 610.
17 Mutai (2007) p. 32.
18 Ostergaard (1993) p. 45.
19 Asante (1997) p. 21.
20 Lee (2002) p. 4.

Coining a precise definition of this term has proven elusive and it has often been concretized by aligning it to economic integration.[21] Indeed, the first part of Lee's above definition incorporates Asante's following classic definition of economic integration as

> a process whereby two or more countries in a particular area voluntarily join together to pursue common policies and objectives in matters of general economic development . . . to the mutual advantage of all the participating states.[22]

From a theoretical point of view, regional integration may take the form of market integration, development integration or neo-functional integration.

Market integration

Market integration is the sequential or linear development by a group of states to an economic union, which progresses through 'integration of goods, labor and capital markets, and eventually monetary and fiscal integration.'[23] Despite its significant challenges, it is Africa's mode of choice.[24] It is achieved through RTAs or Regional Integration Arrangements (RIAs). The classic economic typology of RTAs identifies four kinds of RTAs, namely Free Trade Areas (FTAs), Customs Unions (CUs), Common Markets and Economic Unions.[25] Some scholars add 'total economic integration'[26] or a 'political union'[27] to this list. These terms are defined below. FTAs and CUs are defined with reference to the WTO's General Agreement on Tariffs and Trade (GATT) and General Agreement on Trade in Services (GATS).

An FTA is a 'group of two or more customs territories in which the duties and other restrictive regulations of commerce . . . are eliminated on substantially all the trade between the constituent territories in products originating in such territories.'[28] Rules of origin are put into place in order to prevent non-members of the FTA from seeking to circumvent the trade barriers that apply to them, by routing their wares through a member of the FTA.[29]

A CU is:

> the substitution of a single customs territory for two or more customs territories, so that

21 Afadameh-Adeyemi (2013) p. 15; Akokpari (2008) p. 87; Mutai (2007) p. 31.
22 Asante (1997) p. 19, citing Mutharika (1972) p. 15.
23 Hartzenberg (2011) p. 2. Also see Hartzenberg and Malungisa (2011) p. 62; Lee (2002) p. 1.
24 Lee (2002) p. 1; Ostergaard (1993) p. 27.
25 Perdikis (2007) p. 82–83.
26 Lee (2002) p. 3; Balassa (1961) p. 2.
27 Ostergaard (1993) p. 30.
28 Paragraph 8(b) of Article XXIV of the General Agreement on Tariffs and Trade (GATT) 1994.
29 Perdikis (2007) p. 83.

> (i) duties and other restrictive regulations of commerce . . . [barring some permissible necessary exceptions] are eliminated with respect to substantially all the trade between the constituent territories of the union or at least with respect to substantially all the trade in products originating in such territories, and,
>
> (ii) subject to the provisions of paragraph 9, substantially the same duties and other regulations of commerce are applied by each of the members of the union to the trade of territories not included in the union.[30]

In other words, a CU is one step beyond an FTA because it maintains the FTA and adds to it, a common external tariff that is applicable to trading partners outside the CU.[31]

A Common Market proceeds beyond a CU by adding the unrestrained exchange of capital and labor between its members.[32] An Economic Union is the endgame; it entails fiscal and monetary policy harmonization.[33] The distinction between an Economic Union and total economic integration is that the latter encompasses unification, rather than harmonization, of fiscal and monetary policy.[34]

The laws on the multilateral trading system regulate RTAs. A full purview of these laws is beyond the scope of this work.[35] Suffice it to state that this regulation is necessary because RTAs are inherently discriminatory, which runs contrary to the non-discriminatory fundamental principle of the multilateral trading system.[36] The market integration model has been faulted on various grounds, the primary of which is the fallibility of its underlying assumptions which envisage perfect market conditions, which is sadly not the reality of many developed countries and, more so, of developing countries.[37] Another oft-cited flaw is the model's failure to factor in the reality that due to the different industrial capacities of participating countries, some countries would benefit from integration whilst others would not.[38]

Development integration

Development integration does not focus only on trade like market integration through maximizing production capacity but serves as a catalyst for produc-

30 Paragraph 8(a) of Article XXIV of GATT 1994. For discussion see Viner (1950) and Oslington (2013).
31 Lee (2002) p. 3; Perdikis (2007) p. 83.
32 Lee (2002) p. 3; Perdikis (2007) p. 83.
33 Lee (2002) p. 3; Perdikis (2007) p. 83.
34 Lee (2002) p. 3; Balassa (1961) p. 2.
35 Article XXIV 5GATT. For in depth discussion see Perdikis (2007) pp. 85–87. Also see WTO Understanding on the Interpretation of Article XXIV of the General Agreement on Tariffs and Trade 1994.
36 Perdikis (2007) pp. 84–85.
37 Mutai (2007) p. 36; Ostergaard (1993) p. 31.
38 Mutai (2007) p. 37; Ostergaard (1993) p. 33.

tion capacity, via state intervention fuelled by heightened political co-operation amongst the members of the REC.[39] The uneven distribution of trade profits is rectified through the use of compensatory measures such as transfer tax or budgetary transfers, and corrective measures which afford favorable treatment to the economically weaker countries.[40] Whilst it is clearly more nuanced and better suited to developing states, development integration has been criticized because it does not always succeed in its goal of equitably distributing trade gains.[41] Examples cited in this regard include the first iteration of the EAC that failed and SACU.[42]

Neo-functional integration

Neo-functional integration is a progressive sectoral approach that extends integration to other sectors due to 'political spillover' inspired by preceding successful integration.[43] This spill over may be explained as the development of new political goals motivated by the pressure created by integrated sectors. [44] Such pressure would be generated by affected interest groups and political actors. Like the other theories of integration neo-functionalism is also criticised on a number of grounds. Chief of these for present purposes, is its reliance on the agency of economic and political actors, which is often lacking in Africa.[45]

As stated above, the predominant mode of regional integration in Africa and the core Pan-African approach is market integration. Some historical foregrounding of the Pan-African project is essential, as an introduction to the discussion of the IP regulatory frameworks of some African RECs. Accordingly the following section sets out the Pan-African plan for the establishment of the AEC.

The AU and the AEC

It is beyond the scope of this chapter to fully detail the genesis of Pan-Africanism and the history of its institutionalism through the Organization of African Unity (OAU) that later became the AU.[46] For present purposes, a brief excursus follows.

The OAU was created in 1963 and soon thereafter began to consider means of strengthening Africa's economic status through regionalism, ultimately culminating in the establishment of the AEC. A series of decisions and declarations progressively crystallized this vision, the key of which will be mentioned here. The first of these was the Addis Ababa Declaration, 1973 that strongly recommended the necessity for Africa to take charge of its destiny by crafting its own regional

39 Mutai (2007) p. 38; Ostergaard (1993) p. 34.
40 Ostergaard (1993) p. 35.
41 Ostergaard (1993). pp. 35–39.
42 Mutai (2007) p. 38.
43 Ostergaard (1993) p. 39.
44 Jensen (2013) pp. 62–64.
45 Ostergaard (1993) p. 41.
46 For an overview of this history see Gottschalk (2012) pp. 9–10; Kouassi (2007).

solutions.[47] The Kinshasa Declaration, 1976 articulated the plan to create the AEC within a maximum of 20 years.[48] The OAU Summit adopted this declaration and its accompanying Revised Master Plan in 1977.[49] The commitment to the AEC was confirmed by the Monrovia Declaration of Commitment of the Heads of State and Government, of the OAU on Guidelines and Measures for National and Collective Self-Reliance in Social and Economic Development for the Establishment of a New International Economic Order, 1979.[50] Consequently an extra-ordinary assembly was held in 1980 to pursue this vision and which resulted in the adoption of the Lagos Plan of Action and its annexure, the Final Act of Lagos which committed the OAU to the creation of the AEC by 2000.[51] A major step towards the achievement of that goal was the adoption of the Abuja Treaty Establishing the AEC in 1991, which came into force in 1994.[52] There has been significant commentary on this treaty,[53] which will not be rehashed here as the purpose of this section is to merely present the long-term vision, rather than to interrogate the merits of that vision.

It soon became evident that it would not be possible to realize the AEC by 2000, as originally intended. The OAU then adopted the Sirte Declaration in 1999 that resolved to form the AU to accelerate the implementation of the Abuja Treaty.[54] The AU was formed in July 2001 at Lusaka, Zambia with the adoption of the Constitutive Act of the AU, which came into force on 26 May 2001.[55] Its mandate includes the promotion of sustainable socio-economic and cultural development and the integration of African economies.[56] It also extends to 'co-ordinat[ing] and harmoniz[ing] the policies between the existing and future RECs' and promoting research in science and technology, amongst other fields.[57] A large part of this mandate is being pursued through a strategic program, the New Partnership for Africa's Development (NEPAD) that was established by the AU in 2001[58] and is implemented mostly at REC level.[59] In addition, some AU and NEPAD matters are discussed at regional level to better facilitate final AU collective decisions that are reached at the Assembly of Heads of State and Government (Assembly), the

47 Kouassi (2007) p. 2.
48 Kouassi (2007) pp. 2–3.
49 Kouassi (2007) p. 3.
50 Kouassi (2007) p. 3.
51 Kouassi (2007) p. 3.
52 Kouassi (2007) p. 5.
53 Mutai (2007); Thompson (1993); Mukisa and Thompson (1995).
54 Kouassi (2007) pp. 8–9.
55 Kouassi (2007) p. 9.
56 Article 3(j) Constitutive Act of the African Union.
57 Article 3(l)–(m) Constitutive Act of the African Union.
58 It was officially adopted in 2002 by the African Union Summit through the Declaration on the Implementation of NEPAD (Assembly/AU/Decl. 1 (I)).
59 AU Commission, New Zealand Ministry of Foreign Affairs and Trade/Manat Aorere (2014) p. 98.

highest organ of the AU. To this end, AU member states are organized into five geographic regions, namely central, eastern, northern, southern and western.[60]

The Abuja Treaty sets out an implementation plan of the establishment of the AEC by 2028 through a progressive six-stage process to be achieved within 34 years,[61] with the possibility of an extension to a maximum of 40 years.[62] As stated in Chapter 1, AMU/UMA, CEN-SAD, COMESA, EAC, ECCAS/CEEAC, ECOWAS, IGAD and SADC are intended to merge into the AEC. UMA is currently dormant[63] and ECCAS was dormant for a significant period of time before being operationalized in 1999.[64] The total number of RECs in Africa hovers around 14. This multiplicity poses problems of conflicting obligations for states that have multiple REC memberships. Such conflicts arise from the nuances in REC approaches and the differences in the nature of the RECs themselves. Further, if the ultimate goal is the creation of the AEC through merging 8 RECs, the creation of further RECs is difficult to justify. Consequently, in 2006 the AU placed a moratorium on the recognition of new RECs.[65]

The eight RECs that are listed above have agreed, through a Protocol on how to co-operate with each other and the AU in their progress towards the creation of the AEC.[66] One of the major steps towards this is the creation of inter-REC FTAs that are expected to then merge into the AEC.[67] COMESA, EAC and SADC have created a T-FTA, which is discussed below. Preceding that discussion, the chapter will first provide an overview of individual RECs. In particular, the following sections will focus on ECOWAS, SADC, COMESA, and the EAC for the reasons stated above.

Relational issues between the AU, AEC and RECs surprisingly, remain unaddressed.[68] The Protocol on the Relations between the African Union and the RECs fails to provide for the legal status of RECs within this configuration.[69] The RECs are not members of the AU nor party to the AEC Treaty, therefore they are not obliged to attain the AU's vision of their merging into the AEC.[70] The legal status of the AEC is that it 'form[s] an integral part' of the AU.[71] It has been argued that this means that the AEC will not have separate legal personality but will be

60 Article 1(d) Abuja Treaty; AU Commission, New Zealand Ministry of Foreign Affairs and Trade/ Manat Aorere (2014) p. 14.
61 Article 6(1) Abuja Treaty.
62 Article 6(6) Abuja Treaty; Kouassi (2007) p. 7.
63 Gottschalk (2012) p. 16.
64 AU (n.d.).
65 Mutai (2007) p. 106; AU, Decisions and Declarations – Decision on the Moratorium on the Recognition of Regional Economic Communities (RECs) DOC.EX.CL/278 (IX), AU Doc. Assembly/AU/Dec.111–132 (VII). Assembly of the African Union, Seventh Ordinary Session, 1–2 July 2006, Banjul, The Gambia.
66 Protocol on Relations between the AU and the RECs, 2007.
67 UNECA (2011) p. 6.
68 Oppong (2010) pp. 92–93.
69 Kolbeck (2014) p. 23.
70 Oppong (2010) p. 94.
71 Article 98(1) Treaty establishing the AEC.

subsumed into the AU, which has such personality. Embedding the AEC in the AU in this way has been critiqued as being 'unrealistic in expecting organizations like the [AU] which are primarily concerned with matters of a political nature, to take on the additional technical responsibilities required by the AEC'.[72] Oppong argues that scholarly discourse ought to extend beyond discussions of the legal status of the AEC to a conceptualization of it as a legal system.[73] His main concern pertaining to this system is that whilst its observance is required,[74] there is no express mention of the establishment of such a legal system in the AEC's constitutive treaty.

The relationship between community laws and national laws

It is important to preface the discussion of the IP regulatory framework of RECs with an overview of the import of these frameworks for REC member states. The core question is whether community laws are both binding and enforceable through national courts. This section distinguishes between direct applicability and direct effect. The former refers to when community laws automatically acquire force of law in a party state's jurisdiction upon ratification or accession.[75] The latter refers to instances when community law may be raised by individuals before national courts, typically in pursuit of the enforcement of their rights.[76]

The answer to this question of whether community law is directly applicable or has direct effect depends on the nature of the relevant community law and national approaches to the reception of community laws that encompass constitutional or legislative provisions, 'public awareness', 'legal culture' and 'judicial philosophy'.[77] Some community laws are directly applicable, in which case no positive action is required at national level to receive or translate the law into a particular jurisdiction.[78] The constitutive treaties of the four RECs considered in this chapter do not provide for the direct applicability of their community laws.[79] The treaties provide that member states have to take appropriative affirmative action to domesticate community laws.[80] In contrast, some African states' legislation provides for direct applicability of community laws in their jurisdictions. These are Uganda,[81] Kenya,[82]

72 Mutai (2007) p. 107.
73 Oppong (2006).
74 Article 3(e) AEC Treaty.
75 Oppong (2008) p. 151; Winter (1972) p. 425.
76 Oppong (2008) p. 158; Winter (1972) pp. 425–426.
77 Oppong (2008) p. 149.
78 Oppong (2008) p. 151.
79 Oppong (2008) p. 152.
80 Oppong (2008) pp. 152–154; Articles 5(2) (b), 10 and 12(1) COMESA Treaty; articles 8(2) and 14(5) EAC Treaty; articles 9(6) and 12(4) ECOWAS Treaty; article 6(5) SADC Treaty.
81 East African Community Act, 2002 Act 13 of 2002 (date of entry into force 15 January 2005 per East African Community Act (Commencement) Instrument, 2005); Onoria (2011) p.600; Oppong (2008) p. 153.
82 Section 8 Treaty for the Establishment of the East African Community Act 2 of 2000 (Cap 4C); Oppong (2008) p. 153.

Rwanda[83] and Tanzania.[84] In addition, in EAC member states, community laws are afforded supremacy.[85]

Where laws are not directly applicable, they have to be received or translated into domestic law. The translation of community laws into domestic legal systems is generally regulated by the constitution of the relevant country.[86] The relevant provisions refer broadly to international law, of which community law is a specie. African constitutions usually provide for one or more of the following:[87]

a) express acknowledgment of the RECs to which the country belongs together with an intention to align the state to the community vision and mission;
b) an articulation of the national goal of promoting and abiding by community objectives;
c) the mechanism or process by which international law is to be domesticated or otherwise acquires force of law;
d) the supremacy of the constitution; and
e) how conflicts between international law and national legislation are to be resolved.

In relation to (c) and (e) above, it is important to note that African states tend to fall into either one of two camps depending on their colonial history and post-colonial legal and cultural legacy. Countries formerly colonized by the French are monist; their constitutions usually provide that international law is automatically received into national law upon ratification or accession and also 'has precedence over national laws'.[88] Countries formerly colonized by the British are dualist; their constitutions require affirmative national action to receive international law into national law and in many cases there are no provisions on whether it has precedence over domestic law.[89]

The four RECs considered in this chapter also do not provide for the direct effect of community laws that would enable their enforcement through national courts.[90] However, COMESA, EAC and ECOWAS envisage that community laws would be placed before national courts and consequently provide a procedure through which national courts can refer related issues to community courts.[91]

83 Article 190 of Rwanda Constitution, 2003.
84 Tanzania: Treaty for the Establishment of East African Community Act 2001; Oppong (2008) p. 153.
85 Oppong (2008) p. 155.
86 Oppong (2008) p. 157.
87 Oppong (2008) pp. 158–161.
88 Oppong (2008) p. 159.
89 Oppong (2008) p. 160.
90 Oppong (2008) p. 155.
91 Oppong (2008) p. 155; article 30 COMESA Treaty; article 34 EAC Treaty; article 10(f) Protocol of the ECOWAS Community Court of Justice; article 16 Protocol to the SADC Tribunal and Rules.

Articles 14 and 15 of the SADC Protocol on the Tribunal and Rules of Procedure Thereof provide that domestic remedies must be exhausted before recourse is made to the Tribunal. It is not clear whether national courts can refer matters to it as article 18 provides that a 'competent institution or organ of the Community' may refer matters to the Tribunal. In ordinary parlance, one would not consider a national court to be an institution of the Tribunal. Oppong notes that national courts of the member states of COMESA, EAC and ECOWAS have applied community laws that were neither directly applicable nor domesticated in the relevant jurisdiction to matters placed before them.[92] It is thus difficult to make general statements about the import of community laws in Africa in general. To make an accurate statement about the position in a country, one would have to assess the relevant constitutional provisions as well as any relevant legislation and judicial precedents. It is with this background in mind, that the chapter now turns to a discussion of individual RECs.

COMESA

COMESA was founded in 1994[93] and was the planned outcome of a predecessor Preferential Trade Area (PTA) which had been formed in 1981.[94] COMESA's ultimate goal, like SADC, is the formation of a single currency Monetary Union by 2025.[95] This is preceded by a FTA[96] and a CU[97] which were formed in 2000 and 2009, respectively.

IP regulatory framework

The Treaty Establishing COMESA (COMESA Treaty) provides for co-operation in respect of the regulation of IP. First, article 104(1)(d) provides for information sharing on 'legislation on patents, trademarks and designs'. Further article 128(e) provides that:

> In order to promote co-operation in science and technology development, the Member States agree to jointly develop and implement suitable patent laws and industrial licensing systems for the protection of industrial property rights and encourage the effective use of technological information contained in patents.

92 Oppong (2008) pp. 166–172.

93 The Treaty Establishing the Common Market for Eastern and Southern Africa was signed on 5 November 1993 and came into force on 8 December 1994.

94 Gathii (2011) p. 165.

95 COMESA Treaty Article (4)(4)(a).

96 COMESA Treaty Article 45.

97 COMESA Treaty Article 45.

These clauses focus on industrial property and exclude copyright. Since the conclusion of the COMESA Treaty in 1994, COMESA has not passed any binding regulatory instruments dealing with IP. However, in 2013 it passed an IP Policy, which has been discussed in Chapter 2.

EAC

The EAC was established in 2000[98] by Kenya, Tanzania and Uganda, whilst Rwanda and Burundi joined it in 2007.[99] This small group exhibits diversity and complexity in its legal landscape. For example, Burundi and Rwanda are Francophone civil jurisdictions whilst the other EAC member states are common law jurisdictions. Tanzania comprises the former states of Tanganyika and Zanzibar, which merged politically in 1964. However, legally two systems continue to coexist in Mainland Tanzania and the former Zanzibar. This means that, in effect, whilst there are five EAC member states, there are six legal systems in play. Economically, of the five member states, only Kenya is not an LDC. The EAC's ultimate goal is the creation of a political federation preceded by a monetary union, a common market, and a CU, in reverse order.[100] So far, the CU has been attained,[101] and the common market has been established.[102]

IP regulatory framework

The EAC's regulatory instruments are comprised of protocols, regulations, directives and decisions of the Council that are binding on member states.[103] Of these, the Protocol on the Establishment of the EAC Common Market provides for the co-operation between party states in the area of IP.[104] The details of the nature of this co-operation are spelt out in article 43 of the Protocol that encompasses all areas of IP[105] and re-affirms a commitment to abide by international IP obligations.[106] The two-fold objective of co-operation between the party states is to[107]:

98 The Treaty for Establishment of the East African Community (Treaty establishing the EAC) was signed on 30 November 1999 and entered into force on 7 July 2000.
99 Gathii (2011) p. 181.
100 Gathii (2011) p. 181.
101 Protocol for the Establishment of the EAC CU, 2004 which came into force on 1 January 2005.
102 Protocol on the Establishment of the EAC Common Market, which came into force on 1 July 2010.
103 Article 16 Treaty establishing the EAC.
104 Article 5(3)(k) which provides 'For the purposes of facilitating the implementation of the Common Market, the Partner States further agree to co-operate in the promotion and protection of intellectual property rights.'
105 Article 43(2).
106 Article 43(6).
107 Article 43(1).

(a) promote and protect creativity and innovation for economic, technological, social and cultural development in the Community; and
(b) enhance the protection of intellectual property rights.

To this end the party states are required to[108]:

(a) put in place measures to prevent infringement, misuse and abuse of intellectual property rights;
(b) co-operate in fighting piracy and counterfeit activities;
(c) exchange information on matters relating to intellectual property rights;
(d) promote public awareness on intellectual property rights issues;
(e) enhance capacity in intellectual property;
(f) increase dissemination and use of patent documentation as a source of technological information;
(g) adopt common positions in regional and international norm setting in the field of intellectual property; and
(h) put in place intellectual property policies that promote creativity, innovation and development of intellectual capital.

In particular, the party states are obliged to create regulatory frameworks for[109]:

(a) the legal protection of the traditional cultural expressions, traditional knowledge, genetic resources and national heritage;
(b) the protection and promotion of cultural industries;
(c) the use of protected works for the benefits of the communities in the Partner States; and
(d) the co-operation in public health, food security, research and technological development.

Whilst there is provision for the enactment of directives on co-operation with regard to IP,[110] none have been issued as yet. In the interim some research has been carried out on existing levels of harmonization of IP laws.[111]

In 2009 the EAC member states agreed to aspire to the creation and implementation of a new commonly-held IP regime by January 2014 in anticipation of a bilateral agreement with the EU.[112] The EAC-EU Economic Partnership Agreement (EPA) was finally signed on 16 October 2014.[113]

Motivated by this ambition and by information they received on the 'harmful impacts of counterfeiting and piracy in East Africa' together with the imminent

108 Article 43(3).
109 Article 43(4).
110 Article 43(5).
111 For example Magogo (2013).
112 Blakeney and Mengistie (2011) p. 245.
113 Mwanza (2014).

establishment of the Common Market, the EAC commissioned a report in 2008 on an appropriate policy approach.[114] Following this, the EAC issued a draft policy on Anti-Counterfeiting, Anti-Piracy and other Intellectual Property Rights Violations in 2009[115] and the EAC Anti-Counterfeit Bill in 2010, which has since been revised.[116] The draft policy has not been finalized nor has the bill been enacted. These drafts have been heavily criticized because they espoused a TRIPS-plus position that was, and continues to be, inappropriate for developing countries. Moreso, in the EAC's case because four of its member states are LDCs. This is perhaps not surprising considering that two Nairobi law firms who would be accustomed to view IP matters primarily from a right-holder perspective penned the draft. This is evident from the introductory section of the policy, which makes the usual industry-statistic based arguments about the negative effects of unchecked and widespread counterfeits.[117] In particular, both the policy and bill 'fail to distinguish between various IPR infringements, contain overbroad and imprecise definitions and do not consider the impact of the foreseen measures on access to knowledge, agriculture and public health.'[118]
The Bill (Draft 251011) defines counterfeiting as follows:

(a) the possessing, manufacturing, producing or making, packaging, repackaging or labeling whether in the Community or elsewhere, of any goods whereby those protected goods are imitated in such manner and to such a degree that those other goods are substantially identical copies of the protected goods without the authority of the Owner of any Intellectual Property Right subsisting in the relevant Partner State of Protected Goods;
(b) the possessing, manufacturing, producing or making or applying to goods, whether in the Community or elsewhere, the subject matter of that Intellectual Property Right, or a colourable imitation thereof so that other goods are calculated to be confused with or to be taken as being the Protected Goods of the said Owner or any goods manufactured, produced or made under his license without the authority of the Owner of any Intellectual Property Right subsisting in the relevant Partner State in respect of the Protected Goods.

This definition was then incorporated into EAC Partner states' Anti-Counterfeit legislation.[119] For example, section 2 of Kenya's Anti-Counterfeit Act, Act No. 13 of 2008 provided the following similar definition:

114 Blakeney and Mengistie (2011) p. 258.
115 Draft 260609, prepared by Iseme Kamau & Maema Advocates and Mohammed Muigai Advocates.
116 Draft EAC Anti-Counterfeit Bill, 2011 Draft 251011.
117 Draft Policy paras 2.1–2.12.
118 Health Action International Africa (HAIA) (2010). Also see Musungu (2010), CEHRUD (2010).
119 The Anti-Counterfeit Act, (2008) Kenya; The Counterfeit Goods Bill (Uganda); 2008 Merchandise Marks Regulations in Tanzania [made under Section 18A of the Merchandise Marks Act, Chapter 85 Laws of Tanzania].

> counterfeiting means taking the following actions without the authority of the owner of intellectual property right subsisting in Kenya or elsewhere in respect of protected goods –
>
> (a) the manufacture, production, packaging, re-packaging, labelling or making, whether in Kenya or elsewhere, of any goods whereby those protected goods are imitated in such manner and to such a degree that those other goods are identical or substantially similar copies of the protected goods;
>
> (b) the manufacture, production or making, whether in Kenya or elsewhere, the subject matter of that intellectual property, or a colorable imitation thereof so that the other goods are calculated to be confused with or to be taken as being the protected goods of the said owner or any goods manufactured, produced or made under his licence;
>
> (c) the manufacturing, producing or making of copies, in Kenya or elsewhere, in violation of an author's rights or related rights;
>
> (d) in relation to medicine, the deliberate and fraudulent mislabeling of medicine with respect to identity or source, *whether or not such products have correct ingredients, wrong ingredients, have sufficient active ingredients or have fake packaging* (emphasis added).

A Kenyan High Court held that this definition

> would encompass generic medicines produced in Kenya and elsewhere and thus is likely to adversely affect the manufacture, sale, and distribution of generic equivalents of patented drugs. This would affect the availability of the generic drugs and thus pose a real threat to the petitioners' right to life, dignity and health under the Constitution.[120]

This decision has had a chilling effect and with the exception of Tanzania, none of the EAC Partner States have enacted anti-counterfeiting legislation.

The EAC has a Regional IP Policy on the Utilization of Public Health-Related WTO-TRIPS Flexibilities and the Approximation of National IP Legislation that has been discussed in Chapter 2. In addition to this policy, the EAC has also drafted the Health Protocol on Public Health Related WTO-TRIPS Flexibilities. The Protocol has not yet entered into force because the requisite ratifications have not yet been achieved.

ECOWAS

ECOWAS was formed in 1975. It is currently 'a fully-fledged Customs Union with a Common External Tariff and common trade policy'.[121]

120 *Patricia Asero Ochieng, Maurine Atieno and Joseph Munyi v The Attorney General* HCCC Petition No. 409 of 2009 Para 78.

121 Ngwenya (2015).

IP regulatory framework

Article 27(10) (c) of the ECOWAS Treaty provides that

> In their cooperation in this field, Member States shall harmonize their national technological development plans by placing special emphasis on indigenous and adapted technologies as well as their regulations on industrial property and transfer of technology.

ECOWAS law is contained in Protocols, Regulations and Decisions. It also provides policy guidance through policies. In relation to IP harmonization, ECOWAS states have adopted a TRIPS Policy and Guidelines that have been discussed in preceding chapters. They have not adopted any IP regulatory instruments.

SADC

SADC is the successor to SADCC. It was formed in 1980.[122] SADCC's member states were Angola, Botswana, Lesotho, Malawi, Mozambique, Swaziland, Tanzania, Zambia and Zimbabwe. Its key aim was to 'reduce economic dependence on apartheid South Africa.'[123] It did not have formal legal status nor did it own assets, and sought to achieve its aims through collaborative projects. As the liberation of South Africa appeared to be on the cusp, it was necessary to reconfigure SADCC. In view of this, and to strengthen its capacity, it was decided in 1992 to upgrade SADCC into SADC which had legal status.[124] After the dawn of democracy in 1994, South Africa joined SADC.

Unlike SADCC, SADC's key aims include economic integration, the implementation of which is spelt out in its Regional Indicative Strategic Development Plan (RISDP), 2003 which plans development over a period of 15 years (2005–2020).[125] The core components of the RISDP are the creation of a FTA, CU, Common Market, Monetary Union and ultimately the adoption of a single currency.[126] Of these, the FTA was established, within the planned timeframe, in August 2008 and continues to progress meaningfully.[127] The CU was initially intended for launch in 2010 but this was not achieved.[128] A later implementation date of 2013[129] was then set but it also has not been achieved. The main reasons

122 See SADC (n.d.a); Gathii (2011) p. 211.

123 Hartzenberg (2011) p. 5.

124 Article 3, Declaration and Treaty of the Southern African Development Community, (SADC) 1992 (as amended). For a full historical discussion of this upgrade see Ng'ong'ola (2000) pp. 485–506; Ng'ong'ola (2008).

125 SADC (2011).

126 Hartzenberg (2011) pp. 5–6.

127 Sandrey (2013) p. 2; Gathii (2011) p. 212.

128 Gathii (2011) p. 221.

129 SADC (n.d.a).

for the delay in launching the CU include the complexities brought about by the concurrent membership of numerous RECs (COMESA, EAC and SADC) as well as the Southern Africa CU (SACU)[130] and the COMESA CU by some SADC member states.[131] Each of these CUs has different common external tariffs and tariff schedules. It is hoped that these challenges will be overcome by the creation of a T-FTA which, in turn, will create a CU. As stated above, it is envisaged that these three RECs would then merge with five others to form the AEC.

Regulatory instruments

SADC's legal instruments include Protocols that become binding after ratification by two-thirds of SADC member states.[132] Two of its protocols expressly reference IP. The first of these is the Protocol on Trade of 1996, which entered into force on 25 January 2001. The objectives of this Protocol are the following[133]:

1. To further liberalize intra-regional trade in goods and services on the basis of fair, mutually equitable and beneficial trade arrangements, complemented by Protocols in other areas.
2. To ensure efficient production within SADC reflecting the current and dynamic comparative advantages of its members.
3. To contribute towards the climate for domestic, cross border and foreign investment.
4. To enhance the economic development, diversification and industrialization of the region.

The Protocol therefore establishes a framework within which these objectives may be achieved. In particular, it regulates trade in goods,[134] customs procedures,[135] trade laws,[136] trade related investment matters,[137] trade in services,[138] IP,[139] and competition policy[140] *inter alia*. In the context of its regulation of trade in goods, it prohibits the use of any quantitative import[141] and export[142] restrictions by party

130 The SACU member states are Botswana, Lesotho, Namibia, South Africa, and Swaziland. All five are SADC member states.
131 Gathii (2011) p. 213; Draper, Halleson and Alves (2007).
132 Article 22 Declaration and Treaty of the SADC; see for example Article 16 Protocol on Trade.
133 Article 2.
134 Articles 3–11.
135 Articles 12–15.
136 Articles 16–21.
137 Article 22.
138 Article 23.
139 Article 24.
140 Article 25.
141 Article 7(1).
142 Article 8(1).

states. However, there are wide-ranging general exceptions to these prohibitions, which include IP enforcement. Article 9(d) provides that

> Subject to the requirement that such measures are not applied in a manner which would constitute a means of arbitrary or unjustifiable discrimination between Member States, or a disguised restriction on intra-SADC trade, nothing in Articles 7 and 8 of this protocol shall be construed as to prevent the adopting or enforcement of any measures by a Member State necessary to protect intellectual property rights, or to prevent deceptive trade practices.

Border control IP enforcement measures are thus permissible. These are to be structured within the TRIPS framework as all SADC member states (with the exception of Seychelles which is due to become a member by mid-2015) are also WTO members and, as such, are obliged to be TRIPS compliant. Indeed, the Protocol expressly reminds party states of this obligation in article 24 which provides:

> Member states shall adopt policies and implement measures within the community for the protection of intellectual property rights, in accordance with [the] WTO Agreement on Trade-Related Aspects of Intellectual Property Rights.

Consequently, one of the key harmonization goals of SADC has been articulated as the pursuit of TRIPS compliance by member states in a report commissioned by the UNECA in its provision of assistance to SADC.[143]

The second SADC Protocol that refers to IP is the Protocol on Science, Technology and Innovation, (STI) 2008.[144] Following 12 years after the Protocol on Trade, the Protocol on STI's main purpose is to 'foster co-operation and promote, the development, transfer and mastery of science, technology and innovation in member states' so as to achieve a wide range of related goals.[145] Amongst these is ' the development and harmonization of STI policies in the region'[146] and 'the enhance[ment] and strengthen[ing] of the protection of intellectual property rights.'[147]

143 UNECA (2014).
144 Signed 17 August 2008.
145 Article 2 Protocol on STI.
146 Article 2(c).
147 Article 2(m).

T-FTA

COMESA, EAC and SADC were in talks for a lengthy period of time about the establishment of their T-FTA. Agreement was reached on the establishment of the T-FTA in October 2008.[148] A draft agreement was prepared in 2009[149] and a revised draft was agreed to in 2010.[150] The Tripartite Sectoral Committee of Ministers meeting held in October 2014 decided that the T-FTA would be launched in December 2014 at the Tripartite Summit of Heads of State and Government.[151] However, negotiations under phase 1 of the roadmap were not concluded timeously because of funding constraints and the lack of consensus on some critical substantive issues.[152] Consequently, the Summit was first postponed to February 2015[153] and then further postponed to 7–10 June 2015.[154] The chairperson of the Tripartite Task Force's update to the AU Summit in January 2015 disclosed that negotiations on trade in goods had been concluded and the goods T-FTA would be launched later in the year.[155] As already stated, the T-FTA was launched, as planned, in June 2015 when a declaration and Agreement were signed. The Sharm El Sheikh Declaration Launching the COMESA-EAC-SADC T-FTA was signed by 24 COMESA, EAC and SADC member states. Only Libya and Eritrea did not sign it. Of the 26 member states, only 16 signed the T-FTA Agreement. These signatory members are Angola, Burundi, Comoros, DRC, Djibouti, Egypt, Kenya, Malawi, Namibia, Rwanda, Seychelles, Sudan, Tanzania, Uganda, Swaziland and Zimbabwe. The final Agreement differs to a significant extent from the revised draft Agreement of 2010. In particular, it omits IP related provisions which were included in the revised draft Agreement. These provisions are discussed in the following section to give an indication of what might ultimately emerge from the T-FTA in relation to IP. The tripartite parties will soon commence negotiations on trade in services and other trade-related areas such as competition policy and IP rights.[156] Article 45 of the final Agreement commits signatory states to completing these negotiations within 24 months of its entry into force. Article 39 provides that the Agreement will come into force 'on the thirtieth day after the deposit of the fourteenth instrument of ratification by Member/Partner States of COMESA, EAC and SADC.'

Regulatory framework: tripartite IP agenda

The Revised Agreement contains provisions that set out the tripartite parties' vision for IP, which is known as their IP Agenda. This agenda is more compre-

148 UNECA (2011) p. 5.

149 Agreement Establishing the T-FTA, 2009.

150 Draft Agreement Establishing the COMESA, EAC AND SADC T-FTA, Revised Dec 2010.

151 T-FTA (2014).

152 Mwanza (2014).

153 Mwanza (2014).

154 Bridges Africa (2015).

155 Ngwenya (2015).

156 Cronje (2015); Erasmus (2015); Ngwenya (2015).

hensive than that of the other RECs which have been canvassed above. Article 27 provides:

1. Tripartite Member States shall protect intellectual property rights in a balanced manner that promotes the social economic welfare of society through ensuring that the people of the region meaningfully benefit from and participate in advancements in the arts, and science and technology in accordance with Annex 9 on Intellectual Property Rights.
2. Tripartite Member States shall adopt policies on intellectual property rights including the protection and promotion of cultural industries in accordance with international agreements.
3. Tripartite Member States shall co-operate and develop capacity to implement and utilise the flexibilities in all relevant international agreements on intellectual property rights.

Annex 9 then provides in detail for how these three broad objectives are to be achieved.

Article 1 sets out the tripartite approach to trade and development through a series of 10 undertakings (a)–(j). These undertakings centre around the notion of increasing efforts to reap meaningful rewards from IP protected goods and services through promoting innovation and commercialization. This notion is encapsulated in article 1(a) as follows:

> Tripartite Member States undertake to promote, encourage and facilitate the generation, innovation, creation, development, use, exploitation, commercialization, and licensing of intellectual property rights as well as [their] effective protection.

Some of the undertakings are repetitive. For example (b) and (c) which are reproduced below:

> (b) promote and facilitate the mainstreaming of IP into *all policies*, structures, systems, programs and activities of the Tripartite Member States
> (c) promote and encourage the mainstreaming of IP into the *economic, industrial, technological, social and cultural policies*, systems, structures, programmes and activities of the Tripartite Member States [emphasis added]

When paragraph (b) refers to 'all' policies surely this includes 'economic, industrial, technological, social and cultural' policies and therefore there is no need for two paragraphs as either one of them would have been adequate.

Article 2 entitled 'Trade Negotiations' sets out a common approach to the negotiation of IP related agreements at bilateral, multilateral, regional and international levels in pursuit of ' pro-development outcomes for the region'.[157] There

157 Article 2(a).

is also emphasis on capitalizing on available flexibilities in order to 'increase regional trade' and 'the free flow of IPRs.'[158]

With regard to the IP regulatory frameworks, the Member States undertake to develop an effective 'promotion and protection system' to create opportunities for local innovators or creators and also to attract foreign direct investment (FDI).[159] The latter part of this undertaking reflects belief in the popular notion that a robust IP system attracts FDI. This notion is susceptible to challenge because there are studies that have shown that technology transfer and FDI do not necessarily flow to those developing countries that strengthen their IP regimes.[160] The lesson here is that IP systems should not be made inappropriately robust, to the detriment of local creators and users, in the hope that this will attract FDI. Rather, efforts ought to be made to appropriately calibrate these regimes for local benefit so that even if the aspiration of attracting FDI is not realized, all is not lost.

Article 2 then proceeds to provide for practical matters such as the modes of business collaboration that would stimulate technology transfer to Member States. In this regard, joint ventures, alliances and licensing arrangements are singled out as the preferable approaches that Member States undertake to promote.[161]

Article 3 lists the Member States' undertakings in relation to the cultural and creative industries. The first of these is the creation of 'effective policy and legal frameworks' to secure protection for industry participants and enable them, and presumably society, to extract 'maximum benefits from these industries'.[162] The Member States also commit to the establishment of fora at which dialogue can occur between industry stakeholders and policy makers to enhance the legal and policy framework.[163] They also undertake to promote intra-regional and extra-regional co-operation in relation to these matters.[164]

In pursuit of economic benefits from the cultural and copyright industries, the Member States commit to implementing strategies for production and effective marketing of cultural goods[165] so as to be able to reduce reliance on goods sourced outside the region.[166] Similar to article 2, the rest of article 3 turns to the practical business aspect of promoting local industries through building and using galleries, securing better 'access to foreign markets'[167] so as to enhance their competitiveness on the global plane.[168] One of the first steps towards achieving this is the assessment or audit of the industry so as to get an accurate picture of its economic

158 Article 2(b).
159 Article 2(c).
160 Chang (2001) p. 303; Ncube (2013) p. 372.
161 Article 2(d).
162 Article 3(a).
163 Article 3(g).
164 Article 3(i).
165 Article 3(b).
166 Article 3(c).
167 Article 3(d).
168 Article 3(e).

contribution to Member States.[169] This is reminiscent of the various WIPO studies that have been undertaken to evaluate the economic contribution of the copyright industries to several countries. In addition to national audits, article 8(a) calls upon member states to encourage companies to undertake their own internal IPR audits and to exhort them to use their IPRs for 'raising finance'. Presumably this would be through using them as collateral for loans or for generating licensing revenues. Finally, the article refers to the creation of collective management organizations (CMOs) to handle royalty collection and distribution.[170]

Article 4 of Annex 9 focuses on TK, genetic resources (GR) and folklore. The Member States undertake to promote their use, and to ensure the recognition and reward of their holders.[171] Such recognition and reward would be premised on the protection of TK, GR and folklore that Member States commit to securing through 'IP or sui generis systems'.[172] Such systems would include 'the creation of databases, development of guidelines for access benefit sharing (ABS) and prior informed consent'.[173] In order to ensure that such systems are both meaningful and effective, the Member States undertake to:

- create platforms for interaction between stakeholders and policy makers;[174]
- support and engage in regional and international negotiations on appropriate frameworks;[175] and
- encourage each other to ratify or accede to relevant international treaties that promote the protection of TK and GR.[176]

With regard to effective exploitation of TK and GR, an undertaking is made to draw on biotechnological advances and to use effective business models including joint ventures, and licensing.[177]

Article 5's three undertakings relate to Information and Communications Technology (ICT). First, the Member States commit to the adoption of an appropriate policy and legislative framework to encourage the deployment of ICT by businesses of all sizes.[178] Secondly, they undertake to 'mainstream ICT into the[ir] cultural, social and economic activities'.[179] Thirdly, they pledge to encourage each other to create competition, so as to reduce costs and increase access to ICTs.[180]

169 Articles 3(f) and 8(b).
170 Article 3(g).
171 Article 4(a).
172 Articles 4(b) and 4(d).
173 Article 4(c).
174 Article 4(e).
175 Articles 4(g) and 4(i).
176 Article 4(h).
177 Article 4(f).
178 Article 5(a).
179 Article 5(b).
180 Article 5(c).

Articles 6 and 7 deal with copyright and industrial property respectively and set out five similar undertakings in relation to each. The first of these is the creation of a policy and legislative framework for the protection and promotion of these rights.[181] However, there is a difference in the purpose of the frameworks. The stated objective in relation to industrial property is 'to derive maximum benefits' whilst none is stated in relation to copyright and related rights. A further difference is that article 6 expressly refers to the need to consider 'the balance that exists between . . . [right holders] and the users of the rights' in crafting the framework. No such reference is made in relation to industrial rights.

Second, audits of copyright, copyright industries and industrial property rights will be promoted so as to 'assess their contribution to the cultural, social and economic development' of Member States.[182] Third, collaboration between Member States in respect of the protection and promotion of copyright and related rights and industrial property will be encouraged, particularly in respect of pirated and counterfeit goods.[183] Fourth, the use of existing flexibilities or limitations will be encouraged so as to enable access to copyrighted works and medicines.[184] The fifth and final undertakings are different. In relation to copyright and related rights the Member States undertake to roll out awareness campaigns to educate stakeholders about copyright, whilst in relation to industrial property they undertake to harmonize their legislation.[185]

Conclusion

The above overview has shown the extent to which RECs are involved in IP harmonization or integration. It is clear that the four RECs under discussion have made some progress on this front. This work has to be incorporated into any continental IP integration efforts. Similarly, it has to be framed within the context of the work that has been done by the sub-regional IP organizations that are the subject of Chapter 4. In that regard, the nature of the relationship between the regional IP organizations and the RECs becomes of significance. Currently, such a relationship seems to be rather distant. Their membership consists of the same countries but due to differences in mandate there does not appear to be a close working relationship between them. It is necessary to cultivate such a relationship in order to avoid duplication of efforts and to effectively utilize expertise across the organizations and RECs.

181 Articles 6(a) and 7(a).
182 Articles 6(b) and 7(b).
183 Articles 6(c) and 7(c).
184 Articles 6(d) and 7(d).
185 Articles 6(e) and 7(e).

References

Primary sources

Case law

Patricia Asero Ochieng, Maurine Atieno and Joseph Munyi v The Attorney General HCCC Petition No. 409 of 2009 Para 78.

Legal instruments

AU

Abuja Treaty AEC (1991).

AU Commission, New Zealand Ministry of Foreign Affairs and Trade/Manat Aorere, 2014. *AU Handbook.* Wellington: Ministry of Foreign Affairs and Trade/Manat Aorere.

The Constitutive Act of the African Union, (2000).

Decisions and Declarations – Decision on the Moratorium on the Recognition of Regional Economic Communities (RECs) DOC.EX.CL/278 (IX), AU Doc.Assembly/AU/Dec.111-132 (VII). Assembly of the African Union, Seventh Ordinary Session, 1–2 July 2006, Banjul, the Gambia.

Draft Framework, Road Map and Architecture for Fast tracking The C-FTA (2011).

Monrovia Declaration of Commitment of the Heads of State and Government, of the OAU on Guidelines and Measures for National and Collective Self-Reliance in Social and Economic Development for the Establishment of a New International Economic Order, (1979).

Protocol on Relations between the AU and the RECs (2007).

COMESA

COMESA, 2011. *Official Gazette* Volume 16 (15 October 2011).

COMESA *Report of the Thirtieth Meeting of the Council of Ministers CS/CM/XXX/2 (2011).*

Treaty Establishing the Common Market for Eastern and Southern Africa (1993).

EAC

Draft Anti-Counterfeit Bill 2011 (Draft 251011).

Draft Policy on Anti-Counterfeiting, Anti-Piracy and other Intellectual Property Rights Violations (2009) (Draft 260609).

Health Protocol on Public Health Related WTO-TRIPS Flexibilities (2013).

Protocol for the Establishment of the EAC Customs Union (2004).

Protocol on the Establishment of the EAC Common Market (2009).

Regional Intellectual Property Policy on the Utilization of Public Health-Related WTO-TRIPS Flexibilities and the Approximation of National Intellectual Property Legislation (2013).

Treaty for Establishment of the EAC (1999).

ECOWAS

Economic Community of West African States, Revised Treaty (1993).

SADC

Declaration and Treaty of the SADC (1992).
Protocol on Trade (1996).
Regional Indicative Strategic Development Plan (RISDP) (2003).
RISDP Summary (2011).
SADCC Memorandum of Understanding (1981).
SADC Protocol on the Tribunal and Rules of Procedure Thereof (2000).

COMESA-EAC-SADC TRIPARTITE FTA

Agreement Establishing a Tripartite Free Trade Area Among the Common Market for Eastern and Southern Africa, the East African Community and the Southern African Development Community (2015).
Agreement Establishing the Tripartite Free Trade Area (2009).
Annex 9: Annex on Intellectual Property Rights under Article 27(1) of the Agreement Establishing the Tripartite Free Trade Area (2009).
Draft Agreement Establishing the COMESA, EAC and SADC T-FTA, Revised Dec (2010).
The Sharm El Sheikh Declaration Launching the COMESA-EAC-SADC T-FTA (2015).

UNECA

Assessing Regional Integration in Africa (ARIA V): Towards an African Continental Free Trade Area, (2012).

WTO

Agreement on Trade-Related Aspects of Intellectual Property Rights, Marrakesh Agreement Establishing the World Trade Organization, Annex 1C (1994) 33 I.L.M. 1125, 1197.
General Agreement on Tariffs and Trade (GATT) (1994) 33 I.L.M. 1125, 1154.
General Agreement on Trade in Services (GATS) (1994) 33 I.L.M. 1125, 1167.
WTO Understanding on the Interpretation of Article XXIV of the General Agreement on Tariffs and Trade (1994).

National legislation

Kenya: The Anti-Counterfeit Act, (2008).
Kenya: Treaty for the Establishment of the East African Community Act 2 of 2000 (Cap 4C).
Rwanda: Constitution (2003).
Tanzania: Merchandise Marks Regulations in Tanzania [made under Section 18A of the Merchandise Marks Act, Chapter 85 Laws of Tanzania].

Tanzania: Treaty for the Establishment of East African Community Act 2001.
Uganda: The Counterfeit Goods Bill (2008).

Secondary sources

Afadameh-Adeyemi, A., 2013. *Securing Compliance with African Economic Integration Treaties.* PhD Thesis, University of Cape Town.

Akokpari, J., 2008. 'Dilemmas of regional integration and development in Africa' in Akokpari, J. et al (eds) *The African Union and its Institutions.* Auckland Park, South Africa: Fanele, 85–110.

Asante, S.K.B., 1997. *Regionalism and Africa's Development: Expectations, Reality and Challenges.* London: Palgrave Macmillan.

AU, n.d. 'Economic Community of Central African States (ECCAS)'. Online. Available HTTP: <http://www.au.int/en/recs/eccas>, accessed 6 November 2014.

Balassa, B.A., 1961. *The Theory of Economic Integration.* Homewood, Illinois: Richard Dale, Inc.

Blakeney, M. and Mengistie, G., 2011. Intellectual property and economic development in Sub-Saharan Africa, *Journal of World Intellectual Property*, 14(3/4), 238–264.

Bridges Africa. 2015. 'Launch of African T-FTA now set for June'. 16 March 2016. Online. Available HTTP: <http://www.ictsd.org/bridges-news/bridges-africa/news/launch-of-african-tripartite-fta-now-set-for-june>, accessed 16 March 2015.

CEHRUD, 2010. *Anti-counterfeiting laws and access to essential medicines in East and Southern Africa EQUINET, CEHRUD, TARSC* – Policy brief 22. Harare: EQUINET.

Chang, H-J., 2001. Intellectual property rights and economic development: historical and emerging issues, *Journal of Human Development*, 2, 287–309.

Crawford, J. and Fiorentino, R., 2005. *The Changing Landscape of Regional Trade Agreements.* Discussion Paper No. 8. Geneva, Switzerland: WTO.

Cronje, J.B., 2015. The road ahead for the Tripartite FTA negotiations. Tralac Discussion Paper. 18 June 2015. Online. Available HTTP: <http://www.tralac.org/discussions/article/7567-the-road-ahead-for-the-tripartite-fta-negotiations.html>, accessed 22 June 2015.

Draper, P., Halleson, D. and Alves, P., 2007. *SACU, Regional Integration and the Overlap Issue in Southern Africa: From Spaghetti to Cannelloni?* Johannesburg: The South African Institute of International Affairs.

Erasmus, G., 2015. The Tripartite FTA: Technical Features, Potential and Implementation. Tralac Discussion Paper, 18 June 2015. Online. Available HTTP: <http://www.tralac.org/discussions/article/7568-the-tripartite-fta-technical-features-potential-and-implementation.html>, accessed 22 June 2015.

Fiorentino, R.V., Verdeja, L. and Toqueboeuf, C., 2006. *The Changing Landscape of Regional Trade Agreements: 2006 Update.* Discussion Paper No. 12. Geneva, Switzerland: WTO.

Gathii, J.T., 2010. African regional trade agreements as flexible legal regimes, *North Carolina Journal of International Law and Commercial Regulation*, 35(3), 572–668.

Gathii, J.T., 2011. *African Regional Trade Agreements as Legal Regimes.* Cambridge: Cambridge University Press.

Gottschalk, K., 2012. The African Union and its sub-regional Structures, *Journal of African Union Studies*, 1(1), 9–39.

Haas, E., 1970. The study of regional integration: reflections on the joy and anguish of pre theorizing, *International Organization*, 24(4), 607–646.

HAIA, 2010. *Report of the international meeting on the Proliferation of Anti-counterfeiting Legislation in the East African Community: Addressing Public Health, Copyright and Developmental Concerns.* Arusha, Tanzania: HAIA.

Hartzenberg, T., 2011. *Regional Integration in Africa.* WTO Economic Research and Statistics Division Working Paper ERSD-2011-14. Geneva, Switzerland: WTO.

Hartzenberg, T. and Malungisa, D., 2011. 'Regional integration in Southern Africa: key issues and challenges' in Volz, U. (ed) *Regional Integrations, Economic Development and Global Governance.* Cheltenham, UK: Edward Elgar.

Jensen, C.S., 2013. 'Neo-functionalism' in Cini, M. and Borragan, N. P-S., (eds) *European Union Politics.* 4th ed. Oxford: Oxford University Press, 59–70.

Kaplan, D., 2009. 'Intellectual property rights and innovation in South Africa: a framework' in *WIPO The Economics of Intellectual Property in South Africa.* Geneva: WIPO.

Kolbeck, B., 2014. *Legal Analysis on the Relationship between the AU/AEC and RECs: Africa Lost in a 'Spaghetti Bowl' of Legal Relations?* LLM Thesis. University of Cape Town.

Kouassi, R.N., 2007. the itinerary of the African integration process: an overview of the historical landmarks, *African Integration Review*, 1(2), 1–23.

Lee, M., 2002. Regionalism in Africa: a part of the problem or a part of the solution, *Polis/RCSP/CPSR*, 9, 1–24.

Lee, M., 2003. *The Political Economy of Regionalism in Southern Africa.* Cape Town and Boulder: UCT Press and Lynne Rienner Publishers.

Magogo, T.D.B., 2013. *Harmonization of Copyright within the East African Community: An Analysis of the Kenyan and Tanzanian Copyright Legislation.* Mini-thesis LLM. University of the Western Cape.

Matambalya, F.A.S.T., 2014. 'Integration of industrialisation in sub-regional development agendas: overviews of African Regional Economic Communities', in Matambalya F.A.S.T. (ed.) *African Industrial Development and EU Cooperation: Prospects for a Reengineered Partnership.* Abingdon, Oxfordshire: Routledge.

Matthias, J.H. and Bhagwati, J., 2002. *Regional Trade Agreements in the GATT/WTO: Article XX1V and the Internal Trade Requirement.* The Hague: TMC Asser Press.

Mukisa, R., and Thompson, B., 1995. Prerequisites for economic integration in Africa: an analysis of the Abuja Treaty, *Africa Today*, 42(4), 56–80.

Musungu, S.F., 2010. *The Potential Impact of the Proposed East African Community (EAC) Anti-Counterfeiting Policy and Bill on Access to Essential Medicines.* UNDP BDP HIV Practice/March 2010 Discussion Paper.

Mutai, H.K., 2007. *Compliance with International Trade Obligations: The Common Market for Eastern and Southern Africa.* Netherlands: Kluwer Law International.

Mutharika, B., 1972. *Towards Multinational Economic Cooperation in Africa.* New York: Praeger.

Mwanza, W., 2014. 'Review of trade related developments in 2014' (online).. Stellenbosch: TRALAC. 17 December 2014. Online. Available HTTP: <http://www.tralac.org/discussions/article/6803reviewoftraderelateddevelopmentsin2014.html>, accessed 4 February 2015.

Ncube, C.B., 2013. Harnessing intellectual property for development: some thoughts on an appropriate theoretical framework, *Potchefstroom Electronic Law Journal*, 16(4), 369–487.

Ng'ong'ola, C., 2000. Regional Integration and Trade Liberalization in the Southern African Development Community, *Journal of International Economic Law*,3, 485–506.

Ng'ong'ola, C., 2008. The legal framework for regional integration in the Southern African development community, *University of Botswana Law Journal*, 8, 3–46.

Ngwenya, S., 2015. Statement By Mr Sindiso Ngwenya, Secretary General of COMESA and Chairperson of the COMESA-EAC-SADC Tripartite Task Force, to the African

Union High Level African Trade Committee (HATC): Update On The Tripartite Free Trade Area Negotiations.

Nkomo, M., 2014. Regional integration in the area of intellectual property: The case for Southern African development community involvement. *Law Democracy & Development*, 18, 317–333.

Olivier, G. and Olivier, M., 2004. Models of regional integration: the European Union and the African Union, *SA Public Law (SAPR/PL)*, 19, 351–364.

Oppong, R.F., 2006. Observing the legal system of the community: the relationship between community and national legal systems under the African Economic Community Treaty, *Tulane Journal of International and Comparative Law*, 15, 41–87.

Oppong, R.F., 2008. 'Making regional economic community laws enforceable in national legal systems – constitutional and judicial challenges' in Bosl, A., Breytenbach, W., Hartzenberg, T., McCarthy, C. and Schade, K., (eds) *Monitoring Regional Integration in Southern Africa Yearbook Volume 8*. Stellenbosch: Trade Law Centre for Southern Africa, the Konrad Adenaur Stiftung and the Namibian Economic Unit, 149–178.

Oppong, R.F., 2010. The African Union, the African Economic Community and Africa's regional economic communities: untangling a complex web, *African Journal of International and Comparative Law*, 18, 92–103.

Oppong, R.F., 2011. *Legal Aspects of Economic Integration in Africa*. Cambridge: Cambridge University Press.

Onoria, H., 2011. 'Uganda' in Shelton, D. (ed.) *International Law and Domestic Legal Systems: Incorporation, Transformation, and Persuasion*. Oxford: Oxford University Press, 594–619.

Osiemo, O., 2014. Lost in translation: the role of African regional courts in regional integration in Africa, *Legal Issues of Economic Integration*, 41(1), 87–122.

Oslington, P., 2013. Contextual history, practitioner history, and classic status: reading Jacob Viner's the customs union issue, *Journal of the History of Economic Thought*, 3(4), 491–515.

Ostergaard, T., 1993. 'classical models of regional integration – what relevance for Southern Africa?' in Oden, B. (ed.) *Southern Africa After Apartheid, Regional Integration and External resources*. Uppsala: Nordic Africa Institute, 27–47.

Oyejide, A., Elbadawi, I. and Collier, P., eds. 1997. *Regional Integration and Trade Liberalization in Sub-Saharan Africa: Framework, Issues and Methodological Perspectives*. Basingstoke: Palgrave Macmillan.

Perdikis, N., 2007. 'Overview of trade agreements: regional trade agreements', in Kerr, W.A. and Gaisford, J.D. (eds.) *Handbook on International Trade Policy*. Cheltenham: Edward Elgar.

SADC, n.d.a. 'Customs Union'. Online. Available HTTP: <http://www.sadc.int/about-sadc/integration-milestones/customs-union/>, accessed 10 November 2014.

SADC, n.d.b. 'History'. Online. Available HTTP: <http://www.sadc.int/about-sadc/overview/history-and-treaty/>, accessed 16 February 2015.

Sandrey, R., 2013. An Analysis of the SADC FTA. Tralac Trade Brief D13TB01/2013.

Thompson, B., 1993. Economic integration efforts in Africa: A milestone – The Abuja Treaty, *African Journal of International and Comparative Law*, 5, 743–767.

T-FTA, 2014. 'COMESA, EAC, SADC Ministers Agree to Launch Africa's Largest Free Trade Area' Press Release, 25 October 2014. Online. Available HTTP: <http://www.comesa.int/attachments/article/1355/Tripartite%20Free%20Trade%20Area%20to%20be%20launched%20in%20December.pdf>, accessed 3 January 2015.

UNCTAD, 2011. Global Investment Trends Monitor No 5 (January 2011).

UNECA Southern Africa Office, 2014. *Opportunities and Challenges in Using Intellectual Property*

Systems to Strengthen Regional Cooperation through Policy Harmonization in the SADC Region. ECA-SA/TP.IPR/2014.

UNECA, 2011. *Final Report: Study on the Establishment of Inter-RECs' Free Trade Areas in Africa Drawing on Lessons From the COMESA-SADC-EAC FTA Experience.*

Viner, J., 1950. *The Customs Union Issue.* New York: Carnegie Endowment for International Peace.

Winter, J. A., 1972. Direct Applicability and Direct Effect Two Distinct and Different Concepts in Community Law, *Common Market Law Review*, 9(4), 425–438.

WTO, n.d. 'Regional Trade Agreements Information System (RTA-IS) User Guide'. Online. Available HTTP: <http://rtais.wto.org/UserGuide/RTAIS_USER_GUIDE_EN.html#_Toc201649637>, accessed 3 January 2015.

4 Sub-regional IP co-operation

Introduction

This chapter considers co-operation with respect to IP in specific sub-regional organizations where IP is the sole focus, namely in ARIPO and OAPI. Chapter 3 focused on African states' collaboration with respect to trade through RECs that include IP, amongst other aspects of trade. Many countries are involved in both types of collaboration, and also have multiple REC memberships. This chapter details each sub-regional IP organization's organs and regulatory frameworks in turn. It does not give a detailed overview of all of the substantive content of these frameworks. In order to enable comparative analysis of the two organizations, it only outlines those areas where both organizations have legal instruments in place, namely patents, utility models, industrial designs, trademarks and plant variety protection. OAPI's legal framework is much broader in coverage than ARIPO and it includes annexes on literary and artistic property, geographical indications, trade names, layout designs of integrated circuits and on unfair competition which ARIPO does not have Protocols on. On the other hand, ARIPO's Swakopmund Protocol covers traditional knowledge whilst OAPI does not yet have an equivalent legal instrument.

Whilst the ARIPO and OAPI IP frameworks have significant substantive and procedural differences, which will become apparent below, they co-operate with each other in various ways. For instance, they entered into a quadripartite co-operation agreement in 1985 (with WIPO and the African Regional Centre for Technology) and into a dual co-operation agreement in 1996.[1] Another instance of their co-operation is the joint response of the ARIPO and OAPI Secretariats to the creation of PAIPO announced in April 2014, which is discussed in Chapter 5. In that communiqué they referred to the possibility of an amalgamation between themselves to create a single African IP Office.[2] The chapter concludes with a consideration of the viability of such amalgamation.

1 Chirambo (2002) paras 29–30.
2 ARIPO and OAPI (2014).

ARIPO

As of 1 March 2015, ARIPO had 19 member states, namely Botswana, The Gambia, Ghana, Kenya, Lesotho, Liberia, Malawi, Mozambique, Namibia, Rwanda, Sao Tome and Principe, Sierra Leone, Somalia, Sudan, Swaziland, Tanzania, Uganda, Zambia and Zimbabwe. ARIPO co-operates with the following 12 non-member states who have observer status in the meetings of its main organs: Angola, Algeria, Burundi, Egypt, Eritrea, Ethiopia, Libya, Mauritius, Nigeria, Seychelles, South Africa and Tunisia.[3]

ARIPO was initially known as the Industrial Property Organization for English-speaking Africa (ESARIPO).[4] It was established on 9 December 1976 through the adoption of the Agreement on the Creation of the Industrial Property Organization for English-speaking Africa at a Diplomatic Conference held in Lusaka, Zambia (the Lusaka Agreement). The Lusaka Agreement came into force on 15 February 1978, thereby bringing ESARIPO into operation. It was created with technical and administrative assistance from UNECA and WIPO.[5] Consequently, in article 5 the Lusaka Agreement mandates that ARIPO 'shall establish and maintain close and continuous working relationships' with these two organizations and the African Union.

Upon its establishment, membership of the organization was limited to Anglophone African countries, but in December 1985, article 4 of the Lusaka Agreement was amended in order to expand the pool of states eligible for membership to include all members of UNECA or the OAU (now the AU).[6] The organization's name was then changed to the African Industrial Property Organization (ARIPO) in order to reflect its new membership profile.[7] Whilst the acronym remained constant, ARIPO again changed its full name to the African Regional IP organization in 2004.[8] The original reference to industrial property in the organization's name was a reflection of its initial exclusive focus on industrial property. As will be shown below, its first two protocols dealt with marks, patents and industrial designs. With the passage of time the organization's focus expanded to include other types of IP, necessitating the replacement of industrial property with IP in its name.

The main motivating factor behind the establishment of ARIPO was to more effectively leverage member states' resources and obtain various advantages through collaboration. The preamble to the Lusaka Agreement states that member states are 'aware of the advantage to be derived by them from the effective and continuous exchange of information and harmonization and coordination of their laws and activities in industrial property matters'. ARIPO's objectives are then spelt out in full in article 3 of the Lusaka Agreement. In

3 In terms of Article VI of the Lusaka Agreement.
4 Kongolo (2013) p. 75; Adewopo (n.d.); Nwauche (2003) p. 123.
5 Chirambo (2002) para 6.
6 Chirambo (2002) para 7; Adewopo (n.d.) p. 2.
7 Chirambo (2002) para 7; Adewopo (n.d.) p. 2; Nwauche (2003) p. 128.
8 Kongolo (2013) p. 75; Amendment to the Lusaka Agreement adopted by the Council of Ministers on 13 August 2004.

summary, they pertain to the harmonization of IP frameworks and the sharing of related resources with the intention of achieving technological advancement for economic and industrial development of the member states.

Organs

ARIPO has three primary organs, namely the Council of Ministers, the Administrative Council and the Secretariat.[9] UNECA and WIPO acted as a joint Secretariat of ESARIPO from its inception until 1 June 1981 when ESARIPO established its own Secretariat.[10] The Administrative Council established two more subsidiary organs, namely the Finance Committee and the Board of Appeal in 1993 and 1997 respectively. [11] In addition, the organization now has several technical committees. Each of these organs' composition and principal duties are summarized below.

Council of Ministers

The Council of Ministers is ARIPO's 'supreme organ' and as such bears ultimate responsibility for its policy direction and has oversight of its activities.[12] The membership of the Council of Ministers consists of the Government Ministers responsible for the administration of IP in each member state.[13] Its functions include the receipt of various annual reports, budgets and accounts,[14] resolving disputes and problems that are beyond the Administrative Council,[15] determining any special contributions to be paid by members[16] and determining the location of ARIPO headquarters.[17] Any of these powers may be delegated by the Council of Ministers to the Administrative Council.[18] Ordinary meetings of the Council of Ministers are convened at least once every 2 years[19] and may be attended by accredited observer states.

Administrative Council

The membership of the Administrative Council is comprised of the Heads of Offices dealing with the administration of IP in the member states.[20] However,

9 Article II of the Lusaka Agreement.
10 Chirambo (2002) para 6.
11 Chirambo (2002) para 15.
12 Articles VIbis (2) and (3) (e) Lusaka Agreement.
13 Article VIbis (1) Lusaka Agreement.
14 Article VIbis (3) (a) Lusaka Agreement.
15 Article VIbis (3) (b) Lusaka Agreement.
16 Article VIbis (3) (c) Lusaka Agreement.
17 Article VIbis (3) (d) Lusaka Agreement.
18 Article VIbis (6) Lusaka Agreement.
19 Article VIbis (4)–(5) Lusaka Agreement.
20 Article VII (1) Lusaka Agreement.

a person who does not hold such a position, but who has the requisite IP knowledge, may be nominated to represent a member state.[21] The functions of the Administrative council include the formulation and execution of policy,[22] the approval of ARIPO's program of activities, annual reports, accounts and budgets,[23] the determination of annual and special member contributions[24] and the establishment of the Secretariat and the appointment of the Director General.[25] Any of these powers may be delegated to the Chair and/or Vice-Chairman of the Administrative Council, the Director-General or any subsidiary organ.[26]

The Administrative Council's function in setting special contributions overlaps directly with the Council's exercise of the same function. To avoid a duplication of roles, it might have been better to exclusively reserve the power of setting special contributions for the Council of Ministers. This would leave the setting of annual contributions to the Administrative Council.

Ordinary sessions of the Administrative Council are convened at least once every year and extra-ordinary sessions may be convened as necessary in accordance with internal procedural rules. [27]

Secretariat

The Secretariat is under the management of the Director General who is the 'principal executive officer' of ARIPO and may serve for a maximum of two fixed terms of 4 years each.[28] The Secretariat's functions include the exploration of possible means to achieve ARIPO's objectives, and where appropriate, reporting its findings to the Administrative Council,[29] carrying out any work, studies or services as directed by the Administrative Council,[30] and drafting annual reports, programs of activities, accounts and budgets.[31] In summary, the Secretariat takes charge of the day to day running of the organization. It operates from the seat of the organization in Harare, Zimbabwe.

Board of Appeal

The Board of Appeal was established to hear appeals against the decisions of the ARIPO Office.[32] Its other functions are the review of final administrative

21 Article VII (1) Lusaka Agreement.
22 Article VII (5) (a) Lusaka Agreement.
23 Article VII (5) (b) Lusaka Agreement.
24 Article VII (5) (c) Lusaka Agreement.
25 Article VII (5) (d) Lusaka Agreement
26 Article VII (6) Lusaka Agreement.
27 Article VII (3) Lusaka Agreement.
28 Article VIII (1) Lusaka Agreement.
29 Article VIII (2) Lusaka Agreement.
30 Article VIII (3) Lusaka Agreement.
31 Article VIII (4) Lusaka Agreement.
32 Section 4bis (1) and 4bis (5)(a) Protocol on Patents and Industrial Designs within the Framework of

decisions of the Office pertaining to the implementation of ARIPO Protocols[33] and to make decisions on related or incidental matters.[34] Its membership is comprised of five persons experienced in IP matters, two of whom are required to be patent examiners.[35]

Committees

Article 2 of the Lusaka Agreement provides that the Administrative Council may establish any subsidiary organs it deems fit. It has established several committees, namely the Finance and Audit Committee, the Staff Affairs Committee and technical commitees.[36] The Finance and Audit Committee advises the Director General on financial matters and for the biennium 2014/2015 its members are Sudan, Ghana, Tanzania, Botswana and Zimbabwe.[37] The Staff Affairs Committee deals with matters related to the welfare of ARIPO personnel and for the biennium 2014/2015 the members of this committee are Kenya, Liberia, Malawi, Zambia and Zimbabwe.[38]

In the past ARIPO only had one technical committee that considered all technical issues, a task which is likely to have been overwhelming considering the number of issues that could potentially emerge in the different areas of IP. To ease this burden, the Adminstrative Council established three technical committees on industrial property; copyright and related rights and the protection of new varieties of plants at its 37th Session held in November 2013 in Kampala, Uganda.[39] Each of these technical commitees has a manageable scope and is comprised of experts in the relevant area. Accordingly, they should find it easier to fulfill their mandates.

Regulatory instruments

In addition to its constitutive act, the Lusaka Agreement, ARIPO has four protocols. The first three of these are the Harare Protocol on Patents and Industrial Designs of 1982, the Banjul Protocol on Marks of 1993,[40] and the Swakopmund Protocol on the Protection of TK and Expressions of Folklore of 2010.[41] The

the African Regional Intellectual Property Organization (ARIPO) (adopted by the Administrative Council of ARIPO at Harare, Zimbabwe on 10 December 1982) as amended (Harare Protocol).

33 Section 4bis (5)(b) Harare Protocol.

34 Section 4bis (5)(b) Harare Protocol.

35 Section 4bis (2) Harare Protocol.

36 ARIPO (2014a).

37 ARIPO (2014a).

38 ARIPO (2014a).

39 ARIPO (2014b).

40 Banjul Protocol on Marks within the Framework of the ARIPO, adopted by the Administrative Council of ARIPO at Banjul, The Gambia, on 19 November 1993 as amended.

41 Swakopmund Protocol on the Protection of Traditional Knowledge and Expressions of Folklore within the Framework of the ARIPO, adopted by the Diplomatic Conference of ARIPO at Swakopmund, Namibia on August 9, 2010, not yet in force.

most recent of these protocols, the Swakopmund Protocol, came into force on 11 May 2015, which was three months after the deposit of the sixth instrument of ratification.[42]

These protocols have accompanying regulations.[43] The fourth protocol is the Arusha Protocol for the Protection of New Varieties of Plants (Arusha Protocol) of 2015. It is based on the Draft ARIPO Legal Framework For The Protection of New Varieties of Plants (Draft PVP Protocol).[44] It was adopted on 6 July 2015, at Arusha, Tanzania at a Diplomatic Conference. As already stated in the introduction, only the Harare, Banjul and Arusha Protocols will be briefly outlined below.

The Harare Protocol

The Harare Protocol was adopted by the Administrative Council of ARIPO in Harare, Zimbabwe in December 1982 and entered into force in 1984. Somalia is not a contracting party to the Protocol, so only 18 of the 19 ARIPO member states are parties to it. It empowers ARIPO, through its Secretariat (the Office), to receive and process patent, utility models and industrial design applications on behalf of states party to the Protocol.[45] The duration of protection granted under the protocol is 20 years for patents[46] and 10 years for utility models and industrial designs.[47]

The Harare Protocol requires the filing of the application to be made at a contracting state's industrial property office or at the ARIPO Office.[48] National offices which receive such applications are required to transmit them to the ARIPO Office within 1 month.[49] An applicant for the grant of a patent or the registration of an industrial design or utility model can, by filing only one application, designate any of the contracting states in which he wishes his invention or industrial design or utility model to be accorded protection.[50] After their grant, these rights are designated as ARIPO patents, ARIPO utility models and ARIPO industrial designs respectively.[51] This provision was inserted into the Harare Protocol through its amendment in November 2013.[52] Once granted, these ARIPO industrial property rights are equivalent to national rights granted

42 Section 27(3) Swakopmund Protocol; ARIPO (2015a).

43 For example, Regulations for Implementing the Banjul Protocol on Marks within the Framework of the ARIPO, adopted by the Administrative Council of ARIPO at Kariba, Zimbabwe on 24 November 1995, as amended.

44 The Draft ARIPO Legal Framework for the Protection of New Varieties of Plants within the Framework of the ARIPO, approved by the Council of Ministers at Uganda, November 2013.

45 Section 1(1) Harare Protocol.

46 Section 3. 1(11) Harare Protocol.

47 Section 3ter (10) and Section 4(6) Harare Protocol.

48 Section 2(1) Harare Protocol.

49 Section 2(5) Harare Protocol.

50 Section 1bis Harare Protocol.

51 Section 1(2) Harare Protocol.

52 Amendments to the Harare Protocol 2013.

by the relevant designated contracting state.[53] This provision was also inserted via the 2013 Amendment. Therefore, they are subject to the applicable national law's provisions pertaining to compulsory licenses, forfeiture or the use of patented inventions in the public interest.[54] Similarly, infringements are dealt with under national laws.[55] The following section briefly outlines the Protocol's provision in relation to patents, industrial designs and utility models.

PATENTS

The ARIPO Office, on receipt of the patent application, first establishes whether the application meets formal or procedural requirements and if so, allocates it a filing date[56] and notifies the designated states of the application.[57] If the application does not meet formal requirements, the applicant is given a time period within which to rectify it, failing which the application will be refused.[58] The ARIPO Office then carries out a substantive examination of applications that meet formal requirements to ensure that the invention, which is the subject of the application, is patentable.[59] In other words, that it is new, involves an inventive step and is capable of being applied in industry.[60] If the invention does not meet these requirements, it will be rejected and an applicant may request the Office to reconsider it.[61] If the rejection is upheld, an applicant may then appeal the Office's decision to the Board of Appeal.[62] Alternatively, an applicant may, within 3 months of the notification of the upholding of the rejection by the ARIPO Office, request that any designated state treat his application as an application according its national law.[63]

In 1999, the Harare Protocol was amended to make provision for patent applications involving micro-organisms.[64] Where a patent application that describes or claims a micro-biological process or a related product is filed and its performance requires the use of a micro-organism which is not available to the public on the filing date of the application and which cannot be made or obtained on the basis of the description in the application,[65] the micro-organism made cultures of the mico-organisms have to be deposited.[66]

53 Section 1(3) Harare Protocol.
54 Sections 3(12); 3ter (12) and 4(7) Harare Protocol.
55 Section 3(14)(b) Harare Protocol.
56 Section 3(2)(a) Harare Protocol.
57 Section 3(2)(c) Harare Protocol.
58 Section 3(2)(b) Harare Protocol.
59 Section 3(3) Harare Protocol.
60 Section 3(10) Harare Protocol.
61 Section 3(4) Harare Protocol.
62 Section 3(5) Harare Protocol.
63 Section 3(8) Harare Protocol.
64 In accordance with the Budapest Treaty on the International Recognition of the Deposit of Micro-organisms for the Purposes of Patent Procedures.
65 Section 3 (1)(b).
66 Rule 6bis Regulations for Implementing the Protocol on Patents and Industrial Designs within the Framework of the ARIPO.

When the application complies with the substantive requirements, copies thereof, and search and examination reports (where applicable) are sent to each designated contracting state who may, within 6 months, notify the ARIPO Office if the ARIPO patent would not be valid in their territory.[67] After the expiry of this 6 month period, the ARIPO Office will grant the application.[68]

The Harare Protocol and its Implementing Regulations were amended by the insertion of section 3 bis to create a link between the Protocol and the PCT in 1994.[69] In terms of this amendment any applicant filing a PCT application may designate ARIPO which in turn means a designation of all states party to both the Harare Protocol and the PCT. The ARIPO Office acts as a receiving office under the PCT for such states.

UTILITY MODELS

In the absence of a universally accepted definition of utility models,[70] the Harare Protocol defines a utility model as

> any form, configuration or disposition of elements of some appliance, working tools and implements as articles of everyday use, electrical and electronic circuitry, instrument, handicraft, mechanism or other object or any part thereof in so far as they are capable of contributing some benefit or new effect or saving in time, energy and labour or allowing a better or different functioning, use, processing or manufacture of the subject matter or that gives utility advantages, environmental benefit, and includes micro-organism or other self-replicable material, products of genetic resources, herbal as well as nutritional formulations which give new effects.[71]

It was necessary to provide for such a broad definition in order to cater for the varying national laws of member states.[72]

A patent application can be converted at any time prior to its acceptance or rejection by the ARIPO Office into an application for a utility model.[73] Likewise, an application for a utility model may be converted into a patent application prior to the pronouncement of a decision on the application by the ARIPO Office.[74] Utility models are registered if they are new and industrially applicable.[75] Applications for utility models are dealt with in the same way as those for patents. A formal examination precedes a substantive examination, which in turn

67 Section 3(6) Harare Protocol.
68 Section 3(7) Harare Protocol.
69 By the Administrative Council at its second extra-ordinary session in April 1994. For commentary, see Kongolo (2013) p. 81–82.
70 Aleman (2012).
71 Section 3ter (1) Harare Protocol.
72 ARIPO (n.d.).
73 Section 3(9) Harare Protocol.
74 Section 3ter (11) Harare Protocol.
75 Section 3ter (2) Harare Protocol.

is followed by notification to designated states which may indicate their views on the validity of the models in their territories.[76] Similar to the position with respect to patents, an unsuccessful applicant for the registration of a utility model may ask the office to reconsider an application.[77] If the rejection is upheld then the applicant can lodge an appeal with the Board of Appeal[78] or ask designated states to consider the application under national laws.[79]

INDUSTRIAL DESIGNS

For industrial design applications, only a formality examination is performed.[80] If the application fulfils the formal requirements, the ARIPO Office notifies designated states of the application[81] and affords them a 6 month period within which to respond to the notification.[82] Under s 4(3) the grounds upon which states may reject designs are:

(i) that the industrial design is not new,
(ii) that, because of the nature of the industrial design, it cannot be registered or a registration has no effect under the national law of that State, or
(iii) that, in the case of a textile design, it is the subject of a special register.

After the expiry of this 6 month response period, the ARIPO Office will grant the design and it will be effective in all non-rejecting designated states.

Where the application does not meet the formality requirements and the applicant fails to rectify it, it will be rejected.[83] As with patents and utility models, within 3 months of such rejection, an unsuccessful industrial design applicant may request any designated state to consider the application under national law.[84]

Banjul Protocol on Marks

The Banjul Protocol was adopted by the Administrative Council of ARIPO in December 1993, in Banjul, The Gambia, and entered into force in 1997. Like the Harare Protocol, it was most recently amended in November 2013. The Protocol empowers the ARIPO Office to receive and process trademark applications on behalf of states party to the Protocol.[85] As at 30 June 2013, the following nine countries were parties to the Protocol: Botswana, Lesotho, Liberia, Malawi, Namibia, Swaziland, Tanzania, Uganda and Zimbabwe.

76 Section 3ter (4)–(5) and (7)–(8) Harare Protocol.
77 Section 3ter (6) Harare Protocol.
78 Section 3ter (7) Harare Protocol.
79 Section 3ter (9) Harare Protocol.
80 Section 4(2)(a) Harare Protocol.
81 Section 4(2)(c) Harare Protocol.
82 Section 4(3) Harare Protocol.
83 Section 4(2)(b) Harare Protocol.
84 Section 4(5) Harare Protocol.
85 Section 1.1 Banjul Protocol.

The Banjul Protocol and its implementing regulations do not provide for substantive trademark law. The Protocol merely provides for the duration of trademarks and the possibility of renewal.[86] It provides that trademark applications will be examined in accordance with national laws,[87] which will also govern the cancellation of trademarks.[88]

As under the Harare Protocol, applications under the Banjul Protocol may be filed in a party state or at the ARIPO office[89] and must designate the states in which protection is sought.[90] Where the application is filed in a contracting state, such state is required to transmit the application to the ARIPO office within 1 month.[91] The applicant is required to identify the goods or service for which protection is being sought, as well as the relevant NICE classification.[92] The ARIPO office will then verify the correctness of the applicant's classification, and effect amendments where required, subject to the payment of a classification fee.[93] Certain declarations are required when colour[94] and three-dimensional[95] marks are being applied for. The applicant is also required to declare actual use of the mark or an intention to use the mark or apply to register another person as the user of the mark.[96] The ARIPO office conducts checks for compliance with these formal requirements[97] and affords non-compliant applicants an opportunity to rectify applications, failing which the application will be rejected.[98] An unsuccessful applicant may ask the office to reconsider an application.[99] Where the reconsideration upholds the rejection, the applicant may then lodge an appeal with the Board of Appeal[100] or request designated states to consider the application under their national law.[101]

Where an application passes the formality examination, the ARIPO office notifies designated states[102] that they then have a 12 month response period within which to indicate whether they will afford protection to the mark in their jurisdictions.[103] Designated states undertake substantive examination of the application in order to determine whether they will afford protection to the mark.[104] Where a

86 Sections 7.1–7.2 Banjul Protocol.
87 Section 6.1 Banjul Protocol.
88 Section 8.2 Banjul Protocol.
89 Section 2.1 Banjul Protocol.
90 Section 3.1 Banjul Protocol.
91 Section 2.4 Banjul Protocol.
92 Section 3.2 Banjul Protocol.
93 Section 3.2 Banjul Protocol.
94 Section 3.3 Banjul Protocol.
95 Section 3.4 Banjul Protocol.
96 Section 3.5 Banjul Protocol.
97 Section 5.1 Banjul Protocol.
98 Section 5.2 Banjul Protocol.
99 Section 5bis.1 Banjul Protocol.
100 Section 5bis.2 Banjul Protocol.
101 Section 5.4 Banjul Protocol.
102 Section 5.3 Banjul Protocol.
103 Section 6.2 Banjul Protocol.
104 Section 6.2 Banjul Protocol.

designated state decides to reject an application, it is required to advise the ARIPO office of the grounds under its national laws on which the application has been rejected.[105] These grounds will then be communicated to the applicant,[106] which has the right of reply as well as of appeal or review under the relevant national law.[107]

This procedure is different from that under the Harare Protocol in two important respects. First, the length of the response period extended to designated states is twice as long under the Banjul Protocol. Secondly, the substantive examination for the protection of marks is undertaken by national offices, whereas under the Harare Protocol the substantive examination in relation to patents is undertaken by the ARIPO office. This is why designated states need a longer time for response.

If there has been no written communication to ARIPO from a state to the effect that it will not afford protection to the mark, the mark will be granted protection in designated states after the completion of a further two-stage process. First, the acceptance of the mark will be announced through publication in the Marks Journal.[108] Secondly, after the passage of a 3 month period, during which opposition proceedings may be commenced, the mark will be registered upon payment of the application fee and a registration certificate will be issued.[109] If an opposition is filed during this period, it will be determined in accordance with the relevant national laws.

Registered ARIPO marks will be valid in designated states, which have not rejected the application,[110] and national law will apply to the cancellation of marks[111] as well as to infringement claims. Marks are registered for an initial period of 10 years[112] which is renewable.[113]

Arusha Protocol

The history of the Arusha Protocol dates back to 2009 when the Council of Ministers approved the initiation of work on a PVP protocol and policy.[114] Since then, the draft protocol was prepared with technical assistance from the International Union for the Protection of New Varieties of Plant (UPOV).[115] It was approved by the Council of Ministers at its 14th session in Uganda, November 2013 and by the UPOV Council in April 2014.[116] The next stage was the adoption

105 Section 6.3 Banjul Protocol.
106 Section 6.3 Banjul Protocol.
107 Section 6.4 Banjul Protocol.
108 Section 6bis.1 Banjul Protocol.
109 Sections 6bis.2 and 6bis.4 Banjul Protocol.
110 Section 8.1 Banjul Protocol.
111 Section 8.2 Banjul Protocol.
112 Section 7.1 Banjul Protocol.
113 Section 7.2 Banjul Protocol.
114 Kongolo (2013) p. 104.
115 Kongolo (2013) p. 104.
116 De Jonge (2014) p. 102.

of the Protocol at a Diplomatic Conference in July 2015. The protocol was signed by the The Gambia, Ghana, Mozambique and São Tomé and Príncipe and will remain open for signature by AU member states until 31 December 2015.[117]

The Arusha Protocol is a *sui generis* framework for the protection of new plant varieties,[118] which is based primarily on the UPOV 1991 Act (UPOV 1991).[119] It affords Plant Breeders' Rights (PBR) to plant varieties that are new, distinct, uniform and stable,[120] as does UPOV 1991.[121] The final test of the Arusha Protocol has not been published by ARIPO and the outline that follows is based on the Draft PVP Protocol which has been published by ARIPO. The holder of a PBR has the exclusive right to authorize the following acts in respect of the protected plant variety:[122]

(i) production or reproduction (multiplication),
(ii) conditioning for the purpose of propagation,
(iii) offering for sale,
(iv) selling or other marketing,
(v) exporting,
(vi) importing,
(vii) stocking for any of the purposes mentioned in (i) to (vi), above.

The duration of a PBR is 20 years generally and 25 years for trees and vines.[123] There are exceptions to the PBR, which include acts done privately and for non-commercial purposes and for experimental purposes.[124] PBRs will be exhausted by the sale or other marketing of material or of its derivatives by the breeder or with his consent in the territories of the Contracting States.[125] However, exhaustion does apply where there is 'further propagation of the variety in question' or 'an export of material of the variety, which enables the propagation of the variety, into a country which does not protect varieties of the plant genus or species to which the variety belongs, except where the exported material is for final consumption purposes.'[126]

The administrative arrangements provided for by the Draft PVP Protocol are similar to those in other ARIPO Protocols with the ARIPO Office playing a pivotal role[127] which includes maintaining a register of PBRs.[128] Once the Protocol

117 ARIPO (2015b).
118 Preamble Draft PVP Protocol.
119 International Convention for the Protection of New Varieties of Plants of December 2, 1961, as Revised at Geneva on November 10, 1972, on October 23, 1978, and on March 19, 1991 (UPOV 1991).
120 Article 6(1) Draft PVP Protocol.
121 Article 5(1) UPOV 1991.
122 Article 21(1)(a) Draft PVP Protocol.
123 Article 26 Draft PVP Protocol.
124 Article 22(1) Draft PVP Protocol.
125 Article 23(1) Draft PVP Protocol.
126 Article 23(1) Draft PVP Protocol.
127 Article 4(3) Draft PVP Protocol.
128 Article 5(1) Draft PVP Protocol.

comes into force, it will be possible to file a single application, which, if successful, will secure PBR in all contracting states.[129] Such application can be filed directly with the ARIPO Office or through an NCA[130] that would then transmit it to the ARIPO Office. Applications will be published in the ARIPO Journal.[131] There will then be an opportunity for interested parties to lodge a written objection to the grant of PBRs.[132] The ARIPO Office is required to undertake formality and substantive examinations of applications[133] or to make arrangements for their performance by competent institutions.[134]

There was opposition from civil society organizations (CSOs) to ARIPO's adoption of the UPOV 1991 model.[135] De Jonge crisply summarizes the grounds of such opposition as '1) the fear that biopiracy will be facilitated, 2) the lack of protection of farmers' rights, and 3) the non-appropriateness of the criteria for protection in the context of Sub-Saharan Africa.'[136] The CSOs are rightly concerned that the adoption of the UPOV 1991 model robs developing countries of the opportunity to nuance their PBR systems so that they better cater for farmers and their national socio-economic conditions.[137] He suggests that this might have been achieved by the adoption of a hybrid system, such as those in place in Malaysia, the Philippines and Zambia.[138] Another option would have been to borrow from the AU's African Model Legislation for the Protection of the Rights of Local Communities, Farmers and Breeders, and for the Regulation of Access to Biological Resources of 2000. This model law provides for the *sui generis* protection and has been domesticated by some African states.[139] These valid criticisms and viable alternatives notwithstanding, ARIPO resolved to adopt the draft PVP in October 2013, at a regional workshop on the draft PVP Protocol, hosted in Harare.[140] As stated above, the Arusha Protocol was subsequently adopted in July 2015.

OAPI

The membership of OAPI consists of 17 countries, namely Benin, Burkina Faso, Cameroon, Central African Republic, Chad, Comoros, Congo, Côte d'Ivoire, Gabon, Guinea, Equatorial Guinea, Mali, Mauritania, Niger, Guinea Bissau, Senegal and Togo. Its seat is in Yaoundé, Cameroon.[141]

129 Article 4(1)–(2) Draft PVP Protocol.
130 Article 12(1) Draft PVP Protocol.
131 Article 15(1) Draft PVP Protocol.
132 Article 16(1) Draft PVP Protocol.
133 Article 17 Draft PVP Protocol.
134 Article 18(1) Draft PVP Protocol.
135 Saez (2014).
136 De Jonge (2014) p. 101.
137 De Jonge (2014) p. 104.
138 De Jonge (2014) pp. 106–107.
139 Feris (2004) pp. 252–253.
140 ARIPO (2014c); Alliance for Food Sovereignty in Africa (AFSA) (2014).
141 Article 40 Bangui Agreement.

Prior to their independence, the French National Patent Rights Institute (INPI) met French colonies' patent administration needs.[142] Post their independence, Benin, Burkina Faso, Cameroon, Central African Republic, Chad, Republic of Congo, Côte d'Ivoire, Gabon, Malagasy, Mauritania, Niger and Senegal[143] replaced the INPI by creating the African and Malagasy Office of Industrial Property (l'*Office Africaine et Malgache de la Propriété Industrielle* in French, known as OAMPI) through the adoption of a constitutive agreement[144] at Libreville, Gabon.[145] Like the first iteration of ARIPO, OAMPI focused only on industrial property.

The OAMPI constitutive agreement, known as the Libreville Agreement, was revised on 2 March 1977 at Bangui, Central African Republic.[146] OAPI was created by this revision agreement, the Agreement relating to the creation of an African Intellectual Property Organization, known as the Bangui Agreement. The 1977 Bangui Agreement came into force on 8 February 1982.[147] It was extensively revised in 1999 to ensure compliance with the TRIPS Agreement.[148] The revised text, including Annexes I–IX, came into force on 28 February 2002. The tenth annex came into force on 1 January 2006.

OAPI's member states articulate their main objective in the preamble of the Bangui Agreement as 'to promote the effective contribution of intellectual property to the development of their States on the one hand, and . . . on the other hand to protect intellectual property rights on their territories in as effective and uniform a manner as possible.' The functions and responsibilities of the organization that enable it to realize this objective are set out in full in article 2. In summary they pertain to collaboration with regard to substantive and administrative aspects of IP with a view to furthering the economic development of member states.

Organs

Unlike ARIPO that has four main organs, OAPI only has three, namely the Administrative Council, the High Commission of Appeal and the Directorate General.[149] Each of these organs' composition and principal duties are summarized below.

Administrative Council

The Administrative Council is OAPI's 'supreme organ' and as such is responsible for the organization's general policy and regulates and controls its activities.[150]

142 Adewopo (n.d.) p. 7.
143 Nwauche (2003) p. 105.
144 The Agreement relating to the creation of an African and Malagasy Office of Industrial Property.
145 Kongolo (2013) p. 82; Nwauche (2003) p. 105; Adewopo (n.d.) p. 7.
146 Kongolo (2013) p. 82; Nwauche (2003) p. 105; Adewopo (n.d.) p. 7.
147 WIPO (n.d.).
148 Nwauche (2003) p. 110.
149 Article 27 Bangui Agreement.
150 Article 29 Bangui Agreement.

Its membership consists of one representative of each member state[151] and a member state may ask another to represent it subject to the limitation that a single Council member may not represent more than two states.[152] The functions of the Administrative Council are:[153]

(a) drafting the regulations necessary for the application of the Bangui Agreement and its Annexes;
(b) establishing regulations pertaining to financial matters, fees, the High Commission of Appeal, the general staff and to professional representatives;
(c) supervision of the implementation of these regulations;
(d) approval of the program of activities and the budget, and the control of their implementation;
(e) examination and approval of annual accounts and inventory;
(f) approval of the annual report on the activities of OAPI;
(g) appointment of the holders of unclassified posts and the designation of the auditor of the Organization;
(h) ruling on applications for admission as members or as associated States of the Organization;
(i) setting the amount of any contribution to be made by member States or by associated States;
(j) deciding on the creation of ad hoc committees on specific issues; and
(k) determining the working language or languages.

The Administrative Council also has powers to draft implementing regulations for specified international agreements.[154] It is required to convene one annual ordinary session[155] and 'extraordinary sessions may be convened where necessary by the Chairman at the request of one-third of the membership, or at the request of the Director General.'[156]

High Commission of Appeal

The High Commission of Appeal hears appeals relating to the rejection of applications for titles of industrial property protection; requests for the maintenance or extension of terms of protection and requests for reinstatement and appeals of decisions on oppositions.[157] Its membership consists of three members who are selected by the drawing of lots from a list of representatives designated by the member States.[158] Each State has one designated representative on the list from

151 Article 28(1) Bangui Agreement.
152 Article 28(2) Bangui Agreement.
153 Article 29 Bangui Agreement.
154 Article 30 Bangui Agreement; Nwauche (2003) p. 107.
155 Article 31(1) Bangui Agreement.
156 Article 31(2) Bangui Agreement.
157 Article 33(2) Bangui Agreement.
158 Article 33(1) Bangui Agreement.

which lots are drawn.[159] Unlike with the provisions pertaining to the ARIPO Board of Appeal, there is no express requirement that these members have to have any industrial property technical expertise. However this may only be an illusory problem if in reality suitably qualified persons get put on the list.

The Directorate General

The Directorate General is under the management of the Director General who is the 'highest official' of OAPI and may serve for a maximum of two fixed terms of 5 years each.[160] The Directorate General is seized with the executive work of the Organization.[161] As such it is responsible for the day-to-day management of OAPI. It implements the instructions of the Administrative Council and reports to it.

Unlike the Lusaka Agreement that does not enumerate the duties of the Director General, the Bangui Agreement lists the following duties of the Director General:

- producing drafts for the budget, program and balance sheet and also periodical activity reports which he is required to convey to the member States;[162]
- participation, without voting rights, in all sessions of the Administrative Council at which also he serves as secretary ex officio;[163] and
- the recruitment, appointment and dismissal or termination of the appointments of OAPI staff, with the exception of unclassified staff.[164]

Ultimately, the Director General is answerable for the management of the Organization to the Administrative Council, to which he reports and with whose instructions he is required to comply.[165]

Regulatory instruments

The Bangui Agreement serves as a civil code of IP and has direct application in the member states.[166] It focuses on IP (as opposed to only industrial property as the Libreville Agreement did) and addresses its various aspects in the following ten annexes which are listed in article 4:

Annex I: Patents;
Annex II: Utility models;
Annex III: Trademarks and service marks;
Annex IV: Industrial designs;

159 Article 33(1) Bangui Agreement.
160 Article 35(1)–(2) Bangui Agreement.
161 Article 34 Bangui Agreement.
162 Article 35(3) Bangui Agreement.
163 Article 35(4) Bangui Agreement.
164 Article 35(5) Bangui Agreement.
165 Article 35(2)(b) Bangui Agreement.
166 Kongolo (2013) p. 83.

Annex V: Trade names;
Annex VI: Geographical indications;
Annex VII: Literary and artistic property;
Annex VIII: Unfair competition;
Annex IX: Layout designs of integrated circuits; and
Annex X: New varieties of plant.

As noted in the introduction, the scope of OAPI's legal framework is much broader than that of ARIPO and for purposes of comparison, this section will only outline those annexes that have a counterpart in the ARIPO framework.

Annex I: Patents

Annex 1 begins with a statement of patentability criteria, *viz* novelty, inventive step and industrial applicability.[167] These criteria are as prescribed by the TRIPS Agreement and are therefore the same as those outlined in the Harare Protocol. However there are some important differences between the Harare Protocol and Annex 1. First, the Harare Protocol does not have a general patentability exclusion clause, fashioned along the lines of article 27 (2)–(3) of TRIPS or article 52(2) of the Convention on the Grant of European Patents (EPC). Annex 1 has such an exclusion clause, which excludes the following from patentability:[168]

(a) inventions the exploitation of which is contrary to public policy or morality, provided that the exploitation of the invention shall not be considered contrary to public policy or morality merely because it is prohibited by law or regulation;
(b) discoveries, scientific theories and mathematical methods;
(c) inventions having as their subject matter plant varieties, animal species and essentially biological processes for the breeding of plants or animals other than microbiological processes and the products of such processes;
(d) schemes, rules or methods for doing business, performing purely mental acts or playing games;
(e) methods for the treatment of the human or animal body by surgery or therapy, including diagnostic methods;
(f) mere presentations of information;
(g) computer programs;
(h) works of an exclusively ornamental nature;
(i) literary, architectural and artistic works or any other aesthetic creation.

However, in contrast to article 52(3) of the EPC, the Annex does not qualify the exclusions, to the subject matter 'as such'. Therefore there is an outright prohibition of patent protection for the above listed subject matter.

167 Article 2(1). Expounded in articles 3–5.
168 Article 6.

The Harare Protocol's only provisions pertaining to subject matter exclusions are in relation to biotechnological inventions.[169] These are defined as 'inventions which concern a product consisting of or containing biological material or a process by means of which biological material is produced, processed or used.' The following biotechnological inventions are excluded from patentability:[170]

i. processes for cloning human beings,
ii. processes for modifying the germ line genetic identity of human beings,
iii. uses of human embryos for industrial or commercial purposes,
iv. processes for modifying the genetic identity of animals which are likely to cause them suffering without any substantial medical benefit to man or animal, and also animals resulting from such processes,
v. an embryonic stem cell of an animal, an animal at the various stages of its formation and development such as a germ cell, a zoosperm, an embryo etc belong[ing] to the category of animal variety,
vi. a single plant and its reproductive material (such as seed, etc) which maintains its life by synthesizing carbohydrates and protein from the inorganic substances such as water, carbon dioxide and mineral salts and so on through photosynthesis belong[ing] to the category of plant variety,
vii. inventions that do not possess practical applicability, i.e. cannot easily be reproduced,
viii. the human body, at the various stages of its formation and development, and the simple discovery of one of its elements, including the sequence or partial sequence of a gene, cannot constitute patentable inventions.

In accordance with the TRIPS Agreement, the duration of OAPI patents is 20 years[171] and they afford their holders the usual economic exclusivity over working the invention.[172] Working is defined to mean 'manufacturing, importing, offering for sale, selling and using a patented product or a product manufactured through a patented process, holding it for the purposes of offering it for sale, selling it or using it and using a patented process.'[173] The inclusion of importation in this definition was criticized for the perceived harmful effects that would be wrought by an import monopoly, particularly in relation to essential medicines.[174]

Applications can be filed directly with OAPI or with the ministry responsible for industrial property in member states[175] that would then be required to transmit the

169 Rule 7bis (1)(c) Regulations for Implementing the Protocol on Patents and Industrial Designs within the Framework of the ARIPO.
170 Rule 7bis (3) Regulations for Implementing the Protocol on Patents and Industrial Designs within the Framework of the ARIPO.
171 Article 9 Annex 1, Bangui Agreement.
172 Article 7(2) Annex 1, Bangui Agreement.
173 Article 7(3) Annex 1, Bangui Agreement.
174 Nwauche (2003) p. 111.
175 Article 14(1) Annex 1, Bangui Agreement.

application to OAPI within 5 days of receipt.[176] Where the application pertains to biotechnological inventions and it is necessary to submit a micro-organism, proof of such deposit should be submitted with the application.[177] After the allocation of a filing date,[178] a substantive examination is carried out.[179] Should the invention fail to meet patentability criteria or if the application is defective in any way, the applicant will be afforded an opportunity to rectify the application, failing which, it will be rejected.[180] Appeals of a rejection of a patent application are made to the High Commission of Appeal in accordance with the rules of the organization.[181]

An interested person may bring an application for the invalidation of a patent for sub-patentability.[182] There is provision for the application[183] for issuance of compulsory licenses for non-working,[184] and for dependent patents.[185] The holder of the senior patent may appeal the issue of the license.[186] There is also provision for the grant of *ex officio* licenses where the relevant patent 'is of vital interest to the economy of the country, public health or national defense, or where non-working or insufficient working of such patents seriously compromises the satisfaction of the country's needs'.[187] In such cases, the Minister seized with IP matters or who is competent to do so on other grounds, may make an 'administrative enactment' subjecting the patent to the non-voluntary license regime.[188] The enactment will detail all relevant information such as 'the beneficiary administration or organization, the conditions, term and scope of the non-voluntary license and the amount of royalties payable'.[189] Should the patent holder and the relevant ministry fail to agree on the conditions of the ex officio license, they will be set by a civil court.[190] These compulsory license provisions adopt a TRIPS-plus stance because they exclude importation, thereby eliminating the possibility of parallel importation as a means to obtain access to patented technology such as pharmaceuticals.[191]

Patent infringement may be dealt with as a criminal or civil matter or both subject to the limitation that criminal matters are brought entirely at the discretion of the Office of the Public Prosecutor.[192] Where a conviction is secured, the penalty is 'a fine of 1,000,000 to 3,000,000 CFA francs, without prejudice to the right to

176 Article 19(1) Annex 1, Bangui Agreement.
177 Article 14(2) Annex 1, Bangui Agreement.
178 Article 18 Annex 1, Bangui Agreement.
179 Article 20 Annex 1, Bangui Agreement.
180 Articles 23–24 Annex 1, Bangui Agreement.
181 Article 33(2)(a) Annex 1, Bangui Agreement.
182 Article 43 Annex 1, Bangui Agreement.
183 Articles 48–49 Annex 1, Bangui Agreement.
184 Article 46 Annex 1, Bangui Agreement.
185 Article 47 Annex 1, Bangui Agreement.
186 Article 53 Annex 1, Bangui Agreement.
187 Article 56(1) Annex 1, Bangui Agreement.
188 Article 56(1) Annex 1, Bangui Agreement.
189 Article 56(1) Annex 1, Bangui Agreement.
190 Article 56(2) Annex 1, Bangui Agreement.
191 Musungu, Villanueva and Blasetti (2004) p. 55.
192 Article 61 Annex 1, Bangui Agreement.

compensation'.[193] Where a second conviction is secured against the same defendant within a period of 5 years after the first conviction,[194] a term of imprisonment between 1 to 6 months may be imposed in addition to a fine.[195]

Annex II: Utility Models

The Bangui Agreement affords utility model protection of 10 years' duration[196] that entitles its holder to economic exclusivity over the 'manufacturing, offering for sale, selling and using the utility model, and importing and holding it for the purposes of offering it for sale, selling it or using it.'[197]

Utility models are defined as

> implements of work or objects to be utilized or parts of such implements or objects in so far as they are useful for the work or employment for which they are intended on account of a new configuration, a new arrangement or a new component device, and are industrially applicable.[198]

This definition is much shorter than that provided for in the Harare Protocol, which in addition to implements or objects, also expressly mentions

> any form, configuration or disposition of elements of some appliance [and] working tools . . . articles of everyday use, electrical and electronic circuitry, instrument, handicraft, mechanism or other object or any part thereof in so far as they are capable of contributing some benefit or new effect or saving in time, energy and labour or allowing a better or different functioning, use, processing or manufacture of the subject matter or that gives utility advantages, environmental benefit, and includes micro-organism or other self-replicable material, products of genetic resources, herbal as well as nutritional formulations which give new effects.[199]

Another important distinction between the two protocols is the Harare Protocol's express inclusion of micro-organisms, genetic resources, herbal and nutritional formulations as eligible subject matter for utility model protection.

In order to qualify for protection under Annex 2 of the Bangui Agreement, a utility model must be novel and have industrial applicability. Relative novelty is required and disclosure of a utility model in a territory beyond OAPI member states does not anticipate it for OAPI's purposes.[200] Further, a utility model will

193 Article 58 Annex 1, Bangui Agreement.
194 Article 59(2) Annex 1, Bangui Agreement.
195 Article 59(1) Annex 1, Bangui Agreement.
196 Article 6 Annex 2, Bangui Agreement
197 Article 5 Annex 2, Bangui Agreement.
198 Article 1 Annex 2, Bangui Agreement.
199 Section 3ter (1) Harare Protocol.
200 Article 2(1) Annex 2, Bangui Agreement.

not lose its novelty where disclosure has occurred within OAPI territory by an unauthorized person or by the applicant or an authorized person at an officially recognized international exhibition within a period of 12 months prior to the filing of the application.[201] A utility model will have industrial applicability if 'it can be made or used in any kind of industry' which is 'understood in its broadest sense . . . [and] cover[s] handicraft, agriculture, fishery and services.'[202]

The Annex excludes two categories of subject matter from eligibility for utility model protection. The first category includes objects and implements, or components thereof, that are 'contrary to public policy or morality, public health, the national economy or national defense.'[203] However the mere fact that the exploitation or use of a model is prohibited by law or regulation does not render it contrary to public policy or morality.[204] There have to be other substantive grounds for characterizing it as such.

The second category of excluded utility models pertains to those that have 'already been the subject of a patent or a utility model registration based on a prior application or an application validly claiming an earlier priority.'[205]

The creator of a utility model has the sole right to its registration,[206] which will be jointly held by joint creators,[207] and applicants are deemed to be holders of such rights.[208] This right to registration may be assigned or transferred by succession.[209] The utility model registration operates on a first-to-file basis. Where the same model has been independently developed by two or more persons, the first to file or the one with the earliest validly claimed priority date, will be entitled to the registration.[210] Where a model is developed or created by a person within an employment context, the default position is that the right to registration of the model belongs to the employer.[211] This default position may be varied by contract. In certain instances which are outlined below, an employee will be entitled to additional remuneration for his creation, even if it was created within the course and scope of his employment.

An employer will be entitled to the right of registration even if the relevant employment contract did not require that the employee be involved in inventive activity if the employee used 'data or means' at his disposal by virtue of his employment to create the model.[212] However, in such circumstances the employee would be entitled to remuneration mutually fixed between the parties, failing which it

201 Article 2(2) Annex 2, Bangui Agreement.
202 Article 3 Annex 2, Bangui Agreement.
203 Article 4(1) Annex 2, Bangui Agreement.
204 Article 4(1) Annex 2, Bangui Agreement.
205 Article 4(2) Annex 2, Bangui Agreement.
206 Article 7(1) Annex 2, Bangui Agreement.
207 Article 7(2) Annex 2, Bangui Agreement.
208 Article 7(2) Annex 2, Bangui Agreement.
209 Article 7(4) Annex 2, Bangui Agreement.
210 Article 7(3) Annex 2, Bangui Agreement.
211 Article 8(1) Annex 2, Bangui Agreement.
212 Article 8(2) Annex 2, Bangui Agreement.

would be fixed by a court.[213] This right to remuneration is extended to instances where a utility model is created within the course and scope of an employee's work, where the employee's utility model is 'of very exceptional importance.'[214]

Article 9 of the Annex provides for the following exceptions:

a) once a utility model is brought into the market of an OAPI member state by its owner or with his consent, his rights are exhausted;
b) use of the utility model 'on board foreign aircraft, land vehicles or ships that temporarily or accidentally enter the airspace, territory or waters of an OAPI member State';
c) experimental use of a utility model in the course of scientific and technical research;
d) any use 'by any person who in good faith on the filing date of the application, or where priority is claimed on the priority date of the application on the basis of which the utility model is registered on the territory of a member State, was using the utility model or making effective and genuine preparations for such use, in so far as those acts are not different in nature or purpose from the actual or planned earlier use.'

The right to rely on the fourth exception can only be transferred by its initial holder to a third party if the business or company with which the early or prior use of the model is associated is being transferred to the third party.[215]

Annex III: Trademarks and Service Marks

OAPI acceded to the Madrid Protocol on Marks in December 2014 and the Protocol entered into force for OAPI on 5 March 2015.[216] This has been a controversial move as the Bangui Agreement does not expressly provide for the accession to international legal instruments by OAPI. It has led to some conflict between the organization and some of its agents, which has resulted in the suspension of those agents.[217]

The Annex provides for both substantive and procedural aspects of trademark law. The first part of the annex provides for trademarks and service marks. The second part of the Annex provides for collective marks.[218] As the point has already been made that OAPI administers a unitary registration system, this section will not dwell on the procedural aspects. Suffice it to say that there is provision for both pre-grant opposition procedures,[219] appeals against registration decisions[220] and

213 Article 8(3) Annex 2, Bangui Agreement.
214 Article 8(4) Annex 2, Bangui Agreement.
215 Article 9(2) Annex 2, Bangui Agreement.
216 WIPO (2014).
217 Tita (2015).
218 Articles 32–36, Annex 3, Bangui Protocol.
219 Article 15, Annex 3, Bangui Agreement.
220 Article 18, Annex 3, Bangui Agreement.

for cancellation of registration for non-use.[221] Instead, this section will summarize the substantive aspects in relation to trademarks.

Protection is provided for trademarks and service marks, upon registration, for a term of 10 years, which is renewable.[222] An unusual aspect of such protection is that it extends beyond the goods or services for which the mark is registered and also covers similar goods and services.[223] Article 2(1) defines marks as

> Any visible sign used or intended to be used and capable of distinguishing the goods or services of any enterprise shall be considered a trademark or service mark, including in particular surnames by themselves or in a distinctive form, special, arbitrary or fanciful designations, the characteristic form of a product or its packaging, labels, wrappers, emblems, prints, stamps, seals, vignettes, borders, combinations or arrangements of colors, drawings, reliefs, letters, numbers, devices and pseudonyms.

Article 3 then provides that a mark will not be eligible for registration if:

> (a) it is devoid of distinctiveness, notably owing to the fact that it consists of signs or matter constituting the necessary or genetic designation of the product or the composition thereof;
> (b) it is identical to a mark that belongs to another owner and is already registered, or the filing or priority date of which is earlier, and which relates to the same or similar goods or services, or where it so resembles such a mark that it is liable to mislead or confuse;
> (c) it is contrary to public policy, morality or the law;
> (d) it is liable to mislead the public or business circles, notably as to the geographical origin, nature or characteristics of the goods or services in question;
> (e) it reproduces, imitates or incorporates armorial bearings, flags or other emblems, the abbreviated name or acronym or an official sign or hallmark indicating control and warranty of a State or intergovernmental organization established by an international convention, except where the competent authority of that State or of that organization has given its permission.

Article 6 provides protection for well-known marks. The owner of such a mark may file a court application for invalidation in national courts, where a registered mark is 'liable to be confused' with the well-known mark. Such protection is premised on article 6 bis of the Paris Convention and article 16(2) and (3) of TRIPS. However, where the mark was registered in good faith, it may not be invalidated if five years have passed since the filing of the relevant trademark

221 Article 23, Annex 3, Bangui Agreement.
222 Articles 19 and 23, Annex 3, Bangui Agreement.
223 Article 7(1), Annex 3, Bangui Agreement.

application. The annex provides for both criminal sanctions[224] and civil remedies[225] for infringement.

The key substantive differences between ARIPO's Banjul Protocol and OAPI's Annex III is that ARIPO leaves substantive trademark law to national legislation whilst OAPI makes provision for some aspects as shown above.

Annex IV: Industrial Designs

Industrial designs are defined as 'any arrangement of lines or colors' if it 'gives a special appearance to an industrial or craft product and may serve as a pattern for the manufacture of such a product'.[226] A model is similarly defined as 'any three-dimensional shape, whether or not associated with lines or colors, . . . [that] gives a special appearance to an industrial or craft product and may serve as a pattern for the manufacture of such a product.'[227]

Annex IV provides protection for new[228] industrial designs for a period of 5 years.[229] Industrial designs whose exploitation is contrary to public policy or morality are ineligible for protection.[230] Such protection 'may be renewed for a further two consecutive periods of five years on payment of a renewal fee.'[231] However, such protection cannot be enforced against persons who were already exploiting the said design in an OAPI member state, or had begun preparations to do so, at the time the application for the registration of the industrial design was filed.[232]

Criminal sanctions[233] and civil remedies[234] are provided for.

Annex X: New Varieties of Plant

The Bangui Agreement commits OAPI to implementing UPOV 1991.[235] Consequently Annex X is in compliance with UPOV 1991.[236] This annex came into force on 1 January 2006.[237] OAPI joined UPOV in 2014.[238] As they are modeled on the same international agreement, ARIPO's Arusha Protocol and OAPI's Annex X are substantively the same. OAPI's decision to adopt the UPOV model

224 Articles 37–45 Annex 3, Bangui Agreement.
225 Articles 46–49 Annex 3, Bangui Agreement.
226 Article 1(1) Annex 4, Bangui Agreement.
227 Article 1(1) Annex 4, Bangui Agreement.
228 Article 2(1) Annex 4, Bangui Agreement.
229 Article 12(1) Annex 4, Bangui Agreement.
230 Article 2(4) Annex 4, Bangui Agreement.
231 Article 12(2) Annex 4, Bangui Agreement.
232 Article 7 Annex 4, Bangui Agreement.
233 Articles 25–28 and 30 Annex 4, Bangui Agreement.
234 Articles 29, 31–34 Annex 4, Bangui Agreement.
235 Article 30 Bangui Agreement; Cullet (2001) p. 103.
236 UPOV (2000).
237 Gazaro (2006) p. 129.
238 UPOV (2014).

was critiqued on the same grounds that ARIPO's decision was, as outlined above. Further, as noted in Chapter 1, most OAPI member states are LDCs and were thus not required to be TRIPS compliant at the time they made this decision,[239] as they still are.

Conclusion

From a public interest perspective, it is clear that both organizations have not done as much as they could have to advance their member states' interests. For instance, as shown in Chapter 1, OAPI's decision to become an early adopter of TRIPS standards notwithstanding applicable transition periods is lamentable. Similarly, their choice to adopt the UPOV 91 model instead of the AU's Model Law may be faulted for not taking into account African conditions and needs. However, the *sui generis* protection of TK provided for in ARIPO's Swakopmund Protocol is a commendable development. The organization has the requisite technical expertise amongst its staff to offer assistance to its member states and RECs on IP policy and legislation. Such advice would have the advantage of being informed by current conditions on the continent, which other sources of technical assistance often go without. This is a role that ARIPO ought to embrace in the interest of creating relevant IP systems on the continent. OAPI does not need to play a similar role in relation to the development of its member states' legislation because their laws are unified.

As noted in the introduction, the possibility of the merger of the two sub-regional IP organizations has been raised by the organizations themselves. In addition, some scholars have also mooted this possibility. Some have considered a general merger pertaining to all aspects of IP,[240] whilst others have considered a merger only in relation to trademark matters.[241] The advantages of such a merger would include the leveraging of economies of scale and the ease of obtaining IP protection over a broader coverage of states for applicants who use the central application system.[242]

There are two key hindrances to a general merger. First, substantively their laws are different in some respects as shown above. For example, Annex 1 of the Bangui Agreement contains patentability exclusions that the Harare Protocol does not. Another instance of substantive legal standard differences is that the LDC member states of OAPI have voluntarily become early adopters of TRIPS standards prior to the expiry of relevant transition periods. The second hindrance would be the nature of the two sub-regional IP systems. OAPI has unified its member states' IP laws in a common code, the Bangui Agreement, and has a single registration system that secures the grant of industrial property in all its member states. On the other hand, ARIPO has harmonized the IP laws of its

239 Cullet (2001) p. 103.
240 For example see Kongolo (2013) p. 124; Kongolo (2000); Dean (1994a) and Dean (1994b).
241 Mupangavanhu (2015), (2014) and (2013); Adewopo (2003).
242 Adewopo (2003) p. 475.

member states through Protocols to which its members voluntarily subscribe and thereafter domesticate. Its registration system is not unitary and protection is only granted in designated member states, which have an opportunity to accept or decline an application in a national process, following the initial ARIPO application stage.

References

Primary sources: agreements, decisions and official documents

ARIPO

Agreement on the Creation of the African Regional Intellectual Property Organization, adopted on 9 December 1976, and as amended on 13 August 2004 (Lusaka Agreement).

ARIPO & OAPI. 2014. Communiqué Adopted by the Joint Meeting of the Chairmen of ARIPO AND OAPI, held at the Headquarters of ARIPO on April 10 and 11, 2014, Harare, Republic of Zimbabwe.

Arusha Protocol for the Protection of New Varieties of Plant within the Framework of the ARIPO, adopted Diplomatic Conference that was held in Arusha, the United Republic of Tanzania on July 6, 2015.

Banjul Protocol on Marks within the Framework of the ARIPO, adopted by the Administrative Council of ARIPO at Banjul, The Gambia, on 19 November 1993 as amended.

The Draft ARIPO Legal Framework for the Protection of New Varieties of Plants within the Framework of the ARIPO, approved by the Council of Ministers at Uganda, November 2013.

Protocol on Patents and Industrial Designs within the Framework of the African Regional Intellectual Property Organization (ARIPO), adopted by the Administrative Council of ARIPO at Harare, Zimbabwe on 10 December 1982 as amended.

Regulations for Implementing the Banjul Protocol on Marks within the Framework of the ARIPO, adopted by the Administrative Council of ARIPO at Kariba, Zimbabwe on 24 November 1995, as amended.

Regulations for Implementing the Protocol on Patents and Industrial Designs within the Framework of the ARIPO, 1984.

Swakopmund Protocol on the Protection of Traditional Knowledge and Expressions of Folklore within the Framework of the ARIPO, adopted by the Diplomatic Conference of ARIPO at Swakopmund, Namibia on August 9, 2010.

AU

African Model Legislation for the Protection of the Rights of Local Communities, Farmers and Breeders, and for the Regulation of Access to Biological Resources, 2000.

EU

Convention on the Grant of European Patents (European Patent Convention), of 5 October 1973 as revised by the Act revising Article 63 EPC of 17 December 1991 and the Act revising the EPC of 29 November 2000.

OAPI

The Agreement relating to the creation of an African and Malagasy Office of Industrial Property.

Bangui Agreement Relating to the Creation of an African Intellectual Property Organization, Constituting a Revision of the Agreement Relating to the Creation of an African and Malagasy Office of Industrial Property (Bangui (Central African Republic), adopted on 2 March 1977).

UPOV

International Convention for the Protection of New Varieties of Plants of December 2, 1961, as Revised at Geneva on November 10, 1972, on October 23, 1978, and on March 19, 1991.

International Union for the Protection of New Varieties of Plants, Examination of the Conformity of the Bangui Agreement on the Creation of an African Intellectual Property Organization with the UPOV Convention, UPOV Council, Seventeenth Extraordinary Session, Geneva, 7 April, 2000, Doc. C(Extr.)/17/3.

WIPO

Budapest Treaty on the International Recognition of the Deposit of Micro-organisms for the Purposes of Patent Procedures, adopted at Budapest on April 28, 1977, and amended on September 26, 1980.

Madrid (Marks) Notification No. 203, Protocol Relating to the Madrid Agreement Concerning the International Registration of Marks: Accession by the African Intellectual Property Organization, 2014.

Paris Convention for the Protection of Industrial Property, 1883, 21 U.S.T. 1583, 828 U.N.T.S. 305

Protocol Relating to the Madrid Agreement Concerning the International Registration of Marks, adopted at Madrid on June 27, 1989 ('Madrid Protocol (1989)'), as amended on October 3, 2006, and on November 12, 2007.

WTO

Agreement on Trade-Related Aspects of Intellectual Property Rights, including Trade in Counterfeit Goods, adopted 15 December 1993, entered into force 1 January 1995, (1994) 33 ILM 81 (TRIPS).

Secondary sources

Adewopo, A., 2003. Trademark systems in Africa: a proposal for the harmonization of the ARIPO and the OAPI Agreements on Marks, *The Journal of World Intellectual Property*, 6, 473–484.

Adewopo, A., (n.d.). 'Developments in Intellectual Property In Africa'. Online. Available HTTP: <http://www.atrip.org/Content/Activities/Adewopo%20Dev.%20of%20IP%20in%20Africa.doc>, accessed 20 October 2014.

Aleman, M., 2012. International legal framework for protection of utility models. *WIPO Regional Seminar on the Legislative, Economic and Policy Aspects of Utility Models Protection System,* Kuala Lumpur, Malaysia 3–4 September 2012. WIPO/IP/KUL/12/REF/T2C.

Alliance for Food Sovereignty in Africa (AFSA), 2014. *Appeal to ARIPO and African Union Member States and UNECA for an Effective ARIPO Protocol Supportive of Farmers' Rights and the Right to Food.* Online. Available HTTP: <http://www.ip-watch.org/weblog/wp-content/uploads/2014/11/AFSA-statement.pdf>, accessed 22 December 2014.

ARIPO, n.d. 'Utility models'. Online. Available HTTP: <www.aripo.org/index/php/services/utility-model>, accessed 11 December 2014.

ARIPO, 2014a. *Finance and Audit Committee and the Staff Affairs Committee Meet in Harare.* Online. Available HTTP: <http://www.aripo.org/index.php/news-events/press-room/344-finance-and-audit-committee-and-the-staff-affairs-committee-meet-in-harare>, accessed 11 December 2014.

ARIPO, 2014b. *Official Opening of the 2014 Sessions of the Technical Committee on Industrial Property and Technical Committee on Copyright and Related Rights.* Online. Available HTTP: <http://www.aripo.org/index.php/news-events/press-room/339-official-opening-of-the-2014-sessions-of-the-technical-committee-on-industrial-property-and-technical-committee-on-copyright-and-related-rights>, accessed 11 December 2014.

ARIPO, 2014c. *Regional Workshop on the Draft ARIPO Protocol for the Protection of New Varieties of Plants organized by ARIPO in cooperation with UPOV and with the assistance of the United States Patent and Trademark Office (USPTO).* Harare 29–31 October 2014. ARIPO/HRE/2014/INF/1.

ARIPO, 2015. *Entry into Force of the ARIPO Swakopmund Protocol on the Protection of Traditional Knowledge and Expressions of Folklore.* Online. Available HTTP: <http://www.aripo.org/index.php/news-events/press-room/371-entry-into-force-of-the-aripo-swakopmund-protocol-on-the-protection-of-traditional-knowledge-and-expressions-of-folklore>, accessed 23 April 2015.

Chirambo, M.H., 2002. *The African Regional Industrial Property Organization (ARIPO) as an Example of Regional Cooperation in the Field of Patents.* WIPO/INV/BEI/02/10.

Cullet, P., 2001. Plant variety protection in Africa: towards compliance with the TRIPS agreement, *Journal of African Law*, 45(1), 97–122.

Dean, O.H., 1994a. A unified intellectual property law system for southern Africa. Part 1: International arrangements and European conventions, *Juta's Business Law*, 2(3), 111–114.

Dean, O.H., 1994b. A unified intellectual property law system for southern Africa. Part 2: Multinational registrations in Africa, *Juta's Business Law*, 2(4), 165–169.

De Jonge, B., 2014. Plant variety protection in Sub-Saharan Africa: balancing commercial and smallholder farmers' interests, *Journal of Politics and Law*, 7(3), 100–111.

Feris, L., 2004. Protecting traditional knowledge in Africa: considering African approaches, *African Human Rights Law Journal*, 4(2), 242–255.

Gazaro, W.R., 2006. Plant variety protection: Which system of protection in the member states of OAPI? *World Patent Information*, 28(2), 127–131.

Grosse Ruse-Khan, H., 2012. *The International Legal Framework for the Protection of Utility Models.* Research Paper No. 12–10. Online. Available HTTP: <http://ssrn.com/abstract=2160229>, accessed 11 December 2014.

Kongolo, T., 2000. The African IP organizations – the necessity of adopting one uniform system for all Africa, *The Journal of World Intellectual Property*, 3(2), 265–288.

Kongolo, T., 2013. *African Contributions in Shaping the Worldwide Intellectual Property System.* Surrey and Burlington: Ashgate.

Mupangavanhu, Y., 2013. *The Regional Integration of African Trade Mark Laws: Challenges and Possibilities.* Thesis (PhD). University of the Western Cape.

Mupangavanhu, Y., 2014. The integration of trade mark laws in the European Union: lessons for Africa? *South African IP Law Journal*, 2, 109–130.

Mupangavanhu, Y., 2015. African Union Rising to the Need for Continental IP Protection? The establishment of the Pan-African Intellectual Property Organization, *Journal of African Law*, 59, 1–24.

Musungu, S.F., Villanueva, S. and Blasetti, R., 2004. *Utilizing Trips Flexibilities For Public Health Protection Through South-South Regional Frameworks*. Geneva, Switzerland: South Centre.

Nwauche, E., 2003. An evaluation of the African Regional Intellectual Property Rights Systems, *Journal of World Intellectual Property*, 6(1), 101–118.

Saez, C., 2014. *African IP Body Steps Up Regional Effort to Adopt Plant Protection Protocol*. Online. Available HTTP: <http://www.ip-watch.org/2014/11/13/african-ip-body-steps-up-regional-effort-to-adopt-plant-protection-protocol/>, accessed 22 December 2014.

Sibanda, G.H., 2007. Genesis and development of IP academies: perspectives on organizational modules, structures and activities. *The International Symposium on Intellectual Property Academies*, Rio de Janeiro, Brazil 21–23 March 2007. Online. Available HTTP: <http://www.wipo.int/export/sites/www/academy/en/about/global_network/rio_2007/presentation_sibanda.pdf>, accessed 22 December 2014.

Tita, A.N., 2015. OAPI Suspend Agents. 13 April 2015. Online. Available HTTP: <http://afro-ip.blogspot.com/2015/04/oapi-suspend-agents.html>, accessed 21 April 2015.

UPOV, 2014. *African Intellectual Property Organization (OAPI) Becomes Second Intergovernmental Organization to Join UPOV*. Geneva: UPOV. Press Release 97.

WIPO, n.d. 'Background information on member States of OAPI'. Online. Available HTTP: <http://www.wipo.int/wipolex/en/outline/oapi.html#_ftn4 1/>, accessed 28 November 2014.

5 Continental IP co-operation: PAIPO

Introduction

This chapter considers developments pertaining to the establishment of PAIPO. It provides a historical outline of events that have been publicly disclosed. They are likely to be events and stages in the process that are not canvassed simply because they have not been publicly disclosed by the AU and other relevant parties. The reason for any such non-disclosure is probably that creation of a new organization in a continent where there are already two sub-regional institutions, whose future will be impacted significantly by the new organization, is highly political and involves a lot of diplomacy, which often requires confidentiality.

The chapter also discusses how ARIPO, OAPI and PAIPO can co-operate in the future, in a way that respects their distinct mandates and maximizes efficiency. It suggests that PAIPO may be best placed to lead on the formulation of continental policy direction. Therefore the chapter concludes with some views on the key considerations PAIPO ought to take cognizance of, with respect to such policy.

Historical overview of the AU's efforts to establish PAIPO

Suggestions for the creation of a continental IP organization have been made since the mid-1990s.[1] One of the earliest calls was Kongolo's proposal for the formation of the Folklore and IP Organization of Africa (FIPOA).[2] In more recent years, the proposals have centered on a unified continental trademark system.[3] As will be shown below, the current AU proposal does not envisage any industrial property registration function for PAIPO.

The proposal for the establishment of PAIPO is one of the outcomes of the Pan-African agenda, over which the AU has oversight. A brief overview of the historical development of the AU has been given in Chapter 3. This chapter only canvasses recent developments in the AU that catapulted its conceptualization

1 For example see Dean (1994a) and (1994b).

2 Kongolo (2013) p. 124; Kongolo (2000).

3 Adewopo (2003); Mupangavanhu (2014) and (2013).

of PAIPO. As noted in Chapter 3, the AU's mandate includes the promotion of sustainable socio-economic and cultural development and the integration of African economies.[4] It also extends to 'co-ordinat[ing] and harmoniz[ing] the policies between the existing and future RECs' and promoting research in science and technology, amongst other fields.[5] A large part of this mandate is being pursued through NEPAD. In keeping with its objectives, NEPAD began working on initiatives to promote science and technology which included co-hosting a workshop in 2003 with South Africa's Department of Science and Technology (DST).[6] One of the outcomes of this workshop was the creation of African Ministerial Conference on Science and Technology (AMCOST) which had its first conference in November 2003 at which related AMCOST structures and an *Outline of a Plan of Action* were agreed upon.[7] Following this, the NEPAD and the AU Commission's 2004–2007 Strategic Plan for Human Resources, Science and Technology provided for a series of workshops that were hosted in each of the AU's five regions during the period November 2004 to March 2005.[8] The findings of these workshops together with experts' consultations and studies[9] informed the *AU's Science and Technology Consolidated Plan of Action* which the AU adopted in November 2006. This plan constituted a blueprint for science and technology related activities.

The AU Human Resources, Science and Technology (HRS&T) department together with the AU's General Office and WIPO arranged a meeting of the African Group on IP in May 2006 that recommended the establishment of PAIPO.[10] This led to the preparation of a concept paper for consideration at the AMCOST extra-ordinary conference held in November that year.[11] The brief, four-paged, concept paper identified the key motivations for establishing the organization as 'the lack of continental inclusiveness'[12] and the need to 'sharpen the visibility of IP issues as they relate to economic development . . . [to] add impetus to the leaders' political will and commitment to inventiveness and innovation, thus emphasizing the significance of political leadership in such a 'strategic field of development'.[13] It noted that the benefits that would accrue to AU member states upon the establishment of PAIPO would include cost-saving, information sharing and the availability of a platform to deliberate IP issues and reach consensus on a continental position on these issues.

4 Article 3(j) Constitutive Act of the African Union.
5 Article 3(l)–(m) Constitutive Act of the African Union.
6 National Advisory Council on Innovation (NACI) (2007) p. 20; NEPAD (2006) p.6; Dountio (2013).
7 NACI (2007) p. 20; NEPAD (2006) p. 6; Dountio (2013).
8 NEPAD (2006) p. 6.
9 For example van Gardingen & Karp (2006a, 2006b, 2006c), Oldham, Adeoti & Thomas (2006).
10 AU HRS&T (2006) p. 1; Kongolo (2013) p. 125.
11 AU HRS&T *Establishing A Pan-African Intellectual Property Organization (PAIPO)*. A Concept Paper. Extraordinary Conference of the AMCOST. 20–24 November 2006 Cairo, Egypt. EXT/AU/EXP/ST/8(II) p.1 (Concept Paper).
12 AU HRS&T Concept Paper p.2.
13 AU HRS&T Concept Paper p.2; Kongolo (2013) pp. 125–126.

The concept paper emphasized that what was being sought at that stage was a high level expression of interest and commitment from the AU, ARIPO and OAPI. It was envisaged that the two sub-regional bodies would continue to exist under the 'umbrella' of PAIPO after its establishment, the practicalities of which would be ironed out at a later stage through a series of meetings between these key stakeholders. The objectives of the continental organization would be to:[14]

1. Set IP standards that reflect the needs of Member States;
2. Set benchmarks for best practices on intellectual property;
3. Promote the growth of knowledge-based economies in Africa;
4. Facilitate the rationalization and harmonization of IP standards;
5. Collect, process and disseminate relevant information on intellectual property to Member States;
6. Facilitate the utilization of relevant IP information by Member States;
7. Assist Member States in training and capacity building on a wide range of IP matters.

The above references to standards hint at a normative angle to PAIPO's work that may be implemented through hard or soft law approaches. After the presentation and discussion of the concept paper at an experts meeting at the extra-ordinary conference, it was agreed that PAIPO 'would help Africa participate more effectively in IP production and management of IP processes' and that the 'AU should proceed and accelerate the formation of PAIPO with full participation of ARIPO and OAPI.'[15]

In January 2007 the AU Assembly endorsed work on the creation of PAIPO, which had already commenced, by calling for the AU Commission, RECs, WIPO, OAPI and ARIPO 'to submit to it the texts relevant to the establishment of' the organization.[16] According to a progress report tabled at AMCOST III, in November 2007, the HRS&T department appointed the Scientific, Technical and Research Commission (AU-STRC) as the lead office on all matters relating to PAIPO.[17] In addition, a consultant was appointed to conduct a situation analysis[18] and to draft the Constitutive Articles of PAIPO that would be discussed by stakeholders in 2008. Such discussions took place thereafter with WIPO participation.[19]

14 AU HRS&T Concept Paper pp. 2–3.

15 AU Report of the Meeting of Experts Extraordinary Conference of the AMCOST 20–24 November 2006 Cairo, Egypt.. EXT/AU/EXP/ST/Rpt.(II) p. 9.

16 AU Assembly Decision on the Establishment of PAIPO. Assembly of the African Union Eighth Ordinary Session 29–30 January 2007 Addis Ababa, Ethiopia. Assembly/AU/Dec.138 (VIII) para 2.

17 AU Progress Report on Research Policy Framework, Capacity Building for the African Policymakers and the Formation of the PAIPO. AMCOST III Third Ordinary Session 12–16 November 2007 Mombasa, Republic of Kenya. AU/EXP/ST/11(III) p. 1.

18 Sibanda (2009).

19 WIPO Technical Assistance Database: Experts Group Meeting on PAIPO, Addis Ababa, Ethiopia. 18 May 2009; WIPO Support to NEPAD Period of Report: July 2008 to June 2009.

In March 2010 the then draft constitutive articles were discussed at AMCOST IV, in Cairo, Egypt.[20] After such consideration, the conference recommended that the draft should be revised and further consultations undertaken.

The AU-STRC reports that it then retained two consultants to undertake the review that was followed by a stakeholders' meeting in Dakar, Senegal in September 2011.[21] It is reported that part of the consultants' work entailed drafting an Agreement on the Establishment of the PAIPO and a Business Plan for PAIPO that spans 25 years.[22] Neither of these two documents are publicly available, therefore it is not possible to comment on their content and import. However, the length of the development period reportedly provided for in the business plan, shows that this is a long-term endeavour. In mid-2012 a draft statute became public and reports were that it was intended to be approved by AMCOST V in November of that year. It became the center of much scrutiny as it was the first concrete manifestation of how PAIPO would be operationalized.

Several concerns were raised about the draft statute in online critiques authored by scholars and practitioners, the main of which will be discussed below.[23] In addition, concerns about the Draft PAIPO statute were communicated to the AU member states through a petition.[24] In view of these concerns, when AMCOST V met in Brazzaville, Congo on 12–16 November 2012 the draft was not approved, as had been intended, but it was referred back for further consultation. To this end, a Ministerial Decision was taken, urging the finalization and operationalization of PAIPO by 2013.[25] However, this did not eventuate due to strong opposition based on policy considerations which are discussed below. The 20th Ordinary Session of the AU Summit held in Addis Ababa in January 2013 confirmed AMCOST V's position and indicated that a stakeholders' meeting would be held in May 2013.[26] However, the program of the 21st Ordinary Session of the AU Summit held in May 2013 did not include this meeting. A year later, in April 2014, the ARIPO and OAPI Secretariats issued a joint communiqué calling for this meeting to be convened, with their participation. [27] It is important to emphasize that some ARIPO member states may be supportive of efforts to establish and

20 AU Ministerial Decisions. AU/MIN/ST/Dec.(IV). Fourth Ordinary Session of the AMCOST (AMCOST IV), 10 March 2010, Cairo, Egypt.

21 AU-STRC. Progress report to AMCOST V.). Fifth Ordinary Session of the AMCOST (AMCOST V), Dec, 12–15 December 2012, Brazzaville, Congo p. 2; WIPO (2011); Kongolo (2013) p. 127.

22 Kongolo (2013) p. 127; ARIPO Recent IP Developments in the Africa Region and Proposal for the Harmonization of ARIPO and OAPI. Council of Ministers 13th Session, Accra, Ghana, 1–2 December 2011. ARIPO Doc. No. ARIPO/AC/XIII/13 pp. 2–3.

23 For example see Baker (2012); Olivier (2012); Egbuonu (2012); Ncube (2012); Moyo (2012) and Karjiker (2012).

24 Kawooya and Latif (2012).

25 AU Ministerial Decisions. AU/MIN/ST/Dec.(V). Fifth Ordinary Session of the AMCOST (AMCOST V), Dec, 12–15 December 2012, Brazzaville, Congo.

26 AU Assembly Decision on the Creation of PAIPO. DOC. EX.CL/766(XXII). Assembly/AU/Dec.453(XX) Twentieth Ordinary Session, 27–28 January 2013. Addis Ababa, Ethiopia.

27 ARIPO and OAPI (2014).

operationalize PAIPO, as they were not all represented at the meeting after which the communiqué was issued.

ARIPO and OAPI made this call after a meeting they held on 10–11 April 2014, in Harare at which they discussed their concerns about the creation of PAIPO. This meeting was strategically timed to precede the AMCOST meeting scheduled for 15–18 April 2014. In addition to calling for the stakeholders' meeting, ARIPO and OAPI recommended that the ministries responsible for IP be afforded a leading role in the process of establishing PAIPO. To date, the process has been driven by the ministries of science and technology. The communiqué also suggested the possibility of an amalgamation of the two organizations under the oversight of a unit of the AU Commission, which would be created for that purpose. It emphasized that ARIPO and OAPI should continue to be the sole registrants of IP rights in Africa. Its parting shot was a request that 'the Heads of State and Government should be sensitized on the role ARIPO and OAPI play in the management and coordination of IP in Africa'. This last comment is indicative of the sentiment that the work of these two organizations is being undervalued and not given its due weight in the considerations of the necessity and viability of PAIPO.

When AMCOST met at Brazzaville a few days after the release of this communiqué, it considered a revised draft of the PAIPO Statute and approved it.[28] A related development at that meeting was the approval of the Science, Technology and Innovation Strategy for Africa 2024 (STISA-2024). The STISA-2024 succeeds the AU's Consolidated Plan of Action and is part of the AU's Agenda 2063, which is a 50-year developmental plan for the continent. It lists PAIPO as one of the bodies under the AU Commission and describes it as follows:

> PAIPO is in the process of being established to implement AU policy in the field of Intellectual Property. It will ensure dissemination of patent information, provide technical and financial support to invention and innovation and promote protection and exploitation of research results.[29]

Both the 2013 Draft PAIPO Statute and STISA-2014 were then referred to the AU Assembly's 23rd Ordinary Session held in June 2014. STISA-2024 was adopted[30] and the AU Assembly requested the AU Commission to submit the Draft PAIPO Statute to the Specialized Technical Committee (STC) on Justice and Legal Affairs for its consideration.[31] The Assembly also re-affirmed the pivotal role of ARIPO and OAPI as constituent elements of PAIPO whose support of the endeavor is both necessary and desirable. It endorsed Tunisia as the host of the headquarters and secretariat of PAIPO.[32] Finally, it requested the AU to

28 IST Africa (2014).
29 AU STISA-2014 (2014) p. 36.
30 AU (2014).
31 AU (2014).
32 AU (2014); WIPO (2015) p. 58.

'prepare [a] road map for [the] implementation of PAIPO in coordination with the host country and to report progress in this regard to the [next] Summit'. The next summit to which reference was being made was the 2015 Summit that was held in Addis Ababa in January 2015. It appears that the report was not tabled at the 2015 Summit because the STC on Justice and Legal Affairs had not yet made recommendations on the draft statute. This will probably be done in time for the 2016 AU Summit. The events and decisions outlined here are summarized in the time line below (Table 5.1).

How PAIPO will function

It is necessary to outline in some detail what the proposal for PAIPO entails, in order to contextualize the issues that have been raised pertaining to its mandate and role. The outline that follows is based on the 2013 draft. Cross references will be made to an earlier version published in November 2012 (AU/STRC/522) where appropriate, to show development of the statute. The drafts will be differentiated by their year of publication. However, this outline will be brief, as it is based on a draft, rather than a final document.

The legal nature of PAIPO

This section considers the legal nature of PAIPO and how membership of the organization will be acquired. PAIPO will be a specialized agency of the AU.[33] Specialized agencies are one of the institutional organs of the AU, which it has authority to establish through articles 5(2) of the Constitutive Act of the AU. A specialized agency is defined as

> an independent body established by Member States of the Union outside the managerial and budgetary rules and regulations as well as control of the AU or the Commission to carry out a specific or specialized but related function of the mandate of the AU.[34]

Specialized agencies have autonomy, legal personality, their own budget, managerial independence, separate governance structures, as well as staff and financial rules and regulations.[35] PAIPO will be required to raise its own funds through members' dues and it may accept donations, however, the AUC will fund it 'in its first two phases or to the time that PAIPO is capable to generate resource to sustain itself'.[36] PAIPO, like other specialized agencies, will interface with the AU through a department of the AU Commission or an organ of the AU.[37]

33 Article 2(2) of the 2013 Draft Statute.
34 AU (n.d.) p. 2.
35 AU (n.d.) p. 5.
36 Article 17(iii) of the 2013 Draft Statute.
37 AU (n.d.) p. 3.

Table 5.1 PAIPO timeline: known key events and decisions

2006	2007	2008	2010	2011	2012	2013	2014
	AU Assembly decision on PAIPO Assembly/AU/Dec.138 (VIII)					AU Assembly Decision to create PAIPO Assembly/AU/Dec.453(XX)	AU Assembly Referral to STC Assembly/AU/Dec.522(XXIII)
AMCOST extra-ordinary session PAIPO Concept Paper EXT/AU/EXP/ST/8(II)	AMCOST III PAIPO Progress Report AU/EXP/ST/11(III)		AMCOST IV Ministerial Decision AU/MIN/ST/Dec.(IV)		AMCOST V Ministerial Decision AU/MIN/ST/Dec.(V)		AMCOST extra-ordinary session approves draft
		Preparation of draft, stakeholder consultations		Revision of draft, stakeholder consultation			

The methodology of the creation of AU specialized agencies consists of the following three modes:[38]

a) an agency set up by AU member states, which is then approved by the AU Assembly prior to its operationalization;
b) an agency set up by the AU by an Assembly decision; and
c) an already existing agency that is linked to the AU system post its creation by member states.

PAIPO falls into the second category. As stated above, the AU Assembly passed decisions pertaining to the process of its creation and its establishment in 2007 and 2013, respectively. The specifics of operationalization of the organization were not spelt out in the 2013 decision, because they were contained in the draft statute and the organization's business plan. In a decision adopted in 2014, the Assembly instructed the Commission to submit the draft statute to the STC on Justice and Legal Affairs for review.

Once operationalized, PAIPO will serve AU member states. Article 13 of the 2013 Draft Statute provides that membership shall be 'open to any member of the AU' and article 15 provides that the statute will enter into force on the date of its endorsement by the Assembly of Head of States and Government of the AU. As noted by Moyo, there is no provision for the signature and ratification of, or accession to the statute by member states.[39] Whilst it is clear which states are eligible for membership, it is not clear how this membership is to be acquired. This is in contrast to the Lusaka and Bangui Agreements that provide for these aspects in relation to ARIPO and OAPI respectively.[40] Similarly, the convention establishing the WIPO also provides for signature, ratification and accession to the convention.[41] However, the difference is that these agreements were creating new organizations whilst the PAIPO Statute is creating a specialized agency of an existing organization, the AU. Be that as it may, the reference to the opening of membership to AU member states suggests that there would be a method for taking up such membership. It is this subscription process that is not expressly provided for.

Objectives, functions and organs of PAIPO

As stated above, PAIPO is intended to be a specialized agency of the AU. Its objectives include giving policy direction to the continent on IP matters; promoting the harmonization of IP systems; the provision of unstipulated common services to member states and/or RECs in relation to the administration and management of IP rights; serving as a platform for IP policy discussion and formulation; and

38 AU (n.d) p. 3; Articles 5(2) and 9(1)(d) of the Constitutive Act of the AU.
39 Moyo (2012).
40 Article 25 Lusaka Agreement; article 22 Bangui Agreement.
41 Article 14.

promoting the use of the IP system 'as a tool for economic, cultural, social and technological development of the continent.'[42]

Its functions include setting IP standards; facilitating the 'harmonization of national legislation and regional treaties and IP standards'; assisting member states, upon request, in their IP policy formulation; and strengthening regional organizations and collective management organizations.[43] In addition to these functions, PAIPO was also initially intended to serve as a registration office for industrial property rights.[44] However due to the concerns expressed by the OAPI and ARIPO Secretariats, this function was excised from the 2013 draft statute together with the provisions for the Board of Appeal which would have heard appeals against registration decisions.

The standard setting function raises several questions: Which matters will these standards pertain to, since IP standards have been comprehensively set by several existing international and sub-regional agreements such as TRIPS, the Bangui Agreement and the various ARIPO Protocols? What will be the exact nature of the instruments which contain these standards? Will they have force of law? Will PAIPO have legislative competence, and if so, which of its organs will exercise such competence? What form will they take? Will PAIPO craft agreements, protocols and regulations? It is expected that such questions will be answered by reference to the Constitutive Act of the AU, and any further regulations and rules crafted for PAIPO.

As there are already varying national and sub-regional IP laws in force, PAIPO has been set the ambitious function of harmonizing these. The various modes of harmonization of IP laws and standards that PAIPO would have to consider are canvassed in Chapter 6.

The structure of the organization as set out by article 7 of the 2013 draft consists of a Council of Ministers and its Bureau; an Experts Committee and its Bureau; and the Secretariat or Office. As stated above, the 2012 version of the draft statute included a Board of Appeal. The following section considers how PAIPO is intended to interface with the existing sub-regional IP organizations.

Organizational issues (PAIPO, OAPI and ARIPO)

It has been noted that ARIPO and OAPI were not consulted during the early stages of the formulation of the PAIPO proposal so they were opposed to the concept.[45] It would appear that they were not invited to certain crucial consultative meetings. However, with the passage of time and a change of leadership at ARIPO, the two organizations have found ways of making their views known to the AU, primarily through private diplomatic channels but also publicly, through the joint communiqué they issued in April 2014.

42 Article 5 Draft PAIPO Statute (2013).
43 Article 6 Draft PAIPO Statute (2013).
44 Article 6(ii) Draft PAIPO Statute (2012).
45 Blakeney and Mengistie (2011) p. 251.

The key concerns of the two sub-regional IP organizations pertain to the overlapping of their mandates with PAIPO; duplication of the industrial property registration and other functions and the nature of the relationship between themselves and the continental organization. Each of these is briefly addressed, in turn, below with the caveat that they are difficult to separate from each other because they are interconnected and cascade into each other. The general question of mandate solidifies into concerns about registration of industrial property and policy formulation issues which ultimately goes to the crux of the relationship between the three organizations.

Overlapping mandates

According to the 2013 Draft PAIPO Statute, PAIPO is intended to give continental IP policy, law and administrative direction. To all intents and purposes, it would seek to do what the sub-regional organizations currently do, on the larger continental platform, with what the concept paper dubbed 'continental inclusiveness'. The obvious issue that such an ambition immediately raises, is that of turf – what, if any, role would remain for the sub-regional IP organizations after the establishment of PAIPO? The resolution of this issue indisputably involves careful consultation and negotiation.

Another mandate that PAIPO would be seeking to involve itself in, is the provision of a platform or forum at which African states jointly arrive at common positions to advance at international IP law-making fora. African states have already successfully organized themselves into influential groups through which they jointly advance their views. The African Group has established itself as one of the most active groups at both the WTO[46] and WIPO.[47] Its contributions towards the adoption of the WIPO Development Agenda (WIPO DA) have been outlined in Chapter 1. As there is already a working mechanism for this aspect of PAIPO's intended mandate, it is important to have clarity on how PAIPO would complement or substitute that mechanism. An even more fundamental question is whether there is any need for a formal organizational platform in the first place? However, that enquiry has been rendered academic by events, and as PAIPO is due to manifest in the medium to long- term, perhaps the more relevant question would be the first question raised – that of alignment with the African Group. The 2012 Draft PAIPO Statute completely overlooked the pro-development position of the African Group and failed to reference the WIPO DA which it had been instrumental in securing. The 2013 draft expressly references the WIPO DA. However, the lingering concern is whether this is lip service or whether it embodies a real commitment to the imperatives of the Agenda. This, and other policy matters, are canvassed below. Prior to that discussion, it is important to address issues of functional overlap between ARIPO, OAPI and PAIPO.

46 May (2007) p. 74.
47 Shabalala (2007) p. 32.

As outlined in Chapter 3, OAPI and ARIPO register industrial property rights. In OAPI's case, its members all subscribe to one body of IP law, contained in the Bangui Agreement and its Annexes. When an application is made for registration, the granted rights extend to all the member states' territories. ARIPO's Protocols are not automatically binding on its member states and domestication is required to give them force of law in member states. Further, the ARIPO industrial property registration system does not necessarily result in the grant of rights in every member state's territory. An applicant is required to designate countries in which protection is sought. Thereafter, each designated country is afforded an opportunity to indicate whether or not it wishes to grant the said industrial property rights in its territory. Therefore PAIPO would be seeking to sit atop two asymmetrical sub-regional organizations.

Whilst there have been suggestions of the merger of the two sub-regional organizations, such a merger would be complicated by the above-stated differences between them and the more fundamental common law and civil law distinction between them. However, as discussed in Chapter 3, they are already successfully co-operating to a significant extent. ARIPO and OAPI have stressed their view that they ought to remain the sole regional registrants of industrial property rights. Several commentators are in agreement that PAIPO would be ill-suited to the industrial property registration function.[48] The AU has conceded this point through the revision of the Draft PAIPO Statute as explained above.

The remaining functions of PAIPO pertain to activities that currently fall within the purview of ARIPO and OAPI. For instance, in relation to IP policy formulation, article 6 of the 2012 Draft PAIPO Statute listed the following functions:

> (v) Assist its Member States in formulating policies and addressing current and emerging Intellectual Property issues in conformity with the Objectives of the Organization;
> (xi) To develop updated policy guide lines and training modules to support Member States to achieve world-class IP systems;

The sub-regional IP organizations also render IP policy formulation technical assistance to their member states, although their performance has been faulted. In this regard, it has been pointed out that their policy formulation assistance is hampered because

> they tend to operate outside the broad policy framework on research, technology development and innovation that should inform intellectual property policy formulation . . . [and] the mandates of these organizations are mostly limited to matters of patent grants and examination or registration and do not include issues relating to the exercise of patent rights.[49]

48 Ncube and Laltaika (2013) p. 117; Kongolo (2013) p. 130; Baker (2012).

49 Musungu, Villanueva and Blasetti (2004) pp. 55–56.

Consequently, it has been suggested that African RECs create an Advisory Council on Trade-Related Innovation Policies (ACTRIPS) that would be better suited to lead on policy matters because it would not be constrained by the above-stated limitations that apply to ARIPO and OAPI.[50] The original ACTRIPS proposal was that countries develop their own domestic ACTRIPS that would then dialogue at regional level through REC-hosted ACTRIPS.[51] Against this backdrop, the PAIPO proposal can be viewed as a continental, rather than regional, ACTRIPS. Indeed, it has been persuasively suggested that a better approach to the conceptualization of PAIPO would be to limit it to policy oversight and capacity building at its initial stages and to thereafter consider expanding its functions.[52] It would still be possible to build the national and regional ACTRIPS concept into the continental PAIPO model. As stated above, the AU already organizes its members into five geographical regions. These regions, the regional IP organizations or RECs could be the sponsor of regional ACTRIPS. These three possible configurations are diagrammatically represented below.

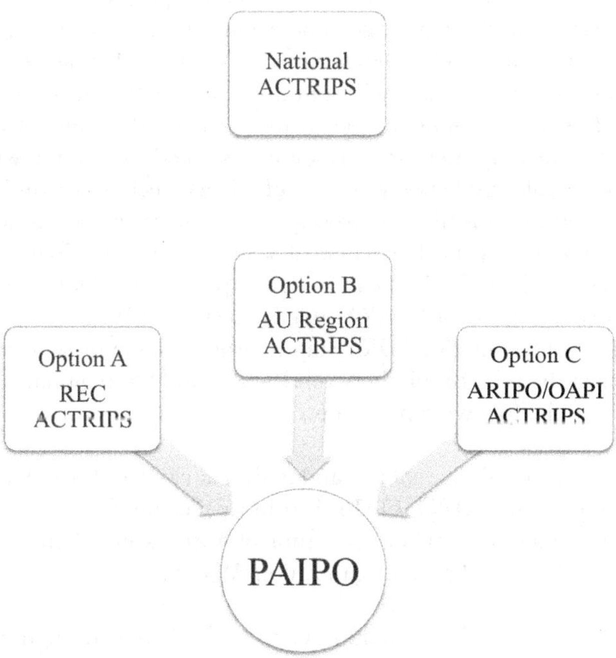

In view of its important continental policy direction function, it is necessary to interrogate the indicators of PAIPO's policy approach, which is done below, after the discussion of the relationship between PAIPO, ARIPO and OAPI.

50 Musungu, Villanueva and Blasetti (2004) pp. 53–54. Also see Reichman (2003) pp. 5–8; Musungu and Dutfield (2003) p. 22.

51 Reichman (2003) p. 5.

52 Blakeney and Mengistie (2011) p. 252.

Relationship between PAIPO, ARIPO and OAPI

The relationship between PAIPO and the two sub-regional IP organizations is also a point of concern. The preambles of both the 2012 and June 2013 versions of the Draft PAIPO Statute state that the AU Heads of states and government both appreciate and respect the autonomy of ARIPO and OAPI and are 'desirous of supplementing and complementing the role played' by them. However, the initial overlooking of the regional organizations in the early consultative stages sent out the unfortunate message that the AU undervalued them and did not fully appreciate their contribution. This impression was compounded by the provision for duplication of the registration function by PAIPO, which, as discussed above, has now been removed. However, it is clear that ARIPO and OAPI are still smarting from this message as evidenced by their call in their joint communiqué for the sensitization of AU heads of state to their significance, quoted above.

Another sore point is the exclusion of ministers of IP in the PAIPO formulation process. Being a creature of AMCOST, its design has been the province of ministers of science and technology. These ministries, whilst being *au fait* with innovation, science and technology, may miss certain IP nuances. Hence the call by ARIPO and OAPI, in their communiqué, for the inclusion of IP ministries in PAIPO deliberations. It goes without saying that these are the ministries with which the two organizations are accustomed to working with and that their involvement, alongside the ministries of science, technology and innovation, would have eased the consultative process. This is necessary because 'the policy impacts of IP go far beyond the realm of science and technology'.[53] Ironically, whilst they were not included in the formulation process, the Draft PAIPO Statute places the implementation of PAIPO under ministries of IP.

Both versions of the Draft PAIPO Statute provide some indicators of how the AU conceives of the relationship between PAIPO and the regional organizations going forward in the following provision:

> The Organization shall establish and maintain close and continuous working relationships with ARIPO, OAPI, World Intellectual Property Organization (WIPO) the International Confederation of Authors and Composers Societies (CISAC) and World Trade Organization (WTO).[54]

In practice such relationships would have to be brokered through co-operation agreements. It is currently unclear as to what in particular such agreements would pertain. However, article 6(iv) of the June 2013 version of the draft statute lists the strengthening of the existing regional organizations as one of PAIPO's functions. It is as yet unclear what form such strengthening may take. However, as shown above, it is likely to relate to policy matters.

53 de Beer (2013) p. 895.

54 Article 15 Draft PAIPO Statute (June 2013); article 16 Draft PAIPO Statute (2012).

Policy imperatives – the PAIPO statute and the WIPO development agenda

This section considers the IP policy stance that is implicit in the Draft PAIPO Statutes. This is an important aspect to consider, because as shown above PAIPO is likely to focus on policy matters. The fairly extensive analysis of the 2012 Draft PAIPO statute referred to above flagged the main concern that its wording did not show that enough regard has been paid to the development imperatives of African states and the hard-won victory of the WIPO DA.[55] For example, I have argued elsewhere that references to effective IP systems juxtaposed to the intent to combat piracy and counterfeiting give the impression of a right-holder centric position that is concerning to those who seek a more equitable position that takes due consideration of user and societal interests.[56]

Similarly, several commentators have pointed out that the 2012 Draft PAIPO Statute's failure to expressly reference the WIPO DA and the issues that confront Africa was a major shortcoming. [57] Fortunately the 2013 version of the draft has now incorporated these considerations. The preamble now states that the AU heads of state and government 'affirm the 45 recommendations of the WIPO DA under world intellectual property rights programmes' and recognize 'international human rights law and international agreements on sustainable development and the protection of indigenous knowledge.'

However, as far as IP and public health are concerned, both the 2012 and 2013 draft statutes neglect to reference the TRIPS flexibilities, the WTO Doha Declaration on the TRIPS Agreement and Public Health and other important decisions such as the Global Strategy and Plan of Action on Public Health, Innovation and IP. It is accepted that draft statute cannot be expected to go beyond a general contextualization of public interest and policy considerations.[58] However, explicit reference to some of these instruments would signal the commitment of the AU to build on existing work in this area. There is solace in the fact that PAIPO ought to be consolidating REC efforts on IP and public health. As shown in Chapters 2 and 3, RECs have made significant progress on this front which hopefully will be taken on board by PAIPO.

Conclusion

There have been several arguments made for and against the establishment of PAIPO.[59] Three of each will be recounted here. First, one of the main arguments made in favor of the creation of the organization pertains to continental

55 For example see Ncube and Laltaika (2013); Kawooya and Latif (2012); Baker (2012); Olivier (2012); Egbuonu (2012); Ncube (2012); Moyo (2012); Karjiker (2012).

56 Ncube and Laltaika (2013).

57 Ncube and Laltaika (2013) p. 116; de Beer (2013) p. 896; Kawooya and Latif (2012).

58 de Beer (2013) p. 896.

59 Mupangavanhu (2015).

geographic, economic and linguistic inclusivity which would be achieved by the creation of an AU organ which potentially would draw in all AU member states.[60] Secondly, the desirability of a continental platform for the consolidation of AU member states views to formulate continental positions of matters of significance has been forwarded as another supportive argument. However, as stated above, African states have to date organized themselves effectively to formulate shared positions at various international fora such as the WTO, WIPO and WHO.

Thirdly, it is argued that having a specialized agency of the AU devoted to IP would elevate IP matters to be a focal point of regional integration efforts.[61] This would be beneficial because it may overcome the challenges faced by ARIPO and OAPI when it comes to crafting policy frameworks that are informed by broader research, technology, innovation and regional economic development concerns. As shown in Chapter 2, to date, only some RECs have concerned themselves with IP. Significant progress has been made in relation to IP by the EAC, ECOWAS and COMESA that have all formulated IP policies. Further, as shown in Chapter 3, IP is one of the key concerns of the T-FTA between COMESA, EAC and SADC as evidenced by the Annex on IP rights which is intended to become part of the T-FTA Agreement after the conclusion of on-going negotiations. This focus on IP will be carried through to the C-FTA, which is intended to progress initially through the merger of the T-FTA and ECOWAS.[62] PAIPO would be well placed to rationalize existing REC initiatives and to stimulate similar activities in the other RECs.

On the other hand, credible concerns have been raised about procedural, institutional and substantive issues. In particular, there is a need to resolve outstanding organizational and relational matters between PAIPO and the existing sub-regional IP organizations. The actual mechanics of the operationalization of PAIPO are not yet clear, although they are reportedly detailed in a 25-year business plan. A phased and incremental approach would be prudent.[63] In addition, the creation of PAIPO will require significant financial overlay which may be beyond the AU and its member states' current economic realities. It would also be vital to ensure that there is no wastage of resources through the unnecessary duplication of functions that are already fulfilled by existing entities. Finally, the nature and status of PAIPO standard setting instruments is not yet clear nor is its efficacy and value as a policy formulation platform indisputable. However, since the AU has committed to the establishment of PAIPO, the real challenge is the efficient operationalization of the organization. It is to this challenge that the next chapter turns, with specific reference to the harmonization objectives of the organization.

60 Ncube and Laltaika (2013) p. 115.

61 Mupangavanhu (2015) p. 4.

62 Ngwenya (2015).

63 Mupangavanhu (2015) p. 24; Blakeney and Mengistie (2011) p. 252.

References

Primary sources

ARIPO

ARIPO and OAPI. 2014. Communiqué Adopted by the Joint Meeting of the Chairmen of ARIPO and OAPI, held at the Headquarters of ARIPO on April 10 and 11, 2014, Harare, Republic of Zimbabwe.

Lusaka Agreement on the Creation of the African Regional Intellectual Property Organization as amended, 2004.

Recent IP Developments in the Africa Region and Proposal for the Harmonization of ARIPO and OAPI. Council of Ministers 13th Session, Accra, Ghana, 1–2 December 2011. ARIPO Doc. No. ARIPO/AC/XIII/13.

Swakopmund Protocol on the Protection of Traditional Knowledge and Expressions of Folklore within the Framework of the ARIPO, adopted by the Diplomatic Conference of ARIPO at Swakopmund, Namibia on August 9, 2010.

AU

Assembly/AU/Dec.453(XX) Twentieth Ordinary Session, 27–28 January 2013. Addis Ababa, Ethiopia.

Assembly Decision on the Creation of PAIPO. DOC. EX.CL/766(XXII).

Assembly Decision on the Establishment of PAIPO. Assembly of the African Union Eighth Ordinary Session 29–30 January 2007 Addis Ababa, Ethiopia. Assembly/AU/Dec.138 (VIII).

Assembly Decision on PAIPO Doc. EX.CL/839(XXV). Assembly/AU/Dec.522(XXIII). Assembly of the Union Twenty-Third Ordinary Session 26–27 June 2014. Malabo, Equatorial Guinea.

Assembly Decision on Strategy For Science Technology and Innovation in Africa 2024. Doc. EX.CL/839(XXV). Assembly/AU/ /Dec.520(XXIII). Assembly of the Union Twenty-Third Ordinary Session 26–27 June 2014. Malabo, Equatorial Guinea.

AU. 2002. Declaration on the Implementation of NEPAD (Assembly/AU/Decl. 1 (I)).

AU HRS&T. Establishing A Pan-African Intellectual Property Organization (PAIPO).

AU-STRC Progress report to AMCOST V. Fifth Ordinary Session of the AMCOST (AMCOST V), Dec, 12–15 December 2012, Brazzaville, Congo.

A Concept Paper. Extraordinary Conference of the AMCOST. 20–24 November 2006 Cairo, Egypt. EXT/AU/EXP/ST/8(II). Report of the Meeting of Experts Extraordinary Conference of the AMCOST 20–24 November 2006 Cairo, Egypt. EXT/AU/EXP/ST/Rpt.(II).

Constitutive Act of the African Union, 2000.

Draft Statute of the Pan-African Intellectual Property Organization (PAIPO), As of June 4 2013.

Final Draft Statute of the Pan-African Intellectual Property Organization (PAIPO), 2012 Ref No: AU/STRC/522.

Ministerial Decisions. AU/MIN/ST/Dec.(IV). Fourth Ordinary Session of the AMCOST (AMCOST IV), 10 March 2010, Cairo, Egypt.

Ministerial Decisions. AU/MIN/ST/Dec.(V). Fifth Ordinary Session of the AMCOST (AMCOST V), Dec, 12–15 December 2012, Brazzaville, Congo.

Press Release N° 29/2010 African Experts on Science and Technology Start Discussion Ahead of AMCOST IV. Online. Available HTTP: <http://storage.globalcitizen.net/data/topic/knowledge/uploads/20110524142120705.pdf>, accessed 2 February 2015.

Progress Report on Research Policy Framework, Capacity Building for the African Policymakers and the Formation of the PAIPO. AMCOST III Third Ordinary Session 12–16 November 2007 Mombasa, Republic of Kenya. AU/EXP/ST/11(III).

OAPI

Bangui Agreement Relating to the Creation of an African Intellectual Property Organization, Constituting a Revision of the Agreement Relating to the Creation of an African and Malagasy Office of Industrial Property (Bangui (Central African Republic), March 2, 1977).

WHO

Global Strategy and Plan of Action on Public Health, Innovation and IP, 2008. Sixty-First World Health Assembly resolution WHA61.21, and resolution WHA62.16.

WIPO

Development Agenda, 2007. WIPO General Assembly Thirty-Fourth (18th Ordinary) Session Geneva, September 24 to October 3, 2007.

WIPO. 2009a. Technical Assistance Database: Experts Group Meeting on PAIPO, Addis Ababa, Ethiopia. 18 May 2009. Online. Available HTTP: <http://www.wipo.int/tad/en/activitydetails.jsp?id=787>, accessed 31 January 2015.

WIPO. 2009b. Support to NEPAD Period of Report: July 2008 to June 2009.

WIPO. 2011. Technical Assistance Database: PAIPO Stakeholders Workshop, Dakar, Senegal. 7–8 September 2011. Available HTTP: <http://www.wipo.int/tad/en/activitydetails.jsp?id=2008>, accessed 31 January 2015.

WIPO. 2015. Assemblies of the Member States of WIPO Fifty-Fourth Series of Meetings Geneva, September 22 to 30, 2014. General Report. A/54/13.

WTO

Doha WTO Ministerial Declaration (adopted 14 November 2001) Doc. WT/MIN(01)/DEC/1 20 November 2001.

Secondary sources

Adewopo, A., 2003. Trademark systems in Africa: A proposal for the harmonization of the ARIPO and the OAPI Agreements on Marks, *The Journal of World Intellectual Property*, 6, 473–484.

AU Commission, New Zealand Ministry of Foreign Affairs and Trade/Manat Aorere, 2014.

AU Handbook. Wellington: Ministry of Foreign Affairs and Trade/Manat Aorere.

Baker, B., 2012. Proposed Pan-African IP Organization a Terrible Idea. 28 September
2012. Online. Available HTTP: <http://infojustice.org/archives/27392?doing_wp_cron=1349607009.5964870452880859375000>, last accessed 6 February 2015.

Blakeney, M. and Mengistie, G., 2011. Intellectual Property and Economic Development in Sub-Saharan Africa, *Journal of World Intellectual Property*, 14(3/4), 238–264.

Dean, O.H., 1994a. A unified intellectual property law system for southern Africa. Part 1: International arrangements and European conventions, *Juta's Business Law*, 2(3), 111–114.

Dean, O.H., 1994b. A unified intellectual property law system for southern Africa. Part 2: Multinational registrations in Africa, *Juta's Business Law*, 2(4), 165–169.

de Beer, J., 2013. Applying best practice principles to international intellectual property lawmaking, *International Review of Intellectual Property and Competition Law*, 44, 884–901.

Dountino, J., 2013. 'Some key events in the early development of the proposal for a PAIPO'. Online. Available HTTP: <http://www.keionline.org/paipo>, accessed 31 January 2015.

Egbuonu, K., 2012. 'Pan-Africa Intellectual Property Organization (PAIPO)'. 8 October 2012. Online. Available HTTP: <http://afro-ip.blogspot.co.uk/2012/10/a-review-of-african-official-ip_8.html>, accessed 6 February 2015.

Gottschalk, K., 2012. The African Union and its sub-regional structures, *Journal of African Union Studies*, 1(1), 9–38.

IST Africa, 2014. 'Science, Technology & Innovation Strategy for Africa (STISA-2024) approved by African Heads of State'. Online. Available HTTP: <https://www.ist-africa.org/home/default.asp?page=news-doc-by-id&docid=8793>, accessed 2 February 2015.

Karjiker, S., 2012. 'Sizing up the 'ill-conceived' PAIPO Draft Statute 6 November 2012. IP Watch Insider Views'. Online. Available HTTP: <http://www.ip-watch.org/2012/11/06/sizing-up-the-ill-conceived-paipo-draftstatute/?utm_source=post&utm_medium=email&utm_campaign=alerts#bio>, accessed 6 February 2015.

Kawooya, D. and Latif, A.A., 2012. 'A new course for The Pan African Intellectual Property Organization is urgently needed'. 18 October 2012. Online. Available HTTP: <https://www.change.org/p/a-new-course-for-the-pan-african-intellectual-property-organization-is-urgently-needed>, accessed 6 February 2015.

Kongolo, T., 2000. The African IP Organizations – the necessity of adopting one uniform system for all Africa, *The Journal of World Intellectual Property*, 3(2), 265–288.

Kongolo, T., 2013. *African Contributions in Shaping the Worldwide IP System.* Surrey and Burlington: Ashgate Publishing.

May, C., 2007. *The World Intellectual Property Organization: Resurgence and the Development Agenda.* Oxford: Routledge.

Moyo, C., 2012. 'Furthering debate on PAIPO'. 31 October 2012. Online. Available HTTP: <http://afro-ip.blogspot.com/2012/10/moyo-furthers-debate-on-paipo_31.html>, accessed 6 February 2015.

Mupangavanhu, Y., 2013. *The Regional Integration of African Trade Mark Laws: Challenges and Possibilities.* PhD Thesis. University of the Western Cape.

Mupangavanhu, Y., 2014. The integration of trade mark laws in the European Union: lessons for Africa? *South African IP Law Journal*, 2, 109–130.

Mupangavanhu, Y., 2015. African Union Rising to the Need for Continental IP Protection? The Establishment of the Pan-African Intellectual Property Organization, *Journal of African Law*, 59, 1–24.

Musungu, S. and Dutfield, G., 2003. *Multilateral Agreements and a TRIPS-plus World: The World Intellectual Property Organization (WIPO).* QUNO, Geneva/QIAP, Ottawa.

Musungu, S.F., Villanueva, S. and Blasetti, R., 2004. *Utilizing Trips Flexibilities For Public Health Protection Through South-South Regional Frameworks.* Geneva: South Centre.

NACI, 2007. *Corporate Business Plan 2007/8.* Pretoria: NACI.

Ncube, C.B., 2012. 'Piping up on PAIPO'. 16 October 2012. Online. Available HTTP: <http://afro-ip.blogspot.co.uk/2012/10/piping-up-on-paipo.html>, accessed 6 February 2015.

Ncube, C.B. and Laltaika, E., 2013. A new intellectual property organization for Africa? *Journal of Intellectual Property Law and Practice*, 8(2): 114–117.

NEPAD, 2006. *Africa's Science & Technology Consolidated Plan of Action*. Online. Available HTTP: <http://www.unesco.org/new/fileadmin/MULTIMEDIA/HQ/SC/pdf/sc_plan_action_en.pdf>, accessed 4 July 2015.

Ngwenya, S., 2015. Statement By Mr Sindiso Ngwenya, Secretary General of COMESA and Chairperson of the COMESA-EAC-SADC Tripartite Task Force, to the African Union High Level African Trade Committee (HATC): Update on the T-FTA Negotiations.

Oldham, G., Adeoti, J., & Thomas, S.M., 2006. *Designing a Model for the African Science and Innovation Facility to implement the Science and Technology Consolidated Plan of Action*. Pretoria: NEPAD Office of Science and Technology.

Olivier, D., 2012. 'South-South agenda timely as PAIPO receives criticism'. 8 October 2012. Online. Available HTTP: <http://afro-ip.blogspot.co.uk/2012/10/south-south-agenda-timely-as-paipo.html>, accessed 6 February 2015.

Reichman, J., 2003. 'Managing the Challenges of a Globalized Intellectual Property Regime'. *The Second Bellagio Series of Dialogues* 18 to 21 September 2003 Bellagio. Online. Available HTTP: <http://www.iprsonline.org/unctadictsd/bellagio/docs/Reichmann_Bellagio2.pdf>, accessed 5 February 2015.

Shabalala, D., 2007. *Citizen's Guide to WIPO*. Geneva: Center for International Environmental Law.

Sibanda, M., 2009. IP Situation in Africa – A profile. *Techno Africa Policy Monitor* (4), AU-STRC.

van Gardingen, P.R. and Karp, A., 2006a. *International Experience on Regional Programmes for Science and Technology: Lessons For Africa's Science and Technology Consolidated Plan of Action*. Edinburgh: The University of Edinburgh.

van Gardingen, P.R. and Karp, A., 2006b. *International Overview of Arrangements For National Support Of R&D. Options for African Nations*. Edinburgh: The University of Edinburgh.

van Gardingen, P.R. & Karp, A., 2006c. *International Survey of Options to Fund Regional Science and Technology in Africa*. Edinburgh: The University of Edinburgh.

6 Key considerations in the development of IP harmonization models

Introduction

Whilst the title of this chapter expressly references harmonization, its coverage is broader than that and extends to co-operation and unification, which are considered as alternatives to harmonization. Chapter 4 has considered existing regional economic integration and IP sub-regional integration through OAPI and ARIPO, which employ unification and harmonization, respectively. Chapter 5 has outlined the AU's continental vision for PAIPO. This chapter considers the prospects for IP co-operation, harmonization and unification at regional and sub-regional level with a view to garnering lessons for PAIPO. From its current approach to various issues, it is evident that the AU's preferred approach is harmonization.

As argued in Chapter 5, IP harmonization is a challenge that the AU is not yet ready to tackle in the short to medium term because it is more prudent to focus on policy issues during this period and the reconciliation of PAIPO's mandate with that of ARIPO and OAPI. However, in the long term, IP harmonization may indeed become a viable option for the AU. It is with this future prospect that this chapter is concerned. It conceptualizes the available possibilities as being on a spectrum of the degrees of regional cohesiveness or conformity to IP law standards. Three nodes can be plotted on this spectrum. The first is IP co-operation that embodies concerted efforts to enable the sharing of administrative and enforcement resources without a regional substantive legal framework. It is followed by harmonization which aspires to such a framework in a way that leaves some room for national nuancing and finally, at the other end of the spectrum, there is unification which has a regional substantive legal framework that leaves no room for national divergence.

This chapter considers each of these options with reference to existing regional and sub-regional entities. IP co-operation is embodied by the approach of the Association of Southeast Asian Nations (ASEAN), the Asia-Pacific Economic Co-operation (APEC) forum and the BRICS. The Southern Common Market (MERCOSUR) and the EU use IP harmonization. However, the EU is better classified as having a hybrid approach because it employs both harmonization directives and unification by regulations.[1] Certain aspects of patent, design and trademark laws have been unified by the supplementary protection certificate for medicinal and plant protection regulations, the Community Design Regulation and the Community Trademark Regulation respectively.[2] To date, the EU has primarily used harmonization with respect to copyright[3] but there are calls to turn to unification due to the uneven regulatory landscape caused by harmonization.[4] OHADA employs unification, as does OAPI. OAPI's legal framework has been outlined in Chapter 3 and only OHADA's will be discussed below.

IP co-operation

This section presents the IP co-operation schemes chronologically rather than alphabetically because the first two regional configurations have overlapping membership and it is helpful to view their development in sequence.

ASEAN

ASEAN was established in 1967 and is pursuing the creation of an economic community, which it intends to achieve 'by the end of 2015'.[5] Its membership comprises the founding states of Indonesia, Malaysia, Philippines, Singapore and Thailand together with the latter joiners, Brunei Darussalam, Vietnam, Lao People's Democratic Republic (Lao PDR/Laos), Myanmar and Cambodia.[6] It is a good comparator for the AU because the membership of the two organizations includes states at markedly different levels of development. In this respect, ASEAN's membership is classified into two groups.[7] The first of which is the more prosperous ASEAN-6 group of Indonesia, Malaysia, Philippines, Singapore, Thailand and Brunei Darussalam. The second group consists of the less prosperous Cambodia, Lao PDR, Myanmar and Vietnam, commonly referred to as CMLV.

ASEAN member states' work on upgrading their IP laws was necessitated by their TRIPS obligations.[8] This work soon expanded to encompass the creation of a regional IP framework. Although ASEAN was faced with significant challenges such as the disparate national socio-economic contexts referred to above and the 'absence of a common framework of substantive laws',[9] it has made notable progress.[10] The ASEAN regional IP framework is grounded in its Framework Agreement on IP

1 Zirnstein (2005); Hugenholtz (2012).
2 Kur and Drier (2013) pp. 62–63, 65–66.
3 Kur and Drier (2013) pp. 63–64.
4 New (2015); European Copyright Society (2014).
5 ASEAN (2014) p. 35; Ng (2013) p. 1.
6 Ng (2013) p. 131
7 OECD (2013) p. 241.
8 Endeshaw (1999) p. 3.
9 Endeshaw (2004) p. 146.
10 Endeshaw (2010) pp. 7, 57–80.

Co-operation of 1995.[11] The development of the framework was driven by the ASEAN Working Group on IP Co-operation (AWGIPC) which was formed in 1996.[12] ASEAN member states initially intended to fully harmonize their IP systems by 2020 but have now set their sights on achieving regional co-operation by 2015. The Hanoi Plan of Action (1999–2004) contained the first iteration of how harmonization would be achieved.[13] Further details of implementation were detailed in the ASEAN IPR Action Plan (2004–2010) and the Work Plan for ASEAN Co-operation on Copyright (2005). This plan was updated when it was realized that full harmonization was not practicable due to the varying degrees of economic development of member states.[14] It was realized that a more reasonable approach would be to seek co-operation in a way that allowed member states to meet their diverse national goals whilst at the same time pursuing regional interests and imperatives. In addition, the program was accelerated by 5 years and a new plan known as the ASEAN IPR Action Plan 2011–2015 was developed.[15] According to its website, the AWGIPC will publish a follow-on plan, the ASEAN IPR Action Plan 2016–2020.[16]

The essence of the ASEAN IP co-operation approach is internal co-operation between member states progressing on parallel tracks with external co-operation with significant trading partners.[17] With regard to the first rung, that of internal co-operation, ASEAN has achieved the following:

1. ASEAN Patent Search and Examination Cooperation (APSEC) which enables participating states to reference each other's national IP Offices' findings on substantive patent examination;[18]
2. ASEAN IP Direct[19] which serves as 'an online directory' of participating states' IP frameworks;[20]
3. ASEAN member states' accession to key international agreements which include the Berne Convention, the Paris Convention, PCT, and the Madrid Protocol. All the member states are bound by TRIPS, by virtue of their WTO membership.

With regard to the second rung, Ng notes that the key achievements of ASEAN member states include co-operation with the EU[21] and Japan.[22] In addition,

11 Ng (2013) pp. 137–138.
12 Ng (2013) p. 137; Kuanporth (2013) p. 306. See the AWGIPC website at <http://www.aseanip.org/>.
13 Ng (2013) pp. 139–142.
14 Barraclough (2004–2005) p. 14.
15 Ng (2013) pp. 146–149.
16 AWGIPC (n.d.).
17 Ng (2013) p. 137.
18 Ng (2013) pp. 149–150; Kuanporth (2013) p. 307.
19 IP Office Singapore (2013). See website at <http://www.ipos.gov.sg/AboutIP/IPResources/UsefulLinks/RegionalOrganisations/ASEANIPDirect.aspx>.
20 Ng (2013) pp. 150–151; Kuanporth (2013) pp. 307–308.
21 Ng (2013) pp. 154–155.
22 Ng (2013) pp. 157–158.

ASEAN has entered into an FTA with Australia and New Zealand that includes provisions on IP.[23] In particular, it requires accession to and compliance with the PCT, the Patent Law treaty and the Budapest treaty.[24] It also covers trademarks, geographical indications, traditional knowledge and folklore.[25]

Co-operation has proven to be the more prudent option for ASEAN, following its unsuccessful attempts to harmonize. It may very well be that in the future, harmonization may progressively be achieved from this bedrock of co-operation. The lesson then, for the AU may be to first establish a firm co-operative framework and to thereafter build on that towards harmonization.

APEC

APEC was founded in 1989[26] and has been characterized as following the contested open regionalism model because it has not adopted classic linear market integration but has chosen open economic co-operation instead.[27] This approach intentionally and expressly shunned the creation of a trading bloc[28] in order to appease ASEAN concerns about institutional rivalry.[29] APEC's membership consists of the following 21 member economies: Australia, Brunei, Darussalam, Canada, Chile, China, Chinese Taipei, Hong Kong, Indonesia, Japan, Korea, Malaysia, Mexico, New Zealand, Papua New Guinea, Peru, Philippines, Russia, Singapore, Thailand, United States, and Vietnam.

In 1994 APEC adopted the Bogor Declaration which set out its economic co-operation aspirations. This declaration, which predates TRIPS, did not expressly mention IP. It provided two achievement deadlines, depending on the developmental status of member economies. Developing states committed to achieving free and open trade and investment in the region by 2020 whilst developed states committed to the earlier deadline of 2010.[30] APEC's 1995 Osaka Action Agenda which sets out the implementation of the Bogor Declaration provides for IP co-operation, primarily to secure conformity with TRIPS and address the challenges faced by its member economies. The objectives are stated as follows:[31]

> APEC economies will:
> a. in conformance with the principles of the TRIPS Agreement:
> – ensure adequate and effective protection, including legislation, administration and enforcement of intellectual property rights,

23 Kuanporth (2013) p. 309.
24 Kuanporth (2013) p. 310.
25 Kuanporth (2013) pp. 310–313.
26 For a historical overview of its formation see Sutton (2007) pp. 135–138; Elek (2005) and (1991).
27 Sutton (2007) pp. 138–142; Taubman (2004) pp. 162, 189–192.
28 Bogor Declaration, 1994; Osaka Action Agenda, 1995; APEC Ministerial Declarations 1997 and 1999.
29 For a discussion of these concerns see Akashi (1997) p. 3.
30 APEC (2010) pp. 3–4.
31 Para 7 Osaka Action Agenda, 1995.

- foster harmonization of intellectual property rights systems in the APEC region,
- strengthen public awareness activities and
- promote dialogue on emerging intellectual property policy issues, with a view to further improve intellectual property rights protection and use of the intellectual property rights systems for the social and economic benefit of members.

b. address the challenges for intellectual property rights arising from the rapid growth and developments of the New Economy by:

- establishing legal frameworks to promote creative endeavor and encourage online activity;
- ensuring a balance between the different rights and interests of copy right owners, users and distributors;
- establishing an appropriate balance among all stakeholders, including content providers and ISPs in terms of the liabilities for infringing intellectual property online; and
- providing incentives for innovation without sacrificing the community's interest in reasonable access to information.

In addition, the Osaka Action Agenda provides for the following guidelines for individual and collective action by member economies:

Guidelines
Each APEC economy will:
a. ensure that intellectual property rights are granted through expeditious, simple, and cost-effective procedures;
b. ensure that adequate and effective civil and administrative procedures and remedies are available against infringement of intellectual property rights; and
c. provide and expand bilateral technical cooperation in relation to areas such as patent search and examination, computerization and human resources development in order to ensure adequate intellectual property right protection in compliance with the TRIPS Agreement.

Collective Actions
APEC economies will take the following collective actions:
a. Deepening the Dialogue on Intellectual Property Policy;
b. Support for Easy and Prompt Acquisition of Rights:
  (i) Participation in International IP-related Systems
  (ii) Establishing Internationally Harmonized IPR Systems
  (iii) Cooperation on Searches and Examinations;
c. Electronic Processing of IPR-related Procedures:
  (i) Electronic Filing Systems
  (ii) Dissemination of Information by Electronic Means;
d. Appropriate Protection of IPR in New Fields:
  (i) Protection for Biotechnology and Computer-related Inventions

   (ii) Protection for Geographical Indications
   (iii) Electronic commerce;
e. Cooperation for Improvements to the Operation of IP System;
f. Establishing Effective Systems for IPR Enforcement:
   (i) Establishment of Enforcement Guidelines
   (ii) Exchange of Information Concerning IPR Infringement
   (iii) Cooperation with other fora/authorities
g. Promoting IP Asset Management in APEC Economies;
h. Raising Public Awareness;
i. Facilitation of Technology Transfer through Ensuring IP Protection.

Pursuant to the above objective and guidelines the Committee on Trade and Investment (CTI) established an Intellectual Property Rights Get Together (IPR-GT) in 1996.[32] Its objective was 'to ensure adequate and effective protection, through legislative, administrative and enforcement mechanisms, of IP rights in the Asia Pacific region' as required by TRIPS 'and other related agreements.'[33] In 1998 the IPR-GT was converted into an official organ and renamed the IPR-Experts Group (IPEG).[34] Taubman points out that this tentative evolution of IPEG is 'a telling instance of the pragmatic value of APEC's constitutional flexibility in combination with a deeply-rooted consensus ethic.'[35] This group's program of action has proceeded cautiously over the years to involve a number of initiatives on IP including an Anti-Counterfeiting and Piracy Initiative that led to the adoption of the following IPR Guidelines to:[36]

1. Reduce trade in counterfeit and pirated goods.
2. Protect against unauthorized copies.
3. Prevent the sale of counterfeit and pirated goods over the internet.
4. Provide effective public awareness campaigns on IPR.
5. Secure supply chains against counterfeit and pirated goods.
6. Strengthen IPR capacity building.

The IPEG has also completed a survey on PVP protection in some member economies[37] and prepared a document on Effective Practices for Addressing Unauthorized Camcording.[38]

In addition to the IPEG's work, the APEC Sub-Committee on Customs Procedures (SCCP), which was created in 1994, has also engaged with IP matters. In particular, it produced IP Rights Enforcement Strategies in 2006 and the

32 APEC (n.d.).
33 APEC (n.d.).
34 APEC (n.d.).
35 Taubman (2004) p. 187.
36 APEC (n.d.).
37 APEC (2009).
38 APEC (2011b).

APEC Guidelines for Customs Border Enforcement, Counterfeiting and Piracy, which were endorsed by the 2011 APEC Ministerial Meeting.[39]

APEC's IP activities are co-operative in nature and lack a normative basis primarily because of its nature as a regional configuration of economies, rather than states.[40] Taubman's evaluation of its success to date, is that it is 'barely successful' in relation to the creation of an internal regulatory framework or providing policy direction beyond its regional reach.[41]

BRICS

The theorization of regionalism in Brazil, Russia, India, China and South Africa (BRICS) is beyond the scope of this section. Suffice it to say that due to its unique features, this configuration has been characterized as a 'new regionalism' of 'emerging economies'[42] and a 'nominal rudimentary "non-regionalism" grouping and [an] "inexact" imitation . . . in the management of contemporary global geopolitics and international relations'.[43] To put it colloquially, BRICS does not fit in nicely with existing conceptualization of regionalism. Be that as it may, what is of relevance to this chapter is its member states' approach to IP co-operation, to which the next paragraph turns.

In March 2013 the BRICS Ministers of Trade agreed on a Trade and Investment Cooperation Framework that provided for the following with respect to IP:[44]

1. Enhancing information exchange on IPR legislation and enforcement through meetings or seminars.
2. Jointly developing capacity building programs in the IPR area.
3. Promoting cooperation among IPR offices.

In addition, in May 2013 the BRICS' heads of the IP Offices agreed on an IP co-operation road map for their IP offices.[45] This road map lists the following 'co-operation streams':

- Training of IP office staff
- IP/patent processes and procedures including search, classification and translation services
- Promotion of public awareness on IP in BRICS countries
- National IP Strategy and IP Strategy for enterprises

39 APEC (2011a).
40 Taubman (2004) p. 191.
41 Taubman (2004) p. 195.
42 Shaw, Grant and Cornelissen (2011) p. 5.
43 Tsheola (2014) p. 195.
44 Clause 4.
45 New (2013).

- Information services on IP e.g. exchange of patent documentation taking account of local legislation
- Collaboration in International Forums as required and subject to consensus
- Examiner exchange program

There has been a follow-on BRICS Trade and Investment Facilitation Plan which was endorsed by the Ministers of Trade at their meeting at Fortaleza in 2014. This plan does not expressly reference IP co-operation. There is no public information on how the BRICS IP Offices have operationalized their co-operation streams.

In addition to the above initiatives of the Ministers of Trade and the Heads of IP Offices, the BRICS ministers of Science, Technology and Innovation have also engaged with IP matters. They signed a Memorandum of Agreement at their meeting in Brasilia in March 2015. This memorandum provides for the following with regard to their management of IP:[46]

> 1. The parties will ensure adequate and effective protection and fair allocation of intellectual property rights of a proprietary nature that may result from the cooperative activities under this Memorandum of Understanding, according to their respective national laws and regulations and their international obligations.
> 2. The condition for the acquisition, maintenance and commercial exploitation of intellectual property rights over possible products and/or processes that might be obtained under this Memorandum of Understanding will be defined in the specific programmes, contracts or working plans of the activities of cooperation.
> 3. The specific programmes, contracts or working plans relating to the activities of cooperation mentioned in Paragraph 2 of this Article will set out the conditions regarding the confidentiality of information whose publication and/or disclosure might jeopardize the acquisition, maintenance and commercial exploitation of intellectual property rights obtained under this Memorandum of Understanding. Such specific programmes, contracts or working plans related to the activities of cooperation will establish, where applicable, the rule and procedures concerning the settlement of disputes on intellectual property matters under this Memorandum of Understanding.

IP co-operation in the BRICS has so far been mostly on a practical level, with an emphasis on the capacity building of IP Offices. However, there is some normative engagement to the extent that national IP strategies were expressly included in the IP Offices' co-operation streams. Due to a lack of information, it is not possible to evaluate the success of such co-operation.

46 Clause 7, Memorandum of Understanding on Cooperation in Science, Technology and Innovation Between the Governments of the Federative Republic Of Brazil, the Russian Federation, the Republic of India, the People's Republic of China and the Republic of South Africa, 2015.

Harmonization

Harmonization is an oft-cited panacea to regional and sub-regional integration challenges. The promise it offers lies in the conformity of economic and legal conditions that are expected to promote trade and foster the adoption of common positions on a variety of international matters. It is argued that a harmonized region or sub-region with a common economic and legal framework is better able to present a united front at international law-making fora. Harmonization is pursued on a variety of levels, namely sub-regional, regional and global. In its earlier manifestations, when it was limited to certain regions, it was dubbed 'regionalism in disguise', however as it became broader in its reach and became more globally inclusive, it was characterized as 'universalism' and in recent times when regional organizations have become active in international harmonization efforts, it has been classified as 'inter-regionalism'.[47]

Harmonization exists across a spectrum of strictness or tightness which is determined by 'the strictness of judicial review of compliance . . . and the extent to which the harmonization instruments constrained regulatory space at both ends of the policy spectrum'.[48]

Methods of harmonization

Goode enumerates the following nine ways of effecting harmonization:[49]

1) a multilateral Convention without a Uniform Law as such;
2) a multilateral Convention embodying a Uniform Law;
3) a set of bilateral Treaties;
4) Community legislation – typically, a Directive;
5) a Model Law;
6) a codification of custom and usage promulgated by an international nongovernmental organization;
7) international trade terms promulgated by such an organization;
8) model contracts and general contractual conditions;
9) restatements by scholars and other experts.

Other classifications cluster the above modes into three groups, namely:

1) legislative means through binding (hard) or non-binding (soft) law;
2) explanatory means through guidelines for practitioners; and
3) contractual means through formulating standard contractual clauses or industry norms.[50]

47 Faria (2009) p. 7.
48 Dinwoodie (2013) p. 3 note 6.
49 Goode (1991) p. 57.
50 Ndulo (1997) pp. 213–214; Faria (2009) p. 8.

This tri-fold categorization captures items (1)–(8) from Goode's list. The following paragraphs discuss these three clusters and Goode's item 9 in the realm of IP law.

Legislative means

There are numerous conventions or treaties that provide for hard IP law, at global, bi-lateral, regional or regional community levels. These conventions and community laws may provide for the resolution of a conflict of laws or for uniform substantive law.[51] Generally, conventions and community laws are subject to an accession or ratification procedure and thereafter have to be domesticated in order to acquire force of law. The exception to this is a community instrument that is enacted to be directly applicable to community members such as the EU's Regulations.

A conflict of law convention enables the identification of the applicable substantive law in circumstances where two or more national systems are relevant, thus providing certainty for contractual parties and other affected persons. There is no IP specific conflict of laws convention. However, WIPO has shown significant interest in the American Law Institute (ALI)'s project on IP: Principles Governing Jurisdiction, Choice of Law, and Judgments in Transnational Disputes (2008) as evidenced by the joint WIPO-ALI Seminar on IP and Private International Law held January 2015.[52]

On the other hand, there are numerous IP specific substantive law conventions that typically set minimum standards.[53] TRIPS is an example of a minimum standard setting treaty. African RECs, such as SADC, have reinforced their member states' obligation to comply with TRIPS.[54] Similarly, the two sub-regional IP organizations' harmonization efforts are essentially an internalization of TRIPS. As is evident from Chapter 3, the two organizations use differing means to achieve this. OAPI's unification via the Bangui Agreement includes provisions that spell out substantive law. On the other hand, ARIPO's community laws, known as Protocols, leave substantive law to its member states and generally provide only for a common application and administrative procedure. However, in those instances where a common position has not been reached at global level, the regional IP organizations set their own substantive standards in the relevant Protocol or Annex. An instance of this is ARIPO's Swakopmund Protocol that provides for the protection of traditional knowledge.

In addition, where TRIPS leaves various options available, there have been sub-regional initiatives to settle on the adoption of a specific approach. This

51 Shumba (2014) p. 47.

52 WIPO-ILA Seminar on IP and Private International Law, Meeting Code S/IP/GE/15, 16 January 2015.

53 Ruse-Khan (2009) pp. 57–59.

54 Article 23 of the SADC Protocol on Trade provides that member states shall 'adopt policies and implement measures within the Community for the protection of Intellectual Property Rights, in accordance with the WTO Agreement on Trade-Related Aspects of Intellectual Property Rights (TRIPS).'

is evident in relation to the protection of plant varieties where TRIPS article 27(3) b requires countries to 'provide for the protection of plant varieties either by patents or by an effective *sui generis* system or by any combination thereof.' ARIPO,[55] OAPI[56] and SADC[57] have opted to adopt the International Union for the Protection of New Varieties of Plants (UPOV)'s International convention for the protection of new varieties of plants (1991).[58]

Soft or model laws are not binding and are offered as templates for best standards and practices.[59] They may be drafted by a specialized international organization such as United Nations Commission on International Trade Law (UNCITRAL) or under the auspices of a supranational organization like the AU, with the use of necessary expertise. States are then at liberty to domesticate the model law, either partially or wholly. An example of the use of soft law to harmonize IP standards, is provided by the AU's African Model Legislation for the Protection of the Rights of Local Communities, Farmers and Breeders, and for the Regulation of Access to Biological Resources of 2000. This model law provides for the *sui generis* protection of traditional knowledge by providing for community rights in both resources and knowledge[60] and was much maligned by both UPOV and WIPO when it was adopted.[61] However, some African states have domesticated elements of this Model law.[62] However as stated above, countries that belong to OAPI are bound to the UPOV approach. Those countries that are members of ARIPO and SADC will probably adopt the same approach once these bodies finalize their draft Protocols. This situation illustrates one of the major disadvantages of harmonization through soft law, namely that of being overridden by a different approach advanced as hard law. A second example of soft law used in the field of IP is the UNESCO–WIPO Tunis Model Copyright Law for Developing Countries, 1976, mentioned in Chapter 1. Countries such as Ghana adopted this model law.

Explanatory

The second method of harmonization, the provision of legislative guides, is resorted to when reaching consensus through hard or soft law, is unattainable. These guides present states with possible legislative and policy options from which they can select nationally appropriate laws and standards.[63] An example of such guides in the domain of IP law is UNCITRAL's Legislative Guide on Secured Transactions: Supplement on Security Rights in Intellectual Property (2010). It

55 Draft ARIPO Legal Framework for the Protection of New Varieties of Plants (2013).
56 Bangui Agreement, Annex X: New Varieties of Plant.
57 Draft Protocol for the Protection of New Varieties of Plants (Plant Breeders' Rights) in the Southern African Development Community Region (2012).
58 For commentary on the appropriateness of this choice see De Jonge (2014).
59 Faria (2005) p. 13.
60 Feris (2004) pp. 251–253; Ekpere (2003) p. 275.
61 World Bank (2012) p. 453.
62 Feris (2004) pp. 252–253.
63 Faria (2005) p. 15.

was developed in consultation with WIPO and sets out options for the legal regulation of security rights in IP.

Since the adoption of the Marrakesh Treaty[64] in 2013, several guides have been issued by various bodies and organizations for states, libraries and users. Under this category of harmonization techniques, it is the guides prepared for states that are of interest. A case in point is ARIPO's draft domestication guide for its member states.[65] This draft guide contains recommendations pertaining to a suitable legislative approach and includes suggested provisions. Such a guide would be considered to be instructive by ARIPO member states due to its provenance. Guides that are prepared by individuals may also be well-received, particularly if they are penned by acknowledged experts in the area.[66]

Contractual

The third device, formulating standard contractual clauses or industry norms, has also been employed in the IP sphere. For example, WIPO has published the following:

1. Recommended WIPO Contract Clauses and Submission Agreements.[67]
2. Recommended Contract Clauses and Submission Agreements for WIPO Mediation and Expedited Arbitration for Film and Media.[68]

WIPO also maintains a database of Biodiversity-related Access and Benefit-sharing Agreements.[69] These draft clauses may be used by anyone. Other interested parties, such as firms of attorneys and research groupings, have also prepared draft clauses.

Attempts to guide or inform industry norms are typically effected through guides for the affected community that spell out appropriate ways to beneficially utilize the law. Examples include guides prepared for libraries,[70] users[71] and academic institutions.[72] The African regional IP organizations and RECs have not yet employed this harmonization technique.

64 Treaty to Facilitate Access to Published Works for Persons Who Are Blind, Visually Impaired, or Otherwise Print Disabled.

65 ARIPO Draft Guidelines for the Domestication of the Marrakesh Treaty to Facilitate Access to Published Works for Persons who are Blind, Visually Impaired or Otherwise Print Disabled, 2014.

66 For example Band and Jaszi (2013).

67 Available at <http://www.wipo.int/amc/en/clauses/>.

68 Available at <http://www.wipo.int/amc/en/film/clauses.html>.

69 Available at <http://www.wipo.int/tk/en/databases/contracts/list.html>.

70 EIFL (2014).

71 Band (2013); Jaszi and Aufderheide (2015).

72 Association of Research Libraries (ARL) (2012).

Restatements of law

Restatements of law are in extensive usage in the US where the ALI has prepared the following IP relevant restatements:

1. Restatement (Third) of Unfair Competition (1995), and
2. Restatement (First) of Torts § 757 – Liability for Disclosure or Use of Another's Trade Secret – General Principle (2010).

Since the beginning of 2015, the ALI has been working on a restatement of Copyright Law.[73] Restatements of IP Law are not currently in use in Africa. However, the recently established African Institute of International Law[74] may in the future begin work on this front.

As evident from the above, African RECs and regional IP organizations use some, but not all, of the available harmonization modes. Indeed, some of them, such as the provision of model contractual terms and constituency guides, are not typically used by such organizations. Rather, they are prepared by specialized organizations such as UNCITRAL and UNIDRIOT. The following section discusses the pros and cons of harmonization in general as a precursor to the section on specific IP harmonization initiatives in various regional and sub-regional communities.

Advantages of harmonization

Legal harmonization is an important aspect of regional economic integration.[75] Trade is easier to conduct across borders where the legal framework is settled and congruent. Further, as argued in Chapter 1, it will be easier for African states to achieve their public health goals by adopting a harmonized regional approach to using patent-related TRIPS flexibilities. This section proceeds on the premise that the concept of harmonization is generally beneficial but that issues or challenges arise with the employment of specific modes of harmonization. In other words, the core problems lie with the *how* rather than the *what* and *why* of harmonization. Accordingly, this section discusses the advantages that attach to the different modes of harmonization.

Harmonization by hard law is laudable for its ability to set binding international standards that serve the ideals of a cohesive legal environment that is expected to ease transactions across borders or regions and also to encourage the international spread of business due to confidence in a more or less uniform legal system. However, this may be at the cost of national flexibility and it may remove the ability for states to nuance their legal frameworks to suit their domestic conditions. It is for this reason that the treaty negotiation process is often fraught with controversy and delays.

73 Vanderbilt Law School (2014).
74 AU Assembly Decision, Assembly/AU/14(XVIII) Add.5 (2012).
75 Ndulo (1997) p. 211.

In view of these difficulties, harmonization by soft norms may be more beneficial as it enables the necessary national nuancing.[76] If a state decides to domesticate aspects of model law, it is able to adapt those aspects to suit its local conditions. It does so from a sound technical foundation because model laws are prepared with the necessary legal expertise which African states sometimes lack and do not have the financial resources to buy-in. Further, where standard contractual terms are accepted by industry and other relevant constituencies, they bring much needed clarity and certainty to contractual transactions.

Disadvantages of harmonization

The section sets out the challenges that are raised by both hard and soft law approaches, in turn.

There are many challenges that attach to the use of hard law to harmonize the legal framework of a region or sub-region. Several of these are highlighted here. First, when the hard law or treaty model is used the pace of harmonization tends to be quite slow and once agreed, tends to be uneven and may stagnate.[77] This is because reaching agreement at international or regional level on the initial text and on any future amendments is very difficult and may take decades, as is the case with negotiations at the IGC pertaining to the protection of TK. In some cases a treaty never comes to fruition, as happened with the substantive Patent Law treaty. Where a treaty is agreed, the spread of its norms may be uneven when some target states do not ratify it.[78] For those states that choose to ratify it, there is often another lengthy process to see its norms domesticated. Party states have to go through an essentially political accession or signature and ratification process followed by the due process through the national legislature. In those areas where fast changing technologies or innovation are occurring, it may very well be that when these processes are completed, the law is out-stripped by developments and has become obsolete.

Secondly, when agreement on norms is achieved, it is invariably a compromise, and some party states will be disadvantaged to the extent that their needs and preferences are not met satisfactorily. More so, when instances of legislative capture by powerful industry lobbies is evident.[79] Indeed, this has been one of the much-cited flaws of TRIPS in relation to developing countries, as discussed in Chapter 1. Many directives also ratchet-up TRIPS minimum standards, as has been the case in the EU.[80]

A third difficulty raised by the use of hard law is the resolution of what Oppong has identified as 'relational issues', namely the interface between community and national laws, conflict of laws between them, how community and

76 Faria (2009) p. 13.
77 Faria (2009) pp. 8–9.
78 Hugenholtz (2012) p. 6.
79 Faria (2009) p. 10.
80 Hugenholtz (2012) p. 6.

national institutions interact, which of them has jurisdiction over which matters and how citizens or residents of member states can access, and participate in, community institutions.[81] These issues have to be resolved by binding legal provisions or legal precedents that apply to the community and its member states. Care has to be taken to ensure that these provisions are appropriately placed in both community and national law. Typically, such provisions will stipulate the supremacy of community law. They will also expressly state how community law acquires force of law in the member states. It is also necessary to provide guidance on how, if at all, national judicial institutions will interpret, apply and enforce community laws. One way of doing this is by making provision for a procedure through which national courts can refer questions of community law to community or regional adjudicatory bodies. Other matters that need to be resolved include provision for the circumstances under which individuals have access to regional legislatures and adjudicatory structures.[82] With regard to *locus standi* before regional courts, the available options include direct standing as is the case in the EAC and COMESA[83]; the requirement of seeking the leave of national courts as in the case of Caribbean, or the obligation to exhaust domestic remedies prior to advancing to the regional plane which prevails in COMESA and SADC.[84]

The fourth difficulty is the enormity and complexity of the domestication process. Community law typically impacts a host of national legislation and policies that have to be repealed or amended as appropriate to achieve the community standard. For example, it has been reported that Uganda has to amend 54 statutes in order to conform to the EAC's Common Market Protocol and related sector specific Protocols.[85] This is an extensive and expensive exercise for which the retention of the services of consultants is required. It is important to note that this difficulty also attaches to the internalization of model laws. The domestication process also introduces a measure of uncertainty to the national sphere when a regional or sub-regional legal instrument introduces 'new rights or novel terminology'.[86] Such uncertainty persists until a national, sub-regional or regional court resolves it.

The fifth shortcoming is that the legislative process is complex, often lacks transparency and may be driven by obscured political agendas which compromises the quality of the resultant legal instrument.[87]

In addition to the above noted disadvantage, soft law approaches are also beset by the uncertainty that follows from the high levels of flexibility extended to states. Due to this flexibility states select different portions of model laws to adopt and a patchwork of different approaches then applies across the continent

81 Oppong (2011) p. 8.
82 Oppong (2011) p. 52.
83 Tino (2013) p. 151.
84 Tino (2013) p. 152.
85 UNECA SRO-EA (2013) p. 22.
86 Hugenholtz (2012) p. 7.
87 Hugenholtz (2012) p. 7.

or a sub-region.[88] Further, it is not up to states to adopt or apply draft contractual terms and recommended constituency norms. The acceptance of these lies with industry or other relevant constituency. Consequently, it may be that these soft laws are rejected or ignored and that where they are accepted, it is in a haphazard manner.[89] Having laid this context, the following section outlines EU and MECOSUR approaches to harmonization.

Lessons from existing harmonization efforts

EU

The EU is a good comparator for the AU because of the significant commonalities between the two organizations. As noted by Gottschalk, [90] the AEC Treaty's proposal of the creation of an African common market through a phased process spanning over 34 years is modeled on the EU's evolution during the 34 years between the adoption of the Treaty of Rome[91] in 1957 and the adoption of the Maastricht Treaty[92] in 1991.

The EU achieves harmonization primarily through the adoption of Directives which set regional standards but leave some national discretion with regard to implementation within a stipulated time-frame.[93] After the expiry of this period, national laws that are contrary to community standards will be struck down, upon application, by the European Court of Justice (ECJ) (negative harmonization) or over-ridden by the community standard. Unification is achieved through Regulations.

Some of the relevant EU legal instruments that regulate IP are tabulated in Table 6.1 further below.

A discussion of the substantive content of the above legal instruments is beyond the scope of this work.[94] EU's Office for Harmonization in the Internal Market (Trademarks and Designs) (OHIM) administers the Community Trademark (CTM) system and the community design system.[95] The patent system is administered by the European Patent Organization, which comprises the European Patent Office (EPO) and the Administrative Council. Like ARIPO, the EPO administers a single patent application process for designated states, which if successful results

88 Shumba (2014) p. 55.
89 Shumba (2014) pp. 56–58.
90 Gottschalk (2012) p. 16.
91 Treaty establishing the European Economic Community (TEEC), now the Treaty on the Functioning of the European Union (TFEU).
92 The *Treaty on European Union.*
93 Woods and Watson (2014) p. 342.
94 For commentary see Dinwoodie (2010) and (2013); Hugenholtz (2012); Raciti (1996); Max Planck Institute for Intellectual Property and Competition Law (2011); Blakely (2000); Askew (1999); Loewenheim (1996); Blakely (2000).
95 Kur and Drier (2013) p. 163.

Table 6.1

Trademarks	*Designs*	*Patents*	*Copyright*
Trademark Directive (TMD) Community Trade Mark Regulations (CMTR)	Design Directive (DD) Community Design Regulation (CDR)	– European Patent Convention – Biotechnological Inventions Directive – Supplementary protection certificate for medicinal products regulation – Supplementary certificate for plant protection products regulation	– Computer Programs Directive – Rental Rights Directive – Term Directive – Satellite and Cable Directive – Database Directive – Information Society Directive, 2001 – Resale Right Directive – Orphan Works Directive

in the grant of national patents in the designated states.[96] Enforcement is harmonized by the Enforcement Directive of 2004 and infringement litigation is adjudicated by national courts with a right of appeal, ultimately, to the ECJ. In addition, national courts may also refer questions of the meaning of EU legal instruments.[97] In general, the EU's IP harmonization efforts have been very successful due to its nature as a supranational organization.[98] In contrast, the AU has not achieved this status and operates as an intergovernmental organization.[99] This fundamental difference, coupled with the AU's resource constraints and weaker institutions, means that AU harmonization attempts are likely to fall far short of the EU's.

MERCOSUR

MERCOSUR's member states are Argentina, Brazil, Paraguay, Uruguay and Venezuela. Bolivia lodged its Protocol of Accession in 2012 and is in the process of becoming a full member.[100] Its associate states are Chile, Bolivia, Colombia, Ecuador and Peru.[101] Two further states have applied for associate status by concluding framework agreements with MERCOSUR, namely Guyana and Suriname.[102] New Zealand and Mexico have observer status. MERCOSUR was established in 1991 through the adoption of the Treaty of Asuncion and later operationalized in 1994 with the adoption of the Ouro Preto Protocol on

96 Kur and Drier (2013) p. 88.
97 Article 267 TFEU.
98 Fagbayibo (2013) p. 34.
99 Fagbayibo (2013) p. 34; Fagbayibo (2008) pp. 502–503.
100 Mercosur (n.d.a).
101 Mercosur (n.d.b).
102 Guyana-Mercosur Framework Agreement, 2013; Suriname-Mercosur Framework Agreement, 2013.

Institutional Structure.[103] Its end goal is the creation of a common market[104] but it is currently a CU. It is an appropriate comparator for the AU because its membership consists of developing countries and LDCs. Further, individually and collectively, its member states have significant trade relations with African states. For instance, Brazil and South Africa are members of BRICS and trade in that context; while MERCOSUR and SACU concluded a PTA in 2008.[105]

Its legal framework consists of the founding treaty and its annexes, Protocols, Decisions of the Council of the Common Market (CCM),[106] Resolutions of the Common Market Group (CMG)[107] and Directives of the MERCOSUR Trade Commission (MTC).[108] The primary law, namely the founding treaty, its annexes and Protocols, has to be translated into national law in dualist member states.[109] Of the MERCOSUR member states, Argentina is monist.[110] Its secondary law namely decisions, resolutions and directives are binding on member states[111] however only directives are self-executing.[112] In addition, there are also 'atypical' sources of law such as Declarations.[113]

Harmonization of IP is complicated by the differences in the domestic IP laws of the member states[114] and progress has been slow. To date the following legal instruments are in place:

1. Protocol on the harmonization of IP rights in MERCOSUR, relating to trademarks, indications of source and appellations of origin, 1995.
2. Protocol on the harmonization of standards in the field of industrial designs, 1998.
3. CCM Decision No 2/01 on drug policy in MERCOSUR, Bolivia and Chile, 2001.

The protocol on IP rights has only been ratified by Paraguay and Uruguay for whom it came into force on 6 August 2000.[115] This protocol provides the foundation for further regulation on IP in article 24 which provides:

> The states parties undertake to make efforts to conclude, as soon as possible, additional agreements on patents, utility models, industrial designs, copyrights and related fields, and other matters relating to intellectual property.

103 Malamuc (2010) p. 25.
104 Article 1 Treaty of Asuncion.
105 For commentary see Nkomo and Olmos (2013).
106 Article 9 Protocol of Ouro Prerto (POP).
107 Article 15 POP.
108 Article 20 POP.
109 Giupponi (2010) p. 59.
110 Giupponi (2010) p. 65.
111 Giupponi (2010) pp. 60–61; article 41 POP.
112 Giupponi (2010) p. 63.
113 Giupponi (2010) p. 63.
114 Hicks and Holbein (1997) p. 805.
115 Fernandez (2010) p. 321.

The protocol on industrial designs has not been ratified by any of the MERCOSUR member states.[116] This illustrates one of the key shortfalls of harmonization, that of uneven adoption of norms across a sub-region or region. There is no legal instrument that seeks to regulate patents and copyright. The third of the above listed instruments is a policy statement on access to medicines, ensuring the 'quality, safety and efficacy' of medicines, rationalizing their use and supporting R&D in relevant sectors of the region.[117] It expressly references patents and asserts that patent law must be nuanced to promote the health services provision goals of the region.[118] MERCOSUR does not yet have any common IP administrative structure.

Enforcement and dispute resolution is cursorily dealt with in the Protocol on trademarks, indications of source and appellations of origin. Article 25 provides

> The controversies that should arise among the Party States with respect to the application, interpretation or noncompliance of the provisions contained in the Present Protocol shall be resolved by means of direct diplomatic negotiations. If through said negotiations an agreement cannot be reached or if the controversy should be resolved only in part, the procedures established in the controversy resolution system in force in the MERCOSUR shall apply.

The reliance on diplomatic channels to resolve substantive legal issues is unsatisfactory. If this avenue does not yield results the matter is then escalated to the ad hoc arbitration procedure and, if necessary, thereafter to the Permanent Review Court, which is the current dispute resolution framework established by the Olivos Protocol. The protocol provides that states must first attempt to resolve disputes through direct negotiations.[119] Should these fail, within the prescribed period of 15 days, the matter may then be referred to the CMG that will then have 30 days to achieve resolution of the dispute.[120] If resolution is not achieved with the assistance of the CMG, the matter may then be referred to the ad hoc arbitration court,[121] from which a right of review lies to the Permanent Review Court.[122] The Permanent Review Court has jurisdiction to resolve legal disputes as a forum of last resort and deals with referrals of questions of community law from member states.[123] The key shortcoming of applying this dispute resolution mechanism to IP matters is that it is limited to disputes between member states and thus excludes private actor access.[124] Private persons are only permitted to file claims 'in connection with the adoption or application, by any of the state parties, of legal or

116 Fernandez (2010) p. 326.
117 Fernandez (2010) p. 328.
118 Fernandez (2010) p. 329.
119 Article 4 Olivos Protocol.
120 Articles 6–8 Olivos Protocol.
121 Article 9 Olivos Protocol.
122 Article 17 Olivos Protocol.
123 Susani (2010) p. 75.
124 Susani (2010) p. 75.

administrative measures having a limiting, discriminatory or unfair competition effect. . . .'[125] Effectively, the system is unable to deal with substantive IP disputes between private persons. Further, the dispute resolution system lacks exclusive jurisdiction and member states may resort to other available avenues.[126] In view of the above, it is clear that in the decade following its first IP specific protocol, through which it committed to IP harmonization, this goal has not been achieved in MERCOSUR.

Unification in OHADA

OHADA was created in 1993 to harmonize business law in its member states which as at 9 February 2015 comprised of Benin, Burkina Faso, Cameroon, Central African Republic, Chad, Comoros, Cote d'Ivoire, DRC, Gabon, Guinea, Guinea-Bissau, Equatorial Guinea, Mali, Niger, Senegal and Togo.[127] Whilst OHADA's legislative texts exclude IP, its member states' (with the exception of the DRC) IP regimes are unified through OAPI as discussed in Chapter 4. From an IP policy perspective, there is further coverage for Comoros and the DRC through the COMESA IP policy. Nine OHADA members are also members of ECOWAS; Benin, Burkina Faso, Cote d'Ivoire, Guinea, Guinea Bissau, Mali, Niger, Senegal and Togo. None of the OHADA members are members of the EAC.

OHADA and OAPI employ the same model of unification, that of hard law with direct application in their member states. OHADA currently has nine Uniform Acts.[128] Although OHADA's intended scope of regulatory coverage includes IP,[129] it has yet to venture into that domain, possibly because its member states have already unified their IP laws through OAPI's Bangui Agreement. For present purposes, OHADA's law making modus operandi and implementing structure is of relevance.

The Permanent Secretariat, in liaison with member states and the Common Court of Justice and Arbitration, drafts OHADA's Uniform Acts.[130] Sometimes the drafting is undertaken with technical assistance from international agencies. For example, the OHADA draft Uniform Act on Contract Law was drafted with technical assistance from the International Institute for the Unification of Private Law (UNIDROIT).[131] Once drafts are finalized they are referred to the

125 Article 39 Olivos Protocol.

126 Susani (2010) pp. 75–76.

127 For an overview of its historical development see Mouloul (2009) pp. 8–19; Martor et al (2002) pp. 4–7.

128 General Commercial Law (1997); Commercial Companies and Economic Interest Groups (1997); Secured Transactions (1997); Simplified Debt Collection Procedures and Enforcement Measures (1998); Bankruptcy (1998); Arbitration (1999); Accounting (2000); Carriage of Goods by Road (2003); and Cooperative Companies (2010).

129 Beauchard and Kodo (2011) p. 9.

130 Beauchard and Kodo (2011) p. 10.

131 Faria (2009) p. 13.

Council of Ministers for adoption. OHADA's Common Court of Justice and Arbitration serves as a dispute resolution forum. It hears appeals from national courts which may be brought to it by parties to litigation or by national courts. [132] It also serves as an arbitration center but in the last 6 years, this role has remained 'undeveloped.'[133]

OHADA's unification seems to have yielded some success.[134] However, truly serving the public interest requires the adaptation of legal norms and practices to local conditions. This imperative makes unification a less viable option than harmonization because it excludes the policy and legislative space for national nuancing. It may be that countries of a particular region have significant national commonalities but it is improbable that they would have exactly the same local conditions. For example, the member states of both OAPI and OHADA share a common francophone heritage, a similar colonial past and post-colonial legacy which justifies the adoption of a common legal framework. However, there are significant national differences amongst the member states that make unification a contestable choice. The membership of the AU reflects even more diversity, and unification on a continental scale would face the significant hurdle of overcoming a plethora of different legal traditions and cultures. Perhaps it is due to such considerations, that the AU's preferred approach is harmonization.

Conclusion

The above overview of instances of IP co-operation, harmonization and unification provide a number of significant considerations for the AU and its plans for PAIPO. However, it should be borne in mind that a complete legal transplant of another region's scheme would be ill advised because it would overlook the variances in regional conditions. The more appropriate approach would be to evaluate what has worked, and what has not worked, in another region and then select aspects that may be relevant and practicable in Africa. The key learnings from the above synopsis of ASEAN, APEC, BRICS, EU, MERCOSUR and OHADA approaches are summarized in this section.

First, co-operation is the best starting place. Indeed, ASEAN's experience was that seeking full harmonization as an initial goal was overly ambitious hence its retreat from the goal of harmonization to co-operation. In the 10 years since the conclusion of its Framework Agreement on IP Co-operation in 1995, ASEAN has crafted a sound co-operation system that is driven by the AWGIPC according to successive Action Plans. The lesson for the AU in this is that creating a co-operation system is a lengthy process that requires careful negotiation and the establishment of the necessary co-ordinating unit and detailed strategic planning. Therefore it is suggested that PAIPO's first 10 years could be devoted to playing a role similar to that played by ASEAN's AWGIPC to secure regional

132 Fagbayo (2009) p. 341.
133 Fagbayo (2009) p. 341 and (2013) p. 45.
134 Mancuso (2007) p. 177.

IP co-operation. As highlighted in Chapter 4, a major part of this co-ordination needs to be devoted to rationalizing the roles currently fulfilled by ARIPO and OAPI.

APEC's IP co-operation model based on open regionalism has had less success than ASEAN's. APEC's nature is markedly different from any of Africa's sub-regional groupings, thus the wholesale adoption of its brand of IP co-operation is not the best option for the AU and PAIPO. The BRICS' brand of IP co-operation is currently limited to IP office operations and is therefore on a much smaller scale than that conceived of by the AU for PAIPO.

Secondly, harmonization must be considered on the bedrock of successful co-operation. The pros and cons of harmonization have been canvassed above and since the AU has committed itself to IP harmonization through PAIPO, the question is no longer whether it should harmonize IP. Instead, the main consideration is really how to harmonize to the best effect in a way that minimizes the disadvantages of harmonization. This requires a careful consideration of which instruments to use and how to craft the regional harmonized system. As pointed out above, regional legal instruments have to provide for relational aspects and it would be necessary for the AU to provide appropriate technical legal assistance to its member states for the domestication of community IP norms.

Generally speaking, the adoption of a hard law instrument such as a directive is preferable to a soft law approach for the galvanizing effect it would have on AU member states.[135] In addition, if it adopted a loose, rather than tight, approach, it would leave the necessary scope for national divergence to suit local conditions. The EU's experience has shown that the development of a harmonized IP system is a long and expensive process.[136] This is also evident from MERCOSUR's experience that has spanned a decade to date and the region is yet to achieve harmonization. It also has to be IP right specific so that the system caters separately for each IP right through a series of directives. Indeed, there have been calls for Africa to harmonize its trademark laws per the EU model.[137] It may be possible to rationalize the implementation of the system through one or two administrative structures as the EU does with the EPO and OHIM.

The AU's internalization of the above considerations must be taken in the context of ARIPO and OAPI IP systems' substantive legal norms, administrative and enforcement systems. This distinguishes the AU from the EU. The EU system was not built on top of existing sub-regional systems: it only had to contend with national systems. The AU, on the other hand, has to rationalize two entrenched sub-regional IP organizations that intend to continue their IP right registration functions.

Enforcement would also need to be provided for through a hard law instrument. Such an instrument would have to establish a regional judicial structure to adjudicate infringement and other IP related matters such as dealing with the

135 Mupangavanhu (2013) p. 303.

136 Mupangavanhu (2013) p. 306.

137 Mupangavanhu (2015) and (2013); Adewopo (2003) and Dean (1994a) and (1994b).

referral of questions on community IP law from national courts. The existing AU adjudication arrangements are likely to be ill suited for IP matters due to the technical expertise that would be required of the bench. However, a permanent IP specific regional court may be under-utilized because, in reality, IP is not a priority for many African states that are seized with other issues such as food security, security threats and political instability. Therefore a periodic IP Court would be the most prudent option.[138] It would allow for IP judges and experts from across Africa to be seconded to the periodic court for brief periods that would ensure that their expertise is not lost to their home countries but is also extended to the regional plane. However, Africa has had mixed results with sub-regional judiciaries, the most cited failure being that of the SADC Tribunal, whilst she has been somewhat successful with COMESA and EAC courts.[139]

IP unification as embodied in the EU's community IP systems, OHADA and OAPI is not an appropriate option because it will overlook national peculiarities.

References

Primary sources

APEC

APEC Economic Leaders' Declaration for Action, Osaka, November, 1995.
APEC Economic Leaders' Declaration of Common Resolve, Bogor, Indonesia, 15 November, 1994.
APEC Eleventh APEC Ministerial Meeting, Auckland, New Zealand, 9–10 September 1999.
APEC Intellectual Property Rights (IPR) Enforcement Strategies, 2006.
APEC Ninth APEC Ministerial Meeting Joint Statement, Vancouver, 21–22 November 1997.
APEC Osaka Action Agenda: Implementation of the Bogor Declaration, 1995.

ARIPO

ARIPO Draft Guidelines for the Domestication of the Marrakesh Treaty to Facilitate Access to Published Works for Persons who are Blind, Visually Impaired or Otherwise Print Disabled, 2014.
Draft ARIPO Legal Framework for the Protection of New Varieties of Plants, 2013.

ASEAN

ASEAN Framework Agreement on Intellectual Property Cooperation, Bangkok, 15 December 1995.
ASEAN Hanoi Plan of Action 1999–2004.
ASEAN IPR Action Plan 2004–2010.

138 Mupangavanhu (2013) pp. 310–311.
139 For commentary see Tino (2013).

ASEAN IPRs Action Plan 2011–2015.
Work Plan for ASEAN Co-operation on Copyright 2005.

AU

African Model Legislation for the Protection of the Rights of Local Communities, Farmers and Breeders, and for the Regulation of Access to Biological Resources 2000.
AU Assembly Decision, Assembly/AU/14(XVIII) Add.5 On the Establishment of an African Institute of International Law in Arusha, the United Republic of Tanzania 2012.

BRICS

IP co-operation road map, 2013.
Memorandum of Understanding on Cooperation in Science, Technology and Innovation Between the Governments of the Federative Republic Of Brazil, the Russian Federation, the Republic of India, the People's Republic of China and the Republic of South Africa, 2015.
Trade and Investment Cooperation Framework, 2013.

EU

COPYRIGHT

Council Directive 93/83/EEC of 27 September 1993 on the coordination of certain rules concerning copyright and rights related to copyright applicable to satellite broadcasting and cable transmission, [1993] OJ L 248/15 (Satellite and Cable Directive).
Council Directive 2009/24/EC on the legal protection of computer programs, [2009] OJ L/16, originally published as Council Directive 91/250/EEC of 14 May 1991 on the legal protection of computer programs [1991] OJ L 122/42 (Computer Programs Directive).
Directive 96/6/EC of the European Parliament and of the Council of 11 March 1996 on the legal protection of databases, [1996] OJ L 77/20 (Database Directive).
Directive 2001/29/EC of the European Parliament and of the Council of 22 May on the harmonization of certain aspects of copyright and related rights in the information society, [2001] OJ L 167/10 (Information Society Directive).
Directive 2001/84/EC of the European Parliament and of the Council of 27 September 2001 on the resale right for the benefit of the author of an original work of art, [2001] OJ L 272, 13.10.2001, p. 32–36 (Resale Right Directive).
Directive 2006/116/EC of the European Parliament and of the Council of 12 December 2006 on the term of protection of copyright and certain related rights, [2006] OJ L 372/12, originally published as Council Directive 93/98/EEC of 29 October 1993 harmonizing the term of protection of copyright and certain related rights, [1993] OJ L 290/9 (Term Directive).
Directive 2006/115/EC of the European Parliament and of the Council of 12 December 2006 on rental right and lending right and on certain rights related to copyright in the field of IP, originally published as Directive 92/100/EEC: Rental Right and Lending Right Directive (Rental and Lending Right Directive).
Directive 2011/77/EU of the European Parliament and of Council of 27 September 2011 amending Directive 2006/116/EC on the term of protection of copyright and certain related rights, [2011] OJ L 265/1.

Directive 2012/28/EU of the European Parliament and of the Council of 25 October 2012 on certain permitted uses of orphan works [2012] OJ L 299/5 (Orphan works Directive).

DESIGNS

Council Regulation (EC) No. 6/2002 of 12 December 2001 on Community designs [2002] OJ L3, 1–24 (Community Design Regulation).
Directive No. 98/71/EC of the European Parliament and of the Council of 13 October 1998 on the legal protection of designs [1998] OJ L289, 28–35 (Design Directive).

ENFORCEMENT

Directive 2004/48/EC of European Parliament and of Council 29 April 2004 on the enforcement of IP rights, [2004] OJ L 195/16 (Enforcement Directive).

PATENTS

Convention on the Grant of European Patents, adopted 5 October 1973, entered into 7 October 1977, (1973) 13 *ILM* 270 (European Patent Convention).
Directive 95/2008/EC of the European Parliament and the Council to approximate the laws of the Member States relating to trade marks (codified version), [2008] OJ 299/25, originally enacted Directive 104/89/EEC [1989] OJ L 40/1.
Directive 98/44/EC of the European Parliament and of Council of 6 July 1998 on the legal protection of biotechnological inventions, [1998] OJ L 213/13.
Regulation (EC) 469/2009 of 6 May 2009 concerning the creation of a supplementary protection certificate for medicinal products (codified version) [2009] OJ L 152/1.
Regulation (EC) 1610/96 of 23 July 1996 concerning the creation of a supplementary certificate for plant protection products, [1996] OJ 198/30.

TRADEMARKS

Council Regulations 207/2009 on the Community trade mark (codified version), 2009 OJ L 78/1; originally enacted as Council Regulation 40/1994, [1994] OJ L 11/1 (Community Trade Mark Regulations (CMTR)).
Directive 95/2008/EC of the European Parliament and of the Council to approximate the laws of the Member States relating to trademarks (codified version), [2008] OJ L 299/25, originally enacted as Directive 104/89/EEC, [1989] OJ L 40/1.

MERCOSUR

CCM Decision No 2/01 on drug policy in MERCOSUR, Bolivia and Chile, Montevideo, 27 November 2001.
Guyana-Mercosur Framework Agreement, 2013.
Olivos Protocol for the Settlement of Disputes in MERCOSUR.
Protocol of Ouro Preto, 1994.
Protocol on the harmonization of IP rights in MERCOSUR, relating to trademarks, indications of source and appellations of origin, Asuncion, 5 August 1995, CCM Decision No 08/98.

Protocol on the harmonization of standards in the field of industrial designs, Rio de Janeiro, 10 December, CCM Decision No 16/98.
Suriname-Mercosur Framework Agreement, 2013.
Treaty of Asuncion, 1991.

OAPI

Bangui Agreement Relating to the Creation of an African Intellectual Property Organization, Constituting a Revision of the Agreement Relating to the Creation of an African and Malagasy Office of Industrial Property, 1977.

SADC

Draft Protocol for the Protection of New Varieties of Plants (Plant Breeders' Rights) in the Southern African Development Community Region (2012).
SADC Protocol on trade (1996).

UPOV

International convention for the protection of new varieties of plants (1991).
UNCITRAL's Legislative Guide on Secured Transactions: Supplement on Security Rights in Intellectual Property (2010).

WIPO

UNESCO–WIPO Tunis Model Copyright Law for Developing Countries, 1976.

Secondary sources

Adewopo, A., 2003. Trademark systems in Africa: A proposal for the harmonization of the ARIPO and the OAPI Agreements on Marks, *The Journal of World Intellectual Property*, 6, 473–484.

Akashi, Y., 1997. *An ASEAN Perspective on APEC.* The Helen Kellogg Institute for International Studies Working Paper 240. Notre Dame. Hellen Kellogg Institute for International Studies.

APEC, n.d. 'Intellectual Property Rights Experts Group'. Online. Available HTTP: <http://www.apec.org/Groups/Committee-on-Trade-and-Investment/Intellectual-Property-Rights-Experts-Group.aspx>, accessed 1 March 2015.

APEC, 2009. *Report on Survey of Plant Variety Protection Regimes in APEC Economies.* Singapore: APEC Policy Unit.

APEC, 2010. *The Report on APEC's 2010 Economies' Progress Towards the Bogor Goals.* Singapore: APEC Policy Unit.

APEC, 2011a. Ministerial Statement. *APEC Ministerial Meeting*, Honolulu 11 November 2011.

APEC, 2011b. Effective Practices for Addressing Unauthorized Camcording. 2011/AMM/014app05APEC, n.d. Intellectual Property Rights Experts Group. Online. Available HTTP: <http://www.apec.org/Groups/Committee-on-Trade-and-Investment/Intellectual-Property-Rights-Experts-Group.aspx>, accessed 1 March 2015.

ASEAN. 2014. *Thinking Globally, Prospering Regionally – ASEAN Economic Community 2015.* Jakarta: ASEAN Secretariat.

Askew, L.A., 1999. The CJEU, the ICJ and Intellectual Property: Is harmonization the key? *Tulsa Journal of Comparative and International Law* 7, 375–412.

Association of Research Libraries (ARL), (2012). *Code of Best Practices in Fair Use for Academic and Research Libraries.* Washington: ARL.

AWGIPC, n.d. The ASEAN IPR Action Plan 2016-2020. Online. Available HTTP: <http://www.aseanip.org/About-Us/ASEAN-IPR-Action-Plan-2016-2020>, accessed 1 March 2015.

Band, J., 2013. *A User Guide to the Marrakesh Treaty.* Online. Available HTTP: <http://www.librarycopyrightalliance.org/bm~doc/user-guide-marrakesh-treaty-0913final.pdf>, accessed 1 March 2015.

Band, J. and Jaszi, P., 2013. *Model Statute for Implementation of the Marrakesh Treaty to Facilitate Access to Published Works for Persons who are Blind, Visually Impaired, or Otherwise Print Disabled.* Online. Available HTTP: <http://infojustice.org/wp-content/uploads/2013/09/MODEL-STATUTE-FOR-MARRAKESH-IMPLEMENTATION.pdf>, accessed 1 March 2015.

Barraclough, E., 2004–2005. *ASEAN Scales Back IP Plans. Managing Intellectual Property. 1 December 2004.* Online. Available HTTP: <http://www.managingip.com/Article/1255213/News-focus-Asean-scales-back-IP-plans.html>, accessed 1 March 2015.

Beauchard, R. and Kodo, M.J.V., 2011. *'Can OHADA Increase Legal Certainty in Africa?'* World Bank Justice and Development Working Paper Series. Washington, DC: The World Bank.

Blakely, T.W., 2000. Beyond the international harmonization of trade mark law; The Community Trade Mark as a model of unitary transnational trade mark protection, *University of Pennsylvania Law Review*, 149(1), 313.

Bowman, E.E., 2003. Trademark distinctiveness in a multilingual context: Harmonization of the treatment of marks in the European Union and the United States, *San Diego International Law Journal*, 4, 514–542.

Dean, O.H., 1994a. A unified intellectual property law system for southern Africa. Part 1: International arrangements and European conventions, *Juta's Business Law*, 2(3), 111–114.

Dean, O.H., 1994b. A unified intellectual property law system for southern Africa. Part 2: Multinational registrations in Africa, *Juta's Business Law*, 2 (4), 165–169.

De Jonge, B., 2014. Plant Variety Protection in Sub-Saharan Africa: Balancing Commercial and Smallholder Farmers' Interests, *Journal of Politics and Law*, 7 (3), 100–111.

Dinwoodie, G.B., 2010. Editorial: Trade Mark Harmonisation: National Courts and the European Court of Justice, *International Review of Industrial Property and Copyright Law*, 41, 1–3.

Dinwoodie, G.B., 2013. The Europeanisation of trademark law. University of Oxford Legal Research Paper Series Paper No 54/2013 April 2013. Oxford. Online. Available HTTP: <http://ssrn.com/abstract=2260908>, accessed 1 March 2015.

EIFL, 2014. The Marrakesh Treaty: An EIFL Guide For Libraries. Online. Available HTTP: <http://www.eifl.net/news/marrakesh-treaty-eifl-guide-libraries>, accessed 1 March 2015.

Ekpere, J., 2003. 'African model law on the protection of the rights of local communities, farmers and breeders, and for the regulation of access to biological resources' in Nnadozie, K., et al (eds) *African Perspectives on Genetic Resources: A Handbook on Law, Policies and Institutions*, Washington DC: Environmental Law Institute, 275–286.

Elek, A., 1991. Asia Pacific Economic Cooperation (APEC). *Southeast Asian Affairs.* Singapore: Institute of Southeast Asian Studies.

Elek, A., 2005. 'Back to Canberra: founding APEC' in Elek, A. (ed.) *The Evolution of PECC: The First 25 Years.* Singapore: Pacific Economic Cooperation Council, (PECC) 65–92.

Endeshaw, A., 1999. Harmonization of Intellectual Property laws in ASEAN, *The Journal of World Intellectual Property*, 2, 3–23.

Endeshaw, A., 2004. 'The Momentum for review of TRIPS and harmonization of intellectual Property in ASEAN' in Antons, C., Blakeney, M. and Heath, C. (eds.) *Intellectual Property Harmonization Within ASEAN and APEC.* The Hague: Kluwer Law International, 139–158.

Endeshaw, A., 2010. *Intellectual Property in Asian Emerging Economies: Law and Policy in The Post-TRIPS Era.* Surrey and Burlington: Ashgate Publishing.

European Copyright Society, 2014. Letter to Commissioner for Digital Economy and Society. Unification of copyright law. 19 December 2014. Online. Available HTTP: <http://www.ivir.nl/syscontent/pdfs/78.pdf>, accessed 1 March 2015.

Faybayibo, B., 2008. A supranational African Union? Gazing into the crystal ball, *De Jure* 3, 493–503.

Fagbayibo B., 2009. Towards the harmonisation of laws in Africa: Is OHADA the way to go? *CILSA,* 309–322.

Fagbayibo, B., 2013. Common Problems Affecting Supranational Attempts in Africa: An Analytical Overview, *PER / PELJ* 16 (1), 32–69.

Faria, J.A.E., 2005. Model laws as an instrument of legal harmonisation: The experience of UNCITRAL. *ALRAESA Conference*, South Africa, 15–17 March. Online. Available HTTP: <http://www.justice.gov.za/alraesa/conferences/2005sa/papers/s5_faria2.pdf>, accessed 1 March 2015.

Faria, J.A.E., 2009. Future directions of legal harmonization and law reform: stormy seas or prosperous voyage? *Uniform Law Review,* 14, 5–34.

Feris, L., 2004. Protecting traditional knowledge in Africa: Considering African approaches, *African Human Rights Law Journal*, 4(2), 242–255.

Fernandez, F.V., 2010. 'The protection of intellectual property in MERCOSUR' in Filho, M.T.F., Lixinski, L. and Giupponi, M.B.O., eds. *The Law of Mercosur.* Oxford: Hart Publishing, 317–330.

Giupponi, M.B.O., 2010. 'Sources of Law in MERCOSUR' in Filho, M. T. F., Lixinski, L. and Giupponi, M.B.O. (eds.) *The Law of Mercosur.* Oxford: Hart Publishing, 57–71.

Goode, R., 1991. Reflections on the harmonization of Commercial Law, *Uniform Law Review*, os-19(1), 54–74.

Gottschalk, K., 2012. The African Union and its sub-regional Structures, *Journal of African Union Studies*, 1(1), 9–39.

Hicks, L.L. and Holbein, J.R., 1997. Convergence of national intellectual property norms in international trading agreements, *American University Journal of International Law & Policy*, 12(5), 770–814.

Hugenholtz, P.B., 2012. Harmonization or unification of EU Copyright Law, *Monash University Law Review* 38(1), 4–16.

IP Office Singapore, 2013. Asean IP Direct. Online. Available HTTP: <http://www.ipos.gov.sg/AboutIP/IPResources/UsefulLinks/RegionalOrganisations/ASEANIPDirect.aspx>, accessed 1 March 2015.

Jaszi, P. and Aufderheide, J., 2015. *Code of Best Practices in Fair Use for the Visual Arts.* Washington DC: College Art Association.

Kuanporth, J., 2013. 'Patents and the emerging markets of Asia: ASEAN and Thailand' in Abbott, F.M., Correa, C.M. and Drahos, P. (eds.) *Emerging Markets and the World Patent Order*. Cheltenham: Edward Elgar, 305–326.

Kur, A. and Drier, T., 2013. *European IP Law: Text, Cases & Materials*. Cheltenham: Edward Elgar.

Loewenheim, L., 1996. Harmonization and intellectual property in Europe, *Columbia Journal of European Law*, 2, 481–490.

Malamuc, A., 2010. 'Theories of regional integration and the origins of MERCOSUR', in Filho, M.T.F., Lixinski, L. and Giupponi, M.B.O., eds. *The Law of Mercosur*. Oxford: Hart Publishing, 9–27.

Mancuso, S., 2007. Trends on the harmonization of contract law in Africa, *Annual Survey of International & Comparative Law*, 13(1), 157–178.

Martor, B., et al., eds. 2002. *Business Law in Africa: OHADA and the Harmonization Process*. London and Sterling: Kogan Page Limited.

Max Planck Institute for Intellectual Property and Competition Law, 2011. 'Study on the Overall Functioning of the European Trade Mark Systems'. Online. Available HTTP: <http://ec.europa.eu/internal_market/indprop/docs/tm/20110308_allensbach-study_en.pdf>, accessed 1 March 2015.

Mercosur. n.d.a 'En pocas palabras'. Online. Available HTTP: <http://www.mercosur.int/innovaportal/v/3862/2/innova.front/en_pocas_palabras>, accessed 1 March 2015.

Mercosur. n.d.b. 'Preguntas frecuentes'. Online. Available HTTP: <http://www.mercosur.int/innovaportal/v/5837/2/innova.front/preguntas_frecuentes>, accessed 1 March 2015.

Mouloul, A., 2009. Understanding the Organisation for the harmonization of business laws in Africa (OHADA) 2 ed. Online. Available HTTP: <http://www.ohada.com/content/newsletters/1403/Comprendre-l-Ohada-en.pdf>, accessed 1 March 2015.

Mupangavanhu, Y., 2013. *The Regional Integration of African Trade Mark Laws: Challenges and Possibilities*. PhD Thesis. University of the Western Cape.

Mupangavanhu, Y., 2014. The integration of trade mark laws in the European Union: lessons for Africa? *South African IP Law Journal*, 2, 109–130.

Mupangavanhu, Y., 2015. African Union rising to the need for continental IP protection? The establishment of the Pan-African Intellectual Property Organization, *Journal of African Law*, 59, 1–24.

Murithi, T., 2005. *The African Union: Pan-Africanism, Peacebuilding and Development*. Aldershot, Hampshire: Ashgate.

Ndulo, M., 1997. 'The need for the harmonization of Trade Laws in the Southern Africa Development Community (SADC)' in Yusuf, A.A., (ed.) *African Yearbook of International Law*. The Netherlands: African Association of International Law, 195–225.

New, W., 2013. *BRICS Launch their own Plan for IP Co-operation; India Defends Itself.* IP Watch 27 November 2013. Online. Available HTTP: <http://www.ip-watch.org/2013/11/27/brics-launch-their-own-plan-for-ip-cooperation-india-defends-itself/>, accessed 1 March 2015.

New, W., 2015. *Top European Copyright Experts Urge Reform, Unification of Copyright*. IP Watch 5 January 2015. Online. Available HTTP: <http://www.ip-watch.org/2015/01/05/top-european-copyright-experts-urge-reform-unification-of-copyright/>, accessed 1 March 2015.

Ng, E.S.K., 2013. ASEAN IP harmonization: striking the delicate balance, *Pace International Law Review*, 25, 129–160.

Nkomo, M. and Olmos, B., 2013. 'The MERCOSUR-SACU Preferential Trade

Agreement: a step forward in South-South relations?' in du Pisani, A., Erasmus, G. and Hartzenberg, T., (eds.) *Monitoring Regional Integration in Southern Africa Yearbook 2012.* Stellenbosch: Trade Law Centre and the Konrad-Adenauer-Stiftung, 194–211.

OECD, 2013. Overview of development gaps in Southeast Asia: Gaps between ASEAN - 6 and CLM V countries. *In Southeast Asian Economic Outlook 2013: With Perspectives on China and India.* Paris: OECD Publishing, 241–290.

Olivier, G.C. and Olivier, M.E., 2004. Models of regional integration: The European Union and the African Union, *SA Public Law,* 19, 351–364.

Oppong, R.F., 2011. *Legal Aspects of Economic Integration in Africa.* Cambridge: Cambridge University Press.

Raciti, E.P., 1996. The harmonization of trademarks in the European Community: the harmonization directive and the community trademark, *Journal of the Patent and Trademark Office, Society* 78, 51–68.

Ratchlitz, R., 2014. Effective private law harmonisation: A comparative analysis of the EU Draft Regulation on Common European Sales Law and the OHADA Uniform Acts, *Journal of Comparative Law in Africa,* 47–65.

Ruse-Khan, H.G., 2009. Time for a paradigm shift? Exploring maximum standards in international intellectual property protection, *Trade, Law and Development,* 1(56), 56–102.

Shaw, T.M, Grant, J.A. and Cornelissen, S., 2011. 'Introduction and overview: the study of new regionalism(s) at the start of the second decade of the twenty-first century' in Shaw, T.M, Grant, J.A. and Cornelissen, S. (eds.) *The Ashgate Research Companion to Regionalisms.* Surrey and Burlington: Ashgate Publishing, 3–30.

Shumba, T., 2014. *Harmonising the Law of Sale in the Southern African Development Community (SADC): An Analysis of Selected Models.* PhD Thesis, Stellenbosch University.

Stack, A.J., 2008. *International Patent Law: Cooperation, Harmonization and an Institutional Analysis of WIPO and the WTO.* Thesis (SJD). University of Toronto.

Susani, N. 2010, 'Dispute settlement' in Filho, M.T.F., Lixinski, L. and Giupponi, M.B.O. (eds) *The Law of Mercosur.* Oxford: Hart Publishing, 73–85.

Sutton, M., 2007. Open regionalism and the Asia Pacific: implications for the rise of an East Asian Economic Community, *Ritsumeikan International Affairs,* 5, 133–152.

Taubman, A.S., 2004. 'Collective management of TRIPS: APEC, New Regionalism and intellectual property' in Antons, C., Blakeney, M. and Heath, C. (eds) *Intellectual Property Harmonisation within ASEAN and APEC.* The Netherlands: Kluwer Law International, 161–202.

Tino, E., 2013. 'The role of regional judiciaries in eastern and southern Africa' in du Pisani, A., Erasmus, G. and Hartzenberg, T. (eds) *Monitoring Regional Integration in Southern Africa Yearbook 2012.* Stellenbosch: Trade Law Centre and the Konrad-Adenauer-Stiftung, 140–174.

Tsheola , J., 2014. Groping in the dark with the 'non-places' BRICS: geopolitics of the emergence of an Empire or States racing to the bottom? *Mediterranean Journal of Social Sciences,* 5(25), 187–197.

UNECA SRO-EA, 2013. *Domestication and Mainstreaming of Regional Integration Processes Instruments and Decisions into National Policies, Legal and Regulatory Frameworks: Issues, Challenges and Opportunities – The Case of Uganda.* Kigali: UNECA SRO-EA.

Vanderbilt Law School, (2014). 'Daniel Gervais to serve as associate reporter of the American Law Institute's Restatement of Law Copyright'. 4 December 2014. Online. Available HTTP: <http://law.vanderbilt.edu/news/daniel-gervais-to-serve-as-associate-reporter-of-the-american-law-institute%E2%80%99s-restatement-of-law-copyright/>, accessed 14 February 2015.

WIPO-ILA Seminar on IP and Private International Law, Meeting Code S/IP/GE/15, 16 January 2015.

Woods, L. and Watson, L., 2014. 'Harmonisation' in Woods, L., Watson, P., and Steiner, J., 2014. *Steiner & Woods EU law.* 12th ed. Oxford: Oxford University Press, 341–360.

World Bank, 2012. *Agricultural Innovation Systems: An Investment Sourcebook*, Geneva: World Bank.

Zirnstein, E., 2005. 'Harmonization and unification of IP in the EU' in Vodov, Z. (ed.) *Intellectual Capital and Knowledge Management: Proceedings of the 5th International Conference of the Faculty of Management*, Koper, University of Primorska 18–20 November 2004. Koper: University of Primorska Faculty of Management, 293–308.

7 General conclusions

The discussion in previous chapters has shown that African states have embarked on a drive to harmonize their IP regimes either within the framework of a sub-regional IP organization or a REC. On a continental level, the AU is progressing towards the operationalization of PAIPO. The focal point of analysis of these developments is whether they serve individual states' public interest. For purposes of the discussion, the public interest has been characterized as a complex, but useful, concept that seeks to identify a state's socio-economic and human rights or constitutional priorities and then to use them as a guide for policy, legislative and state action decisions. Whilst African states share a lot of commonalities, they are also incredibly diverse, which mitigates against any attempt to coin 'one size fits all' solutions or systems. The adoption of the WIPO DA was motivated by the need to appropriately nuance IP systems in order to meet the needs of such diversity in Africa, and elsewhere, in both the global north and south. African states, together with other developing countries, were instrumental in the adoption of the WIPO DA. Therefore, a litmus test of their commitment and drive is the assessment of whether their harmonization efforts carry forward that vision to attain fine-tuned IP systems.

To conduct a meaningful assessment or to make cogent arguments, conceptualizations of the public interest have to be nuanced by national contexts and IP right. Therefore Chapter 1 focused on TRIPS flexibilities, patents and access to medicines. It found that significant progress has been made by EAC, ECOWAS and SADC towards giving policy direction to their member states on how to domesticate TRIPS flexibilities. In many instances African states' existing patent legislation does not adequately serve the public interest by incorporating flexibilities that would enable more effective access to pharmaceuticals. Rectifying this will require legislative amendments. In response to this need, EAC and ECOWAS have provided legislative guidance through the guidelines and protocols that accompany their TRIPS Policies.

Another important step towards legislative reform is policy realignment. If the policy framework is crafted appropriately, the legislative endeavor is considerably aided by clear policy goals, strategies and timelines. The policy then serves as a blueprint for law-makers. IP is inherently cross-cutting and many state and non-state actors are involved in its development and implementation. IP policies therefore also ensure coherence across different sectors and in relevant government departments. Hence Chapter 2's focus on IP policies in Africa. This chapter mapped IP policy design initiatives across the continent and commented briefly on existing policies. It found that there has been a flurry of IP policy related activity with ten states having already adopted IP policies and at least 19 others currently formulating policies. However, there is a dearth of information and in some cases adopted policies are not publicly available, and there is limited or no information at all about the policy formulation process in other instances.

In most cases, policies have been formulated, or are being formulated, with technical assistance from WIPO. Chapter 2 accordingly discussed the import of technical assistance and argued that it has a significant impact on the content and quality of the resulting national IP policy. Therefore, it is important that the technical assistance be infused with public interest considerations and that it equips states to craft appropriate policies. Unsurprisingly, technical assistance is one of the focal areas of the WIPO DA. The chapter outlined a WIPO DA IP policy project, namely Project DA_10_05, which resulted in the creation and publication of an IP policy formulation toolkit. This project was piloted in six countries, three of which are in Africa. The chapter also considered the WIPO Framework for Developing National IP Strategies for Innovation project, which is located outside the DACD and appears to be still ongoing. Articulation between these two projects is required. Based on its content and coverage, the completed WIPO DA project seems to have made a concerted effort to enable states to craft good IP policies.

In tandem with these WIPO interventions, RECs have also turned their attention to including IP on their agendas. For instance, as mentioned above, the EAC and ECOWAS have adopted TRIPS policies that seek to guide their member states in their domestication of TRIPS flexibilities. COMESA has a general IP policy that is not limited to TRIPS flexibilities. Indeed, it does not engage with them in a meaningful way. These three policies will eventually cross-pollinate through the T-FTA and the C-FTA. The T-FTA's agreement, in particular its propsoed Annex 9, deals with IP. The T-FTA was launched in June 2015. Soon thereafter the TRIPS flexibilities aspect will be consolidated when the T-FTA merges with ECOWAS as the next move towards the C-FTA, which ultimately becomes the AEC.

Chapter 3 considered the IP related legal instruments that have been adopted by the continent's leading RECs, namely COMESA, EAC, ECOWAS and SADC. All of these RECs expressly include IP as part of their integration agenda in their constitutive treaties or protocols. However, only the EAC has attempted to enact an IP specific instrument, namely the Anti-Counterfeit Bill, 2010 which ultimately did not eventuate. This Bill was preceded by a draft policy on Anti-Counterfeiting, Anti-Piracy and other Intellectual Property Rights Violations, 2009. Both the policy and bill fell short of public interest expectations primarily because they were TRIPS-plus. Elements of the policy and bill that made it into Kenyan legislation were struck down by a High Court on account of their negative impact on the availability of generics in the country, which would compromise the constitutional rights to life, dignity and health.

ARIPO and OAPI have to date focused on securing their member states' technical TRIPS compliance, rather than pursuing the attainment of public interest goals through domesticating flexibilities. Indeed, OAPI led its LDC members to the early adoption of TRIPS standards during the subsistence of relevant transition periods. As discussed in Chapter 1, this was a very unfortunate route to take. ARIPO has not unified IP law in the same way that OAPI has, so its member states still have national policy and legislative space within which to calibrate their IP systems. However, even in its limited and largely administrative function, ARIPO could do more to assist its member states to adjust their IP laws in a way that allows them to pursue public interest goals. For instance, the Harare Protocol could be amended in order to provide for pre- and post-grant patent opposition proceedings.

Another sore point is that both ARIPO and OAPI have chosen to adopt the UPOV 91 model of protection of plant varieties and eschewed the more context-sensitive approach of the AU's African Model Legislation for the Protection of the Rights of Local Communities, Farmers and Breeders, and for the Regulation of Access to Biological Resources, 2000. The latter approach would have been more suitable for the continent. On the other hand, ARIPO has done well to take the lead on providing for the *sui generis* protection of TK through its Swakopmund Protocol, which came into force in May 2015.

The creation of PAIPO raises real concerns about draining the continent's resources to replicate already fulfilled functions or to create a structure for policy debate when informal means seem to be serving the continent well. The need to articulate African positions on important IP policy matters is indisputable. What is questionable is the need to create a new organization when it is clear that the African Group is already effectively mobilizing and winning significant victories on global platforms. However, as the decision to create the organization has been made by the AU, it is important to engage with its future work.

PAIPO's future role has to be scrutinized regarding its promotion, or otherwise, of individual states' ability to further their public interest goals. In this regard the initial failure of the 2012 Draft PAIPO Statute to refer to TRIPS flexibilities, the WTO Doha Declaration on the TRIPS Agreement and Public Health and other important decisions such as the Global Strategy and Plan of Action on Public Health, Innovation and IP, was of great concern. It signaled a lack of appreciation of the gains that had been made on the global level to create policy space for states to fine-tune their IP systems. A more recent iteration of the draft statute now refers to some, but not all, of these decisions and documents. It could very well be that in practice, PAIPO's work will be infused with public interest considerations due to its interaction with RECs and leading thinkers amongst the African group, but that remains to be seen. In addition to policy concerns, several organizational aspects pertaining to the acquisition of membership, co-operation and overlapping mandates between PAIPO, ARIPO and OAPI also need to be addressed.

Once operationalized, PAIPO will turn to providing policy direction and to leading the IP harmonization efforts of AU member states. There are various models that it could employ, which have been canvassed in Chapter 6. It is suggested that the most appropriate approach would be first seek IP co-operation following the ASEAN, APEC or BRICS model. This model is decidedly light on normative content and focuses on practical or administrative co-operation that seeks to boost IP office capacity and efficiency. Currently the RECs, ARIPO and OAPI are working to achieve this on the sub-regional level and PAIPO's role would be to extend the reach of these efforts to continental level. Once this level of co-operation is achieved, perhaps normative or substantive harmonization may be sought, following either the incremental EU or MERCOSUR approach. This would entail employing a variety of hard and soft-law approaches as appropriate. The AU has already engaged in IP harmonization through soft law by its Model Law on the Protection of the Rights of Local Communities, Farmers and Breeders, and for the Regulation of Access to Biological Resources, 2000. It has not yet ventured into a hard-law approach but it is clear from the PAIPO statute, that it is intended for PAIPO to set binding IP standards. The key hindrance to such an endeavor would be OAPI's unification of certain TRIPS-plus standards amongst its member states. It would be inappropriate to seek to advise the rest of Africa to follow that lead as much as it is improbable that OAPI member states would abandon their current position. However, perhaps it would be possible to harmonize certain aspects of IP where there is some substantive consensus.

For example, trademark law would be easier to harmonize than patent law. Indeed, it has been suggested that PAIPO should consider crafting a trademark directive and setting up the necessary continental infrastructure to facilitate its implementation. Another possible area of convergence would be in relation to the protection of traditional knowledge. ARIPO has chosen the *sui generis* approach via its Swakopmund Protocol, but OAPI is yet to regulate this area. Whatever IP right PAIPO decides to tackle first, it cannot be emphasized enough that any hard-law venture has to ensure that the resultant legal instrument provides for the necessary policy space to enable national calibration. Just as there is no global 'one size fits all', there is no African 'one size fits all.'

Index

Abbott, F.M. 4, 19
Abdel Latif, A. 45
access benefit sharing (ABS) 89, 156
access to knowledge 52, 81, 90
access to medicines 51, 60, 90, 163, 176; *see also* pharmaceutical industry
Adelman, I. 11
Adelphi Charter 6
Adewopo, A. 7, 8, 98, 110, 121, 126, 166
Afadameh-Adeyemi, A. 70, 71
African Economic Community (AEC) 1, 51, 84, 160, 177; African Union and 73–6
African Group 10, 127, 135, 178
African Intellectual Property Organization (*Organisation Africaine de la Propriété Intellectuelle*, OAPI) 2, 3, 58, 68–9, 97, 109–10, 121, 145, 146, 167, 179; Administrative Council 110–11, 112; Bangui Agreement 3, 20, 110, 112–21, 136, 154, 164; Directorate General 112; High Commission of Appeal 111–12, 115; industrial designs 120; main objective 110; merger with ARIPO 97, 121–2, 136; new varieties of plants 113, 120–1, 155, 178; OHADA 164, 165; PAIPO, ARIPO and 126, 128, 129–30, 133, 134–8, 140, 166; patents 113–16; trademarks and service marks 118–20, 121; TRIPS flexibilities 20, 23, 24, 25, 178; utility models 116–18
African Ministerial Conference on Science and Technology (AMCOST) 127, 129, 130, 138
African Regional IP Organization (ARIPO) 2, 3, 58, 68–9, 97, 98–9, 121–2, 145, 154; Administrative Council 99–101; Banjul Protocol on Marks (1993) 101, 105–7, 120; Board of Appeal 100–1, 103, 105, 106; committees 101; Council of Ministers 99, 100, 107–8; Draft PVP Protocol 102, 107–9, 120, 155, 178; Harare Protocol 28, 101, 102–5, 113, 114, 116, 121, 178; IP policy of Rwanda and 55–6; legislative guide 156; merger with OAPI 97, 121–2, 136; objectives 98–9; PAIPO, OAPI and 126, 128, 129–30, 133, 134–8, 140, 166; regulatory instruments 101–9; Secretariat 100; Swakopmund Protocol (2010) 101–2, 121, 154, 178, 179; TRIPS flexibilities 22, 28
African Union (AU) 1, 2, 11, 21, 51, 139–40, 155, 162, 178; AEC and 73–6; ARIPO and 98, 109, 128, 129–30, 134–8, 140; diversity 165; enforcement 166–7; harmonization 145, 165, 166; historical overview of efforts to establish PAIPO 126–31; intergovernmental 161; legal nature of PAIPO 131–2; OAPI and 128, 129, 130, 134–8, 140; PAIPO and Constitutive Act of 134; plant varieties 109, 121, 178
agriculture 81; chemicals 15; farmers' rights 109
AIDS/HIV 18, 25
Akashi, Y. 148
Akokpari, J. 2, 69, 70, 71
Aleman, M. 104
Algeria 11, 98; IP policy 56–7; technical assistance 48, 50, 56–7
alliances 88
American Law Institute (ALI) 154, 157
Anand, S. 11
Andemariam, S.W. 19
Anderson, J.E. 40
Angola 83, 98; T-FTA 86

anti-competitive activities 16, 28, 29
APEC (Asia-Pacific Economic Cooperation) 148–51, 166
appeals 161; ARIPO 100–1, 103, 105, 106; OAPI: High Commission of Appeal 111–12, 115
Argentina 12, 161, 162
ARIPO *see* African Regional IP Organization
Armstrong, C. 1
Arndt, H.W. 11
Asante, S.K.B. 68, 70, 71
ASEAN (Association of South East Asian Nations) 146–8, 165
Askew, L.A. 160
audit 48, 59, 88–9, 90
Australia 148
Avafia, T. 7

Baker, B. 15, 129, 136, 139
Balassa, B.A. 71, 72
Band, J. 156
Bangui Agreement (1977) 3, 20, 110, 112–21, 136, 154, 164
Banjul Protocol on Marks (1993) 101, 105–7, 120
Bannenberg, W. 30
Barraclough, E. 147
Barry, S. 57
Beauchard, R. 164
Belohlavek, A.J. 5
benchmarking 48, 49, 128
Benin 82, 109, 110, 164
Berger, M. 21
Berne Convention 3, 19, 147
bilateral trade agreements 46
biodiversity 55, 58, 156
Biodiversity-related Access and Benefit-sharing Agreements 156
biopiracy 109
biotechnology 113, 114, 115
Blakely, T.W. 160
Blakeney, M. 14, 47, 80, 81, 134, 137, 140
Boahen, A.A. 1
Bolar exceptions 20, 26, 28, 30
Bolivia 161, 162
Boolell, A. 55
Botswana 83, 98, 101; ARIPO: trademarks 106; IP policy 57; TRIPS flexibilities 24, 26, 31
Box, R.C. 5
Brazil 12, 151–2, 161, 162
BRICS 151–2, 162, 166
Broadman, H.G. 1
BruneiDarussalam 146, 148
Burkina Faso 82, 109, 110, 164
Burundi 51, 78, 79, 86, 98; IP policy 57; TRIPS patent-related flexibilities 23, 24, 26

C-FTA (Continental Free Trade Area) 140, 177
Cambodia 146
Cameroon 109, 110, 164
Canada 19, 25, 148
capabilities approach 11
Cape Verde 82; TRIPS patent-related flexibilities 24, 25
Caribbean region 48, 159
Central African Republic 109, 110, 164; IP policy 57
Chad 109, 110, 164; IP policy 57
Chang, H-J. 88
Chatema, Z. 55
Chile 148, 161, 162
China 148, 151–2; State Intellectual Property Office (SIPO) 58
Chinese Taipei 148
Chirambo, M.H. 97, 98, 99
civic society 44, 46
civil law jurisdictions 79, 136
civil society organizations (CSOs) 109
co-operation schemes, IP 145, 146, 165–6; APEC 148–51, 166; ASEAN 146–8, 165; BRICS 151–2, 166
collective management organizations (CMOs) 89
collective marks 118
Collins, R.O. 1
Colombia 161
colonization 1, 3, 43, 77, 165
common law jurisdictions 79, 136
Common Market for Eastern and Southern Africa (COMESA) 2, 69, 75, 78, 84, 140, 167; IP policy 51–2, 79, 177; IP regulatory framework 78–9; *locus standi* 159; relationship between community laws and national laws 77, 78; T-FTA (Tripartite Free Trade Area) 84, 86–90, 140, 177
common markets 71, 72, 79, 83, 159, 162
Comoros 51, 78, 86, 109, 164
competition policy 85
compulsory licensing 7, 16, 18–19, 25, 28–9; Bangui Agreement 115; Harare Protocol 103

computer programs 113
concept of region 2
conflict of laws 154
consent, prior informed 89
constitutions 9, 77, 82
Continental Free Trade Area (C-FTA) 140, 177
Convention on the Grant of European Patents (EPC) 113
copyright 7; access to learning materials 9; Algeria 56–7; ARIPO 101; COMESA 52, 79; EU 146; MERCOSUR 162, 163; T-FTA 88–9, 90; TRIPS flexibilities 28; Tunisia 56; UNESCO–WIPO Tunis Model Copyright Law for Developing Countries (1976) 4, 155; US restatement of law 157
Correa, C.M. 16, 17, 46
Côte d'Ivoire 82, 109, 110, 164
counterfeiting 80–2, 90, 139, 150, 151, 177
criminal law 5, 115–16, 120
Cronje, J.B. 86
Cullet, P. 120, 121
customs unions (CUs) 71–2, 78, 79, 83, 84, 162

damages 16
de Beer, J. 12, 13, 43, 138, 139
De Jonge, B. 108, 109, 155
de Wet, P. 9
Dean, O.H. 121, 126, 166
Deere, C. 14, 20, 21, 44, 45, 46
Deere-Birkbeck, C. 9, 40, 44, 48, 50, 53
definitions: economic development 11; governance 42–3; plan 41; policy design 42; public policy 40; strategy 41; utility model 104, 116
Democratic Republic of the Congo (DRC) 26, 51, 78, 83, 86, 164
designs: ARIPO and industrial 98, 101, 102–3, 105; COMESA 78; EU 146, 160; MERCOSUR and industrial 162–3; OAPI and industrial 120
development integration 72–3
Dinwoodie, G.B. 153, 160
direct applicability 3, 76–7, 78, 112, 154, 164
discrimination 72
diversity and need for flexible IP systems 10–11
Djibouti 51, 78, 86
Dlamini, T. 59
Doha Declaration on TRIPS Agreement and Public Health 8, 139, 178
Doha Development Agenda 8
Dominican Republic 47–8
Dountio, J. 127
Draper, P. 84
Dreyfuss, R.C. 4, 8, 13
du Plessis, E. 3
dualism 77
Dye, T. 5, 40

East African Community (EAC) 2, 51, 69, 73, 75, 79, 84, 140, 164, 167, 177; IP regulatory framework 79–82; *locus standi* 159; private international law 154; relationship between community laws and national laws 77, 78; supremacy of community laws 77; T-FTA (Tripartite Free Trade Area) 84, 86–90, 140; TRIPS flexibilities 22–3, 24, 25, 26–9, 176, 177
East, Central and Southern Africa Health Community (ECSA-HC) 22
Economic Community of West African States (ECOWAS) 2, 51, 69, 75, 82–3, 140, 164; IP Regulatory Framework 83; relationship between community laws and national laws 77, 78; TRIPS flexibilities 22–3, 24, 25, 26, 29–30, 176, 177
economic development 84, 127; definition of 11; OAPI's LDCs: early adoption of TRIPS standards and 20–1
economic unions 71, 72
economies of scale 121
Ecuador 161
education 9, 52, 55
Egbuonu, K. 59, 129, 139
Egypt 31, 51, 78, 86, 98
Ekpere, J. 155
Elek, A. 148
emergencies, national 25, 28
employees 117–18
Endeshaw, A. 146
Equatorial Guinea 109, 164
Erasmus, G. 86
Eritrea 51, 78, 98; T-FTA 86
Ethiopia 51, 78, 98
European Union (EU) 80, 145–6, 147, 158, 167; harmonization 145–6, 160–1, 166; Regulations 154, 160
ever-greening 17, 23, 30

expertise 45; technical assistance *see separate entry*

Fagbayibo, B. 161, 165
Faria, J.A.E. 153, 155, 158, 164
farmers' rights 109
Feris, L. 109, 155
Fernandez, F.V. 162, 163
flexible IP systems, need for 10–11
food security 80, 167
foreign direct investment (FDI) 13, 88
Frankel, S. 46
free trade areas 71, 75, 78, 83–4; Tripartite Free Trade Area (T-FTA) 84, 86–90, 140, 177
Friedrich, C.J. 5

Gabon 109, 110, 164
The Gambia 82, 98; IP policy 57; TRIPS patent-related flexibilities 24, 25
Gana, R.L. 8
Gathii, J.T. 1, 2, 51, 68, 78, 79, 83, 84
Gazaro, W.R. 120
genetic resources (GR) 27, 57, 58, 80, 89, 104, 116
geographical indications 97, 113, 148, 150
Gervais, D. 8
Ghana 3, 41–2, 82, 98, 101, 155; IP policy 53–4; TRIPS patent-related flexibilities 23, 24, 25, 26
Giupponi, M.B.O. 162
globalization 46
Goode, R. 153, 154
Gottschalk, K. 68, 69, 73, 75, 160
governance, definition of 42–3
Guinea 82, 109, 164
Guinea Bissau 82, 109, 164
Guyane 161

Haas, E. 70
Harare Protocol 28, 101, 102–5, 113, 114, 116, 121, 178
harmonization 2, 72, 90, 99, 128, 133, 134, 145–6, 153, 166; advantages of 157–8; co-operation first 148; contractual 156; disadvantages of 158–60; explanatory means 155–6; legislative means 154–5; lessons from existing efforts 160–4, 178–9; methods of 153–7
Harris, D.P. 8
Hartzenberg, T. 71, 83
health, right to 9, 82, 177
Held, V. 5
Helfer, L. 9
Heywood, M. 18
Hicks, L.L. 162
history of national IP laws 2–5
HIV/AIDS 18, 25
Ho, L.S. 5
Hogwood, B.W. 5, 40
Hong Kong 148
Hopeson, D. 53
Howlett, M. 41, 42–3
Hugenholtz, P.B. 146, 158, 159, 160
Human Development Index (HDI) 11
human rights 4, 9, 139; health, right to 9, 82, 177; life, right to 82, 177

India 151–2
indigenous knowledge *see* traditional knowledge
Indonesia 146, 148
industrial property: ARIPO 98, 101, 102–3, 105, 135, 136; COMESA 78–9; ECOWAS 83; MERCOSUR 162–3; OAPI 110, 111, 112, 114, 120, 121, 135, 136; PAIPO 126, 134, 135, 136; T-FTA 90
information and communications technology (ICT) 89
information sharing: ARIPO 98; BRICS 151; COMESA 78; EAC 80; PAIPO 127, 128
Innovative Pharmaceutical Association of South Africa (IPASA) 9
insider governance 45
inter-governmental organizations (IGOs) 22, 161
inter-regionalism 153
International Union for the Protection of New Varieties of Plants (UPOV) 107–8, 120–1, 155, 178

Jain, T.R. 11
Japan 147, 148; Patent Office (JPO) 58
jargon 44
Jaszi, P. 156
Jensen, C.S. 73
Jensen, E. 1
joint ventures 88, 89
Joireman, S.F. 3

Kahn, T. 9
Kanu, O. 59
Kapczynski, A. 8, 14

Karjiker, S. 129, 139
Kawooya, D. 129, 139
Kenya 22, 51, 78, 79, 86, 98, 101; anti-counterfeit legislation 81–2, 177; direct applicability of community laws 76; IP policy 57; TRIPS patent-related flexibilities 23, 24, 26, 29
Kilic, B. 11
Kolbeck, B. 1, 75
Kongolo, T. 1, 3, 4, 8, 98, 104, 107, 110, 112, 121, 126, 127, 129, 136
Korea 148
Kouassi, R.N. 68, 73, 74, 75
Kuanporth, J. 147, 148
Kur, A. 146, 160, 161

Lao People's Democratic Republic (Lao PDR/ Laos) 146
least developed countries (LDCs) 4, 11, 14, 22, 162; EAC 81; technical assistance 46–7, 48, 60; TRIPS flexibilities 15, 20–1, 24, 60, 121, 178
Lee, M. 68, 70, 71, 72
Lesotho 22, 83, 98; ARIPO: trademarks 106; IP policy 57; TRIPS patent-related flexibilities 26, 30
Liberia 82, 98, 101; ARIPO: trademarks 106; IP policy 54–5; TRIPS patent-related flexibilities 23, 24, 25, 26
Libya 11, 51, 78, 98; T-FTA 86
licensing 88, 89; compulsory 7, 16, 18–19, 25, 28–9, 103, 115
life, right to 82, 177
lobbying 9
locus standi 159
Loewenheim, L. 160
Loren, L.P. 9

Madagascar 51, 78, 83; IP policy 57; TRIPS patent-related flexibilities 24, 26
Magogo, T.D.B. 80
Maksus, K.K. 13
Malamuc, A. 162
Malawi 22, 51, 78, 83, 86, 98, 101; ARIPO: trademarks 106; IP policy 55; TRIPS patent-related flexibilities 24
Malaysia 109, 146, 148
Mali 82, 109, 164; IP policy 58; technical assistance 48
malleable harmonization models 2
Mancuso, S. 165
market integration 71–2, 73
Martor, B. 164
Matambalya, F.A.S.T. 68
Matthews, D. 7
Matthias, J.H. 68
Mauritania 109, 110
Mauritius 11, 22, 51, 78, 83, 98; IP policy 55; TRIPS flexibilities 24, 26, 31
May, C. 12, 135
medicines *see* pharmaceutical industry
MERCOSUR 145, 161–4, 166
Merso, F. 11
Mexico 148, 161
micro-organisms: patents 103, 115; utility models 116
Moldova 47–8
monetary union 78, 79, 83
Mongolia 47–8
monism 77, 162
Motsoeneng, T. 9
Mould Iddrisu, B. 53
Mouloul, A. 164
Moyo, C. 129, 133, 139
Mozambique 83, 98; IP policy 55; TRIPS patent-related flexibilities 24, 26
Mukisa, R. 74
Mupangavanhu, Y. 121, 126, 139, 140, 166, 167
Musungu, S.F. 14, 17, 18, 19, 20, 24, 25, 26, 30, 81, 115, 136, 137
Mutai, H.K. 70, 71, 72, 73, 74, 75, 76
Mutharika, B. 71
Mwanza, W. 69, 80, 81, 86
Myanmar 146

Namibia 83, 86, 98; ARIPO: trademarks 106; TRIPS patent-related flexibilities 24, 26
national defense 115, 117
Ncube, C.B. 6, 9, 19, 52, 53, 59, 88, 129, 136, 139, 140
Ndulo, B.J. 4
Ndulo, M. 153, 157
Neba, A. 55
neo-colonialism 4
neo-functional integration 73
Netanel, N.W. 12, 13, 14, 45
New Partnership for Africa's Development (NEPAD) 74, 127
New, W. 146, 151
New Zealand 148, 161
Ng, E.S.K. 146, 147
Ng'ong'ola, C. 83
Ngwenya, S. 69, 83, 86, 140
Niger 82, 109, 110, 164

Nigeria 69, 82, 98; IP policy 58; TRIPS patent-related flexibilities 23, 24, 25, 26
Nkomo, M. 19, 68, 69, 162
non-discrimination 72
Nwauche, E. 98, 110, 111, 114
Nzomo, V. 57

OAPI (*Organisation Africaine de la Propriété Intellectuelle*) 2, 3, 58, 68–9, 97, 109–10, 121, 145, 146, 167, 179; Administrative Council 110–11, 112; Bangui Agreement 3, 20, 110, 112–21, 136, 154, 164; Directorate General 112; High Commission of Appeal 111–12, 115; industrial designs 120; main objective 110; merger with ARIPO 97, 121–2, 136; new varieties of plants 113, 120–1, 155, 178; OHADA 164, 165; PAIPO, ARIPO and 126, 128, 129–30, 133, 134–8, 140, 166; patents 113–16; trademarks and service marks 118–20, 121; TRIPS flexibilities 20, 23, 24, 25, 178; utility models 116–18
Okediji, R.L. 3, 4, 5, 6, 9, 13
Oldham, G. 127
Olivier, D. 129, 139
Olivier, G. 69
Olowu, D. 42
Oppong, R.F. 68, 75, 76, 77, 78, 158–9
Organization of African Unity (OAU) 73–4
Organization for the Harmonization of Business Laws in Africa (OHADA) 2, 146, 164–5, 167
Osiemo, O. 68
Oslington, P. 72
Ostergaard, T. 70, 71, 72, 73
Outterson, K. 19
overview and history of national IP laws 2–5
Owoeye, O.A. 25
Oyejide, A. 68

Pan-African IP Organisation (PAIPO) 11, 14, 69, 97, 126–40, 145, 165–6, 178–9; functions of 134; historical overview of AU's efforts to establish 126–31; legal nature of 131–3; objectives 133–4; organizational issues (PAIPO, OAPI and ARIPO) 134–8, 166; organs of 134; overlapping mandates 135–7; policy imperatives 139; relationship between PAIPO, ARIPO and OAPI 138
Papua New Guinea 148
Paraguay 161, 162
parallel imports 16, 18, 24; Bangui Agreement 115
Paris Convention 3, 119, 147
Park, C. 17
Patent Cooperation Treaty (PCT) 104, 147, 148
patents 6, 7, 179; access to medicines 9; ARIPO 28, 98, 101, 102–4, 121; capture of national IP policy 9–10; COMESA 78; EU 146, 160–1; exclusions 113–14, 121; MERCOSUR 162, 163; OAPI 113–16, 121; TRIPS flexibilities 15, 16–20, 21–31, 157
Perdikis, N. 68, 71, 72
Peru 148, 161
pharmaceutical industry 9; access to medicines 51, 60, 90, 163, 176; Bangui Agreement 115; ever-greening 17, 23, 30; generic products 20, 24, 25, 28, 30, 82, 177; limited manufacturing capacity 19, 28, 30; technical assistance 47; TRIPS flexibilities 15, 16, 17, 18–20, 21–31
Philippines 109, 146, 148
piracy 80–1, 90, 139, 150, 151, 177; biopiracy 109
plan, definition of 41
plants 56, 58; APEC 150; ARIPO: Draft PVP Protocol 102, 107–9, 120, 155, 178; ARIPO: Harare Protocol 114; EU 146; OAPI 113, 120–1, 155, 178; Plant Breeders' Rights (PBR) 108–9; SADC 155
policy design: definition of 42; factors affecting IP 44–6
policy frameworks, IP 176–7; country profiles 52–60; expertise 45; factors affecting IP policy design 44–6; importance of IP policies 43–4; REC IP policies 51–2; technical assistance 43–4, 46–51; terminology 40–3
private international law 154
public engagement 44
public health 6, 8, 46, 80, 81, 115, 117, 139; health, right to 9, 82, 177; TRIPS flexibilities 16, 23, 25, 29, 82, 157; *see also* pharmaceutical industry
public interest 5–6, 16, 25, 45, 46, 103, 121, 139, 176, 177, 178; global 6–8; national 8–10; OHADA 165

public policy 5, 40; exclusion: contrary to morality or 113, 117; policy frameworks, IP *see separate entry*
Pugatch, M.P. 44, 46

Rachlitz, R. 2
Raciti, E.P. 160
Rahmatian, A. 4, 7
Regional Economic Communities (RECs) 1–2, 22, 51, 60, 68–9, 90, 127, 156, 157, 177; ARIPO 121; AU and AEC 73–6; COMESA *see* Common Market for Eastern and Southern Africa; concurrent membership 84; direct applicability 76–7, 78; direct effect 76, 77; EAC *see* East African Community; ECOWAS *see* Economic Community of West African States; PAIPO 128, 133, 137, 139, 140, 178; relationship between community laws and national laws 76–8; SADC *see* Southern African Development Community; theories of regionalism 69–73
Regional Protocol on Health-Related WTO-TRIPS Flexibilities 29, 82
Reichman, J. 137
Republic of Congo 109, 110
research and experimentation exception 20, 26, 27, 30
restatements of law 157
Rodrigues Jr, E.B. 8
Ruse-Khan, H.G. 154
Russia 148
Rwanda 51, 78, 79, 86, 98; direct applicability of community laws 76–7; IP policy 55–6; TRIPS flexibilities 19, 23, 24, 25, 26, 29, 31

SACU (Southern African Customs Union) 73, 84, 162
SADC *see* Southern African Development Community
Saez, C. 109
Salmon, P. 46
Samuelson, P. 9
Sandrey, R. 84
Sao Tome and Principe 58, 98
Schonwetter, T. 59
Schubert, G. 5
Seleti, Y. 59
Sell, S.K. 12, 13
Sen, A. 11
Senegal 31, 82, 109, 110, 164; IP policy 56
service marks 118–20
Seuba, X. 4
Seychelles 11, 22, 51, 78, 83, 85, 86, 98; IP policy 56; TRIPS patent-related flexibilities 23
Shabalala, D. 10, 135
Shaw, T.M. 151
Shelley, T. 1
Shumba, T. 154, 160
Sibanda, M. 25
Sierra Leone 82, 98; IP policy 59; TRIPS patent-related flexibilities 24, 25
Simon, C.A. 40
Singapore 146, 148
small and medium enterprises (SMEs) 48
Smith, K.B. 5
soft law 128, 153, 155, 158, 159–60, 166, 179
Somalia 98, 102
Sorauf, F. 5
South Africa 8, 18, 69, 70, 83, 98, 151–2, 162; Department of Science and Technology (DST) 59, 127; IP policy 59; patents: capture of national IP policy 9; TRIPS patent-related flexibilities 24, 26
Southern African Customs Union (SACU) 73, 84, 162
Southern African Development Community (SADC) 2, 69, 70, 75, 83–4, 154, 159; plant varieties 155; regulatory instruments 84–5; relationship between community laws and national laws 77–8; T-FTA (Tripartite Free Trade Area) 84, 86–90, 140, 177; Tribunal 77–8, 167; TRIPS flexibilities 20, 22, 22–3, 24, 25, 26, 30–1, 176
standard contractual terms 156, 158
Storing, H.J. 5
strategy, definition of 41
Sudan 51, 78, 86, 98, 101
supranational organization 161
Suriname 161
Susani, N. 163, 164
sustainable development 139
Sutton, M. 148
Swakopmund Protocol (2010) 101–2, 121, 154, 178, 179
Swaziland 22, 51, 78, 83, 86, 98; ARIPO: trademarks 106; IP policy 59; TRIPS patent-related flexibilities 26
Switzerland 53
Sykes, S. 41

T-FTA (Tripartite Free Trade Area) 84, 86–90, 140, 177
Tanzania 22, 79, 83, 86, 98, 101; anti-counterfeiting legislation 82; ARIPO: trademarks 106; direct applicability of community laws 76–7; IP policy 59–60; technical assistance 47–8, 49; TRIPS patent-related flexibilities 23, 24, 26, 29; two legal systems 23, 79
Taubman, A.S. 148, 150, 151
technical assistance: ARIPO 121; PAIPO 128; WIPO 43–4, 45, 46, 47–51, 52, 53, 54, 55, 56–7, 59, 60, 98, 177; *see also* United Nations
technology transfer 7, 13, 58, 83, 88, 150
Thailand 146, 148
Thompson, B. 74
time limits: ARIPO: Draft PVP Protocol 108; Bangui Agreement 116, 117, 119–20; Banjul Protocol 106, 107; compulsory licenses 28; Harare Protocol 28, 102, 103, 104, 105; OAPI patents 114; T-FTA 86; TRIPS implementation 4, 15, 20–1, 27, 121, 178; Zimbabwe: compulsory licenses 25
Tino, E. 159, 167
Tita, A.N. 118
Togolese Republic 82, 109, 164; IP policy 60
trademarks 7, 166, 179; ARIPO 98, 101, 105–7, 120, 121; ASEAN 148; COMESA 78; EU 146, 160; MERCOSUR 162; OAPI 118–20, 121; TRIPS flexibilities 24, 28
traditional knowledge (TK) 6, 27, 55, 56, 57, 58, 59, 80, 89, 97, 155, 179; ARIPO: Swakopmund Protocol (2010) 101–2, 121, 154, 178, 179; ASEAN 148
Tripartite Free Trade Area (T-FTA) 84, 86–90, 140, 177
TRIPS (Trade-Related Aspects of Intellectual Property Rights) Agreement 4, 43, 46, 82, 85, 110, 154–5, 176, 177; APEC 148–9; ASEAN 146, 147; Bangui Agreement 113, 119; compulsory licensing 7, 16, 18–19, 25, 28–9; duration of patents 114; implementation by African states 14–31; parallel imports 16, 18, 24; patent-related flexibilities 16–18, 157; public interest 7–8; research and experimentation exception 20, 26, 27, 30; technical assistance 46–7, 60; transition periods 4, 15, 20–1, 27, 121, 178
TRIPS-plus 81, 115, 158, 177, 179
Tsheola, J. 151
Tunisia 11, 98; IP policy 56

Uganda 22, 51, 78, 79, 86, 98, 159; ARIPO: trademarks 106; direct applicability of community laws 76; IP policy 60; TRIPS flexibilities 23, 26, 29, 31
UNESCO 4; UNESCO–WIPO Tunis Model Copyright Law for Developing Countries (1976) 4, 155
UNIDROIT (International Institute for the Unification of Private Law) 157, 164
unification 2, 72, 145–6, 154, 160, 164–5, 167, 179
United Kingdom: DFID 30
United Nations 4, 21, 46, 50; Commission on International Trade Law (UNCITRAL) 155–6, 157; Development Program (UNDP) 11, 21; Economic Commission for Africa (UNECA) 85, 98, 99
United States 148; American Law Institute (ALI) 154, 157; copyright holders 9; Patent and Trademark Office (USPTO) 58; patents 9; restatements of law 157; technical assistance 53
Universal Copyright Convention 3
universalism 153
Uruguay 161, 162
utility models: ARIPO (Harare Protocol) 102–3, 104–5, 116; definitions 104, 116; MERCOSUR 162; OAPI (Bangui Agreement) 116–18

van Gardingen, P.R. 127
Venezuela 161
Vietnam 146, 148
Viner, J. 72

Washington Declaration on IP and the Public Interest 6
West African Health Organization (WAHO) 29
Wilson, R. 5, 40
Winter, J.A. 76
Woods, L. 160
World Health Organization (WHO) 4, 21, 46, 140

World IP Organization (WIPO) 4, 46, 135, 155, 156; Development Agenda (DA) 4, 8, 10–11, 12–14, 43–4, 45, 47–51, 56, 60, 135, 139, 176, 177; Framework for Developing National IP Strategies for Innovation 50–1, 177; IP Development Plan (IPDP) 41–2, 53, 54, 55, 58; model contractual clauses 156; PAIPO 127, 128, 138, 139, 140; technical assistance 43–4, 45, 46, 47–51, 52, 53, 54, 55, 56–7, 59, 60, 98, 177; terminology 40, 41; WIPO Lex 52, 53, 55
World Trade Organization (WTO) 4, 23, 46, 71, 85, 147; PAIPO 135, 138, 140; *see also* TRIPS (Trade-Related Aspects of Intellectual Property Rights) Agreement

Yu, P.K. 8

Zambia 22, 51, 78, 83, 98, 101; IP policy 56; plant varieties 109; TRIPS flexibilities 24, 25, 31
Zimbabwe 22, 51, 78, 83, 86, 98, 101; ARIPO: trademarks 106; IP policy 60; TRIPS patent-related flexibilities 24, 25, 26, 30
Zirnstein, E. 146